Diversity and Motivation

Raymond J. Wlodkowski

Margery B. Ginsberg

Diversity and Motivation

Culturally Responsive Teaching

JOSSEY-BASS
A Wiley Imprint
www.josseybass.com

Published by Jossey-Bass
A Wiley Imprint
989 Market Street, San Francisco, CA 94103-1741   www.josseybass.com

Jossey-Bass books and products are available through most bookstores. To contact Jossey-Bass directly
call our Customer Care Department within the U.S. at 800-956-7739, outside the U.S. at 317-572-3986
or fax 317-572-4002.

Jossey-Bass also publishes its books in a variety of electronic formats. Some content that appears in
print may not be available in electronic books.

(See page 364 for copyright credits)

Library of Congress Cataloging-in-Publication Data

Wlodkowski, Raymond J.
    Diversity and motivation : culturally responsive teaching for
college / Raymond J. Wlodkowski and Margery B. Ginsberg. — 1st ed.
        p.   cm. — (A joint publication in the Jossey-Bass higher and
adult education, education, and social and behavioral science
series)
        Includes bibliographical references (p.   ) and index.
        ISBN 0-7879-0126-1
        ISBN 0-7879-6742-4 (paperback)
        1. Multicultural education—United States.   2. College teaching—
United States.   3. Minorities—Education (Higher)—United States.
1. Ginsberg, Margery B., date.   II. Title.   III. Series: Jossey-
Bass higher and adult education series.   IV. Series: Jossey-Bass
education series.   V. Series: Jossey-Bass social and behavioral
science series.
LC1099.3.W56   1995
370.19'6—dc20   95-15679

FIRST EDITION
HB Printing   10 9 8 7 6 5
PB Printing   10 9 8 7 6 5 4 3 2

A joint publication in

The Jossey-Bass

Higher and Adult Education Series,

The Jossey-Bass

Education Series,

and

The Jossey-Bass

Social and Behavioral Science Series

Contents

Preface

The student population in postsecondary education has become increasingly and undeniably diverse. This mix goes far beyond race, gender, and class, including ethnicity, sexual orientation, age, language, and disability. Multiculturalism has shifted from a trendy buzzword to a wave of indelible influence on education. There is now the belief among many scholars and a growing number of citizens from the public sector that higher education has a moral obligation to accommodate diversity, to transform itself as the society it serves is being transformed by the vast array of cultures that compose it.

In postsecondary education, multicultural efforts are expanding as colleges increase ethnic studies curricula, attempt to recruit larger numbers of faculty and students of color, and focus on creating more inclusive educational environments. Yet college teaching—how courses are organized and taught on a daily basis—lacks a cohesive approach that consistently embraces diversity to support the motivation of all students.

There exist, however, rapidly growing bodies of literature in a range of areas that offer subtle and profound educational practices to prevent discrimination and affirm diverse student groups—in particular, low-income learners of non-European ethnic minority communities. Educational anthropologists, for example, have examined interactional styles and the ways in which discrimination occurs within classrooms when expected behaviors are normed to middle class, European-American experiences. Social and political theorists have critically assessed "the hidden curriculum" and suggested ways to positively alter everyday routines that manifest the unapparent biases of Western economic imperatives.

Learning strategists present numerous options for diversifying approaches to teaching and for reexamining the limited ways in which we define intelligence. Evaluation and assessment scholars are leading a revolution to change narrow and exclusive assessment standards and practices. Systems theorists support and model ways to locate "dysfunction" within institutional practices rather than within human beings. Researchers and teachers in the evolving area of adult education create linkages between transformational learning and instruction.

When we use a conceptual framework based on theories of intrinsic motivation, we can synthesize much of this information across disciplines and cultures. With this conception of knowledge we propose a culturally responsive pedagogy. The essentials of this approach to teaching are that it (1) respects diversity, (2) engages the motivation of all learners, (3) creates a safe, inclusive, and respectful learning environment, (4) derives teaching practices from principles that cross disciplines and cultures, and (5) promotes justice and equity in society. *Diversity and Motivation* specifically illustrates how this pedagogy can be applied to meet what we believe is the foremost challenge in all of education: *to create learning experiences that allow the integrity of every learner to be sustained while each person attains relevant educational success and mobility.* As this book clearly documents, embracing this challenge is integral to a major purpose of higher education: the intellectual empowerment of all learners to achieve equity and social justice in a pluralistic democratic society.

There are pedagogically sound and comprehensive ways to teach diverse students that consistently, yet respectfully, elicit their involvement. Faculty, instructors, and teaching assistants will find this book to be pragmatic and theoretically substantive. Administrators and department heads will be able to use this text as a resource for planning and developing courses and programs to accommodate cultural diversity. Faculty development specialists can rely on *Diversity and Motivation* as a resource to offer practical assistance to faculty. And anyone who is beginning to teach in a postsecondary setting can survey and consider the many ideas presented to create learning experiences that are sensitive and encouraging to all of their students.

Using extensive examples, illustrations, and the reflections of a variety of faculty we offer a repertoire of flexible and variable teaching approaches. These are organized as a set of integrated norms, procedures, and structures. Each is thoroughly documented from a motivational as well as a multicultural perspective and applied in a postsecondary setting. All suggestions adhere to an intrinsic model of motivation in which people are assumed to be self-determined and motivated from within when they are respected and engaged in relevant and challenging experiences that enhance their effectiveness in what they value. For anyone who wants to see their educational setting become a place where inquiry, reflection, trust, equal participation, and learning are the norm, this book offers many carefully considered ideas.

This was a very difficult and, at times, painful book to write. From reviewing the literature; talking with various scholars, students, and teachers; and conducting our own teaching with the procedures that follow, we more deeply understood our complicity with biased and inequitable institutions and behaviors. We also found that because multicultural issues are permeated by ethical considerations each of us tended to feel morally obliged to our opinions about them. As a result when we had differences, for one or both of us to change our opinion was more difficult and emotionally wrought than we might feel altering a simply theoretical stance. Doubt and anxiety, at times, arose that we might be misrepresenting, diminishing, or trivializing the voices of courageous and forthright scholars and teachers. There were also differences between our own opinions about what we had read or were trying to write. In hindsight and with a bit more humor we now recognize that we were going through what most teachers go through when they

implement culturally responsive teaching. Yet the emotional content of those conflicts could be searing, and the idea of relinquish-
ing the project took hold more than once. Interlude, reflection, and
dialogue (sometimes with others) usually led us out of the impasse.
As the reader proceeds through this book, these notions may prove
useful as well.

Overview of the Contents

Because many of the ideas presented are complex, the book follows
a narrative flow. By that we mean not all major ideas are identified
or defined in the first chapter. They occur and are discussed as they
fit the book's motivational framework. We thought this a way to
avoid making the book too dense and possibly overwhelming for
the reader. Due to our backgrounds and professional experiences,
the orientation and suggestions in this book emphasize such disciplines as language arts, social science, and education. Faculty in the
sciences and professions may find many of these ideas adaptable
to their disciplines. This book is not written as a guide for cross-
cultural teaching where most of the students are from countries
other than the one represented by the teacher. Although it has relevance for such situations, the book is intended for use by teachers
in postsecondary schools in the United States.

We have created a synthesis for a culturally responsive pedagogy. Yet we have attempted not to homogenize the various views.
By employing quotes we have sought to leave the many different
voices in the areas of multiculturalism distinct, building bridges
between them with our framework. Often we use examples from
our own teaching to illustrate the ideas in this book, to validate
through our own experience the value of many of the suggestions
offered in this text.

Chapter One defines and establishes the relationship between
culture and motivation to learn. After a discussion of the role of
culture in society and the classroom, it addresses the question
of how a culturally responsive pedagogy can meet the challenges of
multiculturalism. As the theoretical core for culturally responsive

teaching, motivation is presented as being inseparable from culture, learning, and equity.

This chapter also introduces the motivational framework for culturally responsive teaching. A graphic model and a teaching example illustrate its four motivational dimensions or goals: establishing inclusion, developing attitude, enhancing meaning, and engendering competence. In addition, we list the educational practices necessary for achieving the four motivational goals as part of a course-planning scenario. Since resistance and conflict are common impediments to implementing culturally responsive teaching, the chapter ends with discussions of racial identity development theories, intellectual development theories, and belief systems as ways of understanding and constructively reacting to challenges that emerge with issues of diversity.

Chapters Two through Five provide the central content of the book. Each of these chapters is devoted to the comprehensive treatment of a specific motivational goal from the framework: establishing inclusion is covered in Chapter Two, developing attitude in Chapter Three, enhancing meaning in Chapter Four, and engendering competence in Chapter Five. These chapters pragmatically and theoretically describe how each motivational goal can be understood as the embodiment of two related criteria, following this order: *respect* and *connectedness* for inclusion, *self-determination* and *relevance* for attitude, *engagement* and *challenge* for meaning, and *authenticity* and *effectiveness* for competence. Within each of these chapters is an actively defined and exemplified set of norms (values and purposes), procedures (learning strategies and processes), and structures (rules of operation) to accomplish the identified motivational goal. From a teaching standpoint the norms, procedures, and structures are the heart and soul of the culturally responsive pedagogy proposed in this book.

Chapter Six describes how to implement culturally responsive teaching. Readers can reflect on a set of eight guidelines for revising a syllabus, creating an action plan, forming a cooperative collegial group, or identifying a new role to carry out culturally responsive teaching. All of the guidelines offer concrete teaching examples based on a summary of the norms, procedures, and structures of the preceding four chapters. In addition, there is a discussion of good practices in faculty development in the area of multicultural education, with references to programs found on campuses across the United States. The ending of the chapter reflects our thoughts about what higher education can become as it responds to cultural diversity in its service to students and society.

Acknowledgments

This book is the result of numerous conversations, continual encouragement, and the generosity of people sharing their resources, talents, and perspectives. In this regard we are cordially indebted to Suzanne Benally and Barbara McCombs. For helping us to find new ways to teach and other ways to understand we extend our warm appreciation to the students and faculty at Antioch University, Seattle. We also want to express our gratitude to Gale Erlandson, senior editor of Higher and Adult Education at Jossey-Bass, who has been a patiently supportive and critically insightful colleague throughout the creation of this book. In addition we want to thank Sharon Baumann for her expertise in creating and organizing the final manuscript.

This book is lovingly dedicated to our children, who believe in possibilities more than probabilities, making idealism both necessary and joyful.

July 1995   RAYMOND J. WLODKOWSKI
                                                       Boulder, Colorado

                                                       MARGERY B. GINSBERG
                                                       Denver, Colorado

The Authors

RAYMOND J. WLODKOWSKI is director of the Center for the Study of Accelerated Learning in the School for Professional Studies at Regis University, Denver. He is a licensed psychologist who has taught in urban universities for four decades. He specializes in motivation, adult learning, diversity, and professional development. He received his B.S. degree (1965) in social science and his Ph.D. degree (1970) in educational psychology, both from Wayne State University in Detroit.

Wlodkowski conducts seminars for colleges and organizations throughout North America and abroad. Three of the books he has authored have been translated into Spanish, Japanese, and Chinese. Among his publications is *Enhancing Adult Motivation to Learn*, which received the Phillip E. Frandson Award for Literature. He has worked extensively in video production and is the author of six professional development programs, including *Motivation to Learn*, winner of the Clarion Award as the best training and development video program of 1991. His most recent video is *Encouraging Motivation Among All Students* (created with Dr. Margery B. Ginsberg). He has been the recipient of numerous awards including the University of Wisconsin, Milwaukee Award for Teaching Excellence and the Faculty Merit Award for Excellence at Antioch University, Seattle.

MARGERY B. GINSBERG is an independent researcher and consultant in Boulder, Colorado. She has a background as a teacher on two Indian reservations, university professor, and Texas Title I technical assistance contact for the United States Department of Education. She works nationally and internationally to provide support for comprehensive school renewal anchored in a culturally responsive and motivationally significant pedagogy. Her work has been the foundation for several comprehensive school reform demonstration designs, including one of two high schools to receive the 1999–2000 United States Department of Education "Model National Professional Development Award."

Dr. Ginsberg's other books are *Creating Highly Motivating Classrooms for All Students: A Schoolwide Approach to Powerful Teaching with Diverse Learners* (Jossey-Bass, 2000) and *Educators Supporting Educators: A Guide to Organizing School Support Teams* (Association for Supervision and Curriculum Development, 1997). She has a Ph.D. in bilingual/multicultural/social foundations of education from the University of Colorado-Boulder.

Despite all, go on.
       —Maya Angelou

Chapter One

Understanding Relationships Between Culture and Motivation to Learn

> In recognizing the humanity of our fellow beings,
> we pay ourselves the highest tribute.
> —*Thurgood Marshall*

How can culturally diverse people fairly and respectfully learn well together? To answer this question raises a lifetime's worth of other questions and requires society to examine the history of its own past and present actions. As teachers, to reply honestly, we have to engage students on a deeper level than is usual in conventional educational practices. The view across our classrooms reflects significant change in the last fifteen years. Most of us are European-Americans, and many if not most of our students are people of color (American Council on Education, 1993). We have more learners than ever before who perceive and believe differently, not only from ourselves but from one another as well.

Our best experiences in teaching are those where we connect with our learners and are of genuine assistance to them. Being able to encourage diverse people to actively learn is not just a matter of pragmatism or of professional survival but also a means by which we personally thrive and find precious value in our work.

That is why when we consider school graduation rates for people of color, it is both a matter of social concern and, for us, an issue of professional integrity. African-American, Latino, and American

Indian high school completion rates, college participation, and degree attainment continue to be disproportionately lower than those of European-American students (Carter and Wilson, 1991). Just 3.1 percent of all bachelor's degrees awarded in the United States in 1990 went to Latinos, who make up 8.4 percent of the adult population. That compares with 5.8 percent for African Americans, who make up 11.3 percent of the adult population, and 84.3 percent for European Americans, who comprise 84.8 percent of the adult population (Celis, 1993). While the enrollment of African-American students in college has been increasing, their graduation rates have dropped to the levels of the mid 1970s (American Council on Education, 1993).

We know from experience as teachers that how learners feel about the setting they are in, the respect they receive from the people around them, and their ability to trust their own thinking and experience powerfully influence their concentration, their imagination, their effort, and their willingness to continue.

People who feel unsafe, unconnected, and disrespected are unlikely to be motivated to learn. This is as true in college as it is in elementary school. Such a conclusion does not explain all the issues and barriers related to the progress of people of color in postsecondary educational settings, but it is fundamental to what happens among learners and teachers wherever they meet. In education, perhaps more so than in work, it is the day-to-day, face-to-face feelings that make people stay or go. This book is committed to understanding how students and teachers who differ from one another in ways that are often more complex than ethnicity and race can create a reality that holds them together in the pursuit of learning. In our opinion, to do so means that those with the most power in the classroom, those often in the majority, must take the greater responsibility for initiating the process.

The task is a difficult one. As Lisa Delpit eloquently states, "We do not really see through our eyes or hear through our ears, but through our beliefs. To put our beliefs on hold is to cease to exist as ourselves for a moment—and that is not easy. It is painful as well, because it means turning yourself inside out, giving up your own sense of who you are, and being willing to see yourself in the unflattering light of another's angry gaze . . . we must learn to be vulnerable enough to allow our world to turn upside down in order to allow the realities of others to edge themselves into our consciousness" (1988, p. 297).

This may mean raising questions about discrimination or scrutinizing one's own power, even if that power stems merely from being in the majority. Certainly what follows in this book, when taken in the light of what typically goes on in many learning settings in postsecondary education, asks for and sometimes demands that kind of questioning.

Making direct suggestions for change was a challenge for us, because we do not pretend to know what is best, but we have very strong beliefs about what might be better. We ask the reader to keep in mind at least two sensibilities while reading this book. First, acknowledge what can and should be done as soon as possible and earnestly pursue it. Second, identify the larger, long-term changes that require resources and collective action and begin to discuss these with others to create the means to make them happen.

This book is not a blueprint. What is considered motivating varies across cultures and among individual human beings. People are experts on their own lives. Using a multidisciplinary approach that includes but is not limited to philosophy, anthropology, communications, critical theory, feminist theory, adult learning theory, multicultural studies, and linguistics as well as psychology, we offer an interpretive and process-based approach, more in keeping with the metaphor of a compass than a map. There are essential directions to take because all people are intrinsically motivated to learn and share a common humanity, but the cultural terrain of each individual's life so varies that the path to understanding another person is beyond the precision of any modern-day mental cartographer.

The Influence of Culture

The cultural composition of today's postsecondary learners differs markedly from that of thirty years ago, when many of today's college teachers were beginning their careers or still in school. If we look only from the perspective of ethnicity and language, we realize that the wave of immigration absorbed by the United States during the 1980s was the largest in seventy years and that today at least one out of every seven people in this country grew up or are going to grow up speaking a first language other than English (Barringer, 1993).

It is not surprising that we as faculty may be uncomfortable with learners coming from underrepresented racial, ethnic, and linguistic backgrounds at the same time as women are questioning a predominantly male perspective and older adults are returning to formal schooling from family or occupational experiences (Marchesani and Adams, 1992). Taking a closer look at the concept of culture helps us to understand why culturally diverse classrooms frequently challenge the resources of all teachers, even those who are earnest and experienced. Quite simply, what seems to have once worked for us in the classroom may now be clearly inadequate, whether in the area of encouraging motivation, initiating humor, or helping people to learn effectively.

As a society we are only one generation removed from legally sanctioned educational segregation, and many of us who now teach grew up in what appeared to be monocultural schools and communities. It is likely that we were socialized in our formative years with an unexamined set of traditions and beliefs about ourselves and a limited knowledge about others (Bowser and Hunt, 1981). Being socialized and living in the dominant culture often lessens our awareness that our beliefs and behaviors reflect a particular racial group, ethnic heritage, or gender affiliation. This is especially so if we are white, European, and male. We can easily think of these attitudes and norms as universally valued and preferred (Sandler,

1987). We may not imagine that we hold negative assumptions or stereotypes toward those with other values or beliefs (Marchesani and Adams, 1992). In fact, it may feel like heresy (Butler, 1993) to acknowledge that Anglo-Americans and ultimately Western norms enjoy a position of privilege and power in this country's educational system that has diminished other norms as valuable as cooperation (versus competition) and interdependence (versus independence).

Although culture is taught, it is generally considered implicit and conveyed unsystematically (Schein, 1992). That is one of the reasons why it is difficult for anyone to describe in explicit terms who they are culturally. Our own norms, values, and usual patterns of interaction most often work subconsciously. It is no surprise then that the times we are likely to experience uniqueness as cultural beings occur when we are in the presence of those who appear different from ourselves. For example, a person from a family and community that value and model emotionally demonstrative behavior as a sign of open and honest communication may befuddle or embarrass a person whose family and community of origin contain emotion as an understood reverence for that which is greater than oneself. When we meet others whose family and/or community norms vary from our own, it is akin to holding a mirror up to ourselves, provoking questions we might not otherwise think to ask. Contrast and dissonance awaken important assumptions and make it possible to deepen and expand the discovery of who we are, who others may be, and ideally, the rich variation within and between cultural groups.

The most obvious cultural characteristics that people observe are physical. Ethnicity, race, gender, and physical ability are often the antecedents to recognizing possible differences in experiences, beliefs, values, and expectations. Physical characteristics, however, provide a cursory sense of who we are. Our families, friends, jobs, organizational ties, and lifestyles draw upon a repertoire of behaviors, obstructing a clear view of who we might be culturally. Similarly, our unique personal histories and psychological traits interact dynamically to distinguish us from other members of our own cultural groups. The subtle complexity of who we are makes it difficult to define human beings according to narrow, static lists of expected characteristics.

It is a mistake to second-guess a person's cultural identity when the sole criteria are observable characteristics and behaviors. The influences of ethnicity, race, gender, sexual orientation, physical ability, age, and social class do not, in and of themselves, give meaning to the fullest definition of our cultural being.

At the same time, it is important to be aware that when we do not acknowledge the variation and distinction among cultural groups we may think in terms of a single set of cultural norms. These norms typically represent the values, beliefs, and behaviors of the historically dominant European-American middle class. When we accept these norms as universal, we are likely to see deficit rather than difference within the rich variation of human beings. For example, some students have learned the cultural norm that respect for one's teachers is demonstrated by deferring to the information they present. If a teacher expects students to actively question a lecture or interact eagerly about seminar material, students who reserve judgment out of respect may be misjudged as, for instance, linguistically or cognitively limited, underprepared, lacking in initiative, easily intimidated, or arrogant. The presumption of deficit in human beings who fail to conform to expectations and standards that are commonly associated with the dominant culture is one of the key factors accounting for dropout in kindergarten through postsecondary education. Throughout the literature on retention and attrition, these phenomena are attributed to a broad range of institutional barriers that fail to take into account the expectations and experiences of students from various cultural backgrounds (Smith, 1989; Butler and Walter, 1991; Adams, 1992a).

Amid the often perplexing ambiguity of how to correctly understand and respect unique cultural characteristics as well as common human qualities, most theorists agree that culture is the deeply learned confluence of language, values, beliefs, and behaviors that pervade every aspect of a person's life, and that it is continually undergoing minor changes. *What it is not* is an isolated, mechanical aspect of life that can be used to directly explain phenomena in the classroom or that can be learned as a series of facts, physical elements, or exotic characteristics (Ovando and Collier, 1985). In the words of Geertz (1973), "The human being is an animal suspended in webs of significance she or he has spun. I take culture to be those webs, and the analysis of it to be therefore not an experimental science in search of a law, but an interpretive one in search of meaning" (pp. 5, 29).

Geertz's perspective is fundamental to this book. There are few hard and fast rules about people, especially those who are culturally different from ourselves. Similarly, there are rarely any hard and fast rules about the ways in which we might work and learn together.

As teachers, being aware and open to the meaning that is created in interaction with another person will help us to avoid stereotyping. Stereotyping is rooted in our assumptions about the "average characteristics" of a group. We then impose those assumptions upon all individuals from the group. For example, some people believe that all European Americans are individualistic because, as a group, they are commonly considered to be more individualistic than other groups (Sue, 1991). All cultural groups exhibit a great deal of heterogeneity. "Seek first to understand" is a bit of wisdom whose genesis lies within many ethnic and religious communities.

We, as well as our learners, will have beliefs and values regarding learning and the roles of teacher and learner. These are culturally transmitted through such avenues as history, religion, mythology, political orientation, and familial and media communication. The ways in which we experience a learning situation are mediated by such cultural influences. No learning situation is culturally neutral. If we teach as we were taught, it is likely that we sanction individual performance, prefer reasoned argumentation, advocate impersonal objectivity, and condone sports-like competition for testing and grading procedures. Such teaching represents a distinct set of cultural norms and values that for many of today's learners are at best culturally unfamiliar and at worst a contradiction to the norms and values of their gender or their racial and ethnic backgrounds. Just one of several possible examples: many learners find themselves in a dilemma if they have been socialized toward values such as modesty and cooperation in their families and communities but within educational settings are expected to be self-promoting and competitive.

Few of us in postsecondary settings would care to admit that the way we teach compromises the learning of members of certain cultural groups. Yet to avoid or remain insensitive to the cultural issues and influences within our teaching situations under the guise, for example, of maintaining academic standards or treating everyone alike is no longer acceptable. Such a stance excludes or constrains particular groups of learners. Our commitment to educational access and opportunity requires us to acknowledge the cultural variation within our professional settings and to examine how we teach. Such an examination, of course, is not limited to the application of literature focusing specifically on educational equity. As microcosms of the broader society and the broader institution, college courses implicitly and explicitly perpetuate larger systems of inequality. Although the scope of this text is classroom pedagogy, we encourage educators to also examine policy and structural issues on campus that may undermine the conditions for change within classrooms.

We also encourage educators to become familiar with various interpretations of the term *diversity*. It is a word whose meanings are dependent on the context within which it is being understood. An anthropological approach to diversity would provide a comparative view of human groups within the context of all human groups. A political approach would analyze issues of power and class. Applied to a learning situation and to the purpose of this text, diversity conveys a need to respect similarities and differences among human beings and to go beyond "sensitivity" to active and effective responsiveness. This requires constructive action to change ideas and attitudes that perpetuate the exclusion of underrepresented groups of students and that dampen their motivation to learn.

In addition to the various academic connotations of the word *diversity*, its general use is seen, by some, as platitudinal or euphemistic. Although we use the words *diversity* and *cultural diversity* interchangeably, there is the belief that language associated with cultural differences must acknowledge issues of racism, discrimination, and the experience of exclusion. This argument implicates "diversity" as a way of diluting or skirting critical issues by implicitly representing all forms of difference—including individual differences and heterogeneity—within personal identities (Nieto, 1992; Geismar and Nicoleau, 1993). The term *cultural diversity* is seen by some, then, as more closely connected to issues of prejudice, economic discrimination, and political marginalization. Our point here is to acknowledge that each of us has beliefs and understandings that guide and challenge our work within a pluralistic society. Despite the earnestness with which we use language, we are frequently implicated through the meanings we are trying to express.

With respect to cultural diversity, this text offers a macrocultural pedagogical framework. Our framework is built upon principles and structures that are meaningful across cultures, especially with students from families and communities who have not historically experienced success in higher education. Rather than comparing and contrasting groups of people from a microcultural perspective, one that, for example, identifies a specific ethnic group and prescribes approaches to teaching according to assumed characteristics and orientations, our approach emerges from literature on and experience with creating a more equitable pluralistic framework that elicits the intrinsic motivation of all learners. The complicated interaction of history, personality, cultural transmission, and cultural transformation is yet another worthy area of exploration outside the scope of this book. We prefer not to risk reducing dynamic groups of people to sets of stereotypic characteristics. Our emphasis is on creating multiple approaches from which teachers and learners may choose in order to support the diverse perspectives and values that learners bring to the classroom.

Ironically, a most important step in learning this pedagogy is to appreciate that many of the factors that influence our students also affect us. Learning more about these influences will inform our own development. As with all human beings, while we feel the profound impact of culture we can only tenuously grasp its meaning until time and experience reveal its deeper nature.

Personal Appreciation of the Concept of Culture

Unless we, as educators, understand our own culturally mediated values and biases, we may be misguided in believing that we are encouraging divergent points of view and providing meaningful opportunities for learning to occur when we are, in fact, repackaging or disguising past dogmas. It is entirely possible to believe in the need for change, to learn new language and technique, and to, just the same, subtly overlay new ideas with old biases and frames of reference. It is possible to diminish the potential and the needs of others at our most subconscious levels and in our most implicit ways without any awareness that we are doing so. Mindfulness of who we are and what we believe culturally can help us to examine the ways in which we may be unknowingly placing our good intentions within a dominant and unyielding framework—in spite of the appearance of openness and receptivity to enhancing motivation to learn among all students.

One of the most useful places to begin the exploration of who we are culturally and the relevance of that identity is to ask, What values do I hold that are consistent with the dominant culture? This question allows us to be cognizant not only of our dominant-culture values but also of the distinctions we hold as members of other groups in society. This is particularly important for fourth-, fifth-, and sixth-generation Americans of European descent. For many descendants of European Americans, one's family's country or countries of origin can be only marginally useful in understanding who we are *now* as cultural people in the United States. The desire and ability to assimilate, as well as affiliations with numerous other groups in this country (religious, socioeconomic, regional, and so forth), can create confusion about what one *believes* culturally. Further, culture is a dynamic and changing concept for each of us, regardless of country of origin. Our cultural identities are constantly evolving or changing, and, consequently, values, customs, and orientations are equally fluid. Because we, as educators, exert a powerful influence over classroom norms, we ought to make explicit those values that are most often implicit and that profoundly affect all learners.

There are several approaches that can help to personalize the concept of culture. One place to begin is with a list compiled by sociologist Robin M. Williams, Jr. (1970, pp. 454–500). Williams's fifteen cultural themes and orientations that generally reflect the Anglo-Saxon influence on the culture of the United States allow us at least a cursory identification of cultural norms that may or may not be operative in our classrooms as a consequence of our own belief systems. As we scan Williams's list, it is useful to consider other perspectives on each theme and the degree to which we allow for alternative cultural perspectives and related approaches to learning in our classrooms. These themes are condensed below (Locke, 1992). We offer along with them examples of alternative perspectives that may reflect the beliefs and values of some or many students in our classrooms.

1. *Achievement and success:* There is an emphasis on rags to riches stories.
   Alternatives: Personal generosity is the highest human value; conspicuous consumption represents greed and self-interest;

"rags to riches" is rooted in cultural mythology that overlooks the social, political, and economic forces that favor certain groups over others. Thus, achievement has at least as much to do with privilege as personal desire and effort.

2. *Activity and work:* This is a land of busy people who stress disciplined, productive activity as a worthy end in itself.
Alternatives: Caring about and taking time for others is more important than "being busy"; discipline can take many forms and should be equated with respect, moral action, and social conscience; a means-ends orientation has been the justification for such things as cultural genocide and environmental disaster; sustenance is a higher value than productivity.

3. *Humanitarian mores:* People spontaneously come to the aid of others and hold traditional sympathy for the "underdog."
Alternatives: People are selective about whom they will help, especially the large number of people who believe that others get what they deserve; in the dominant culture, contrary to this beneficent norm, personal gain generally takes precedence over kindness and generosity; human emotion makes many people feel vulnerable and inept—it is something to be avoided.

4. *Moral orientation:* Life events and situations are judged in terms of right and wrong.
Alternatives: There is no objective "right" or "wrong," only dominant perspectives that tend to favor and protect the most privileged members of society; human beings are not in a position to judge others or to use judgments as a rationale for domination and control; finding meaning in life events and situations is more important than judging.

5. *Efficiency and practicality:* There is an emphasis on the practical value of getting things done.
Alternatives: Process is more important than product and

makes the strongest statement about what we value; living and working in a manner that values equity and fairness is practical as well as just.

6. *Progress:* An optimistic view is held that things will get better. *Alternatives:* Progress assumes that human beings can and should control nature and everything that happens to us; we ought to acknowledge, respect, and care for that which we have been given, that which is greater than ourselves, and that which is—like life—cyclical. (Interestingly, many languages in North America and around the world do not have a word for "progress.")

7. *Material comfort:* Emphasis is placed on the good life. Many are conspicuous consumers. *Alternatives:* The idea that life will be good if one owns many possessions leads to insatiable, exploitive, and ostentatious behaviors; a good life is defined by sharing and giving things away.

8. *Equality:* There is a constant avowal of the commitment to equality. *Alternatives:* When we espouse this notion, it may imply that the voice of the majority is correct simply because all citizens can participate equitably, which they cannot; the wisdom of elders may take precedence over personal experiences and the lessons of peers; the appeal to a higher form of consciousness may be more judicious than a reasoned argument among mortal beings.

9. *Freedom:* The belief in individual freedom takes on almost a religious connotation. *Alternatives:* Freedom without justice is dangerous; limiting freedom is necessary for equality; accepting the limitations of personal freedom is a sign of respect for your or someone else's culture.

10. *External conformity:* There is great uniformity in matters of dress, housing, recreation, manners, and even the expression of political ideas.
    Alternatives: Conformity creates a comfortable anonymity, especially among people whose differences have caused suspicion or ridicule. The anger that can undergird conformity is becoming increasingly visible as urban youth, second language speakers, low-income students, students of color, and other underrepresented members of society boldly cultivate and embrace their identities.

11. *Science and secular rationality:* There is esteem for the sciences as a means of asserting mastery over the environment.
    Alternatives: The notion of scientific objectivity is based on the mistaken presumption that human beings are capable of value-neutral beliefs and behaviors; science has become a rationale for conquering and exploiting the environment in a manner consistent with the Western belief in "man against nature"; the earth is a sacred gift to be revered and protected.

12. *Nationalism-patriotism:* There exists a strong sense of loyalty to that which is called "American."
    Alternatives: Functionally, "American" has meant conformity to Anglo-European values, behaviors, and appearances; "American" needs to be redefined in the spirit of pluralism and with respect for other global identities; the rightness of that which is commonly seen as "American" has been an excuse for indoctrinating United States citizens with imperialism and greed; the way in which the word *American* is commonly used to describe a single country on the *continent* of the Americas is presumptuous and arrogant.

13. *Democracy:* There is a belief that every person should have a voice in the political destiny of the country.
    Alternatives: Democracy is an illusion that perpetuates the domination of society's most privileged members; people must have

the means and ability to use their voices—this requires access to multiple perspectives on issues and confidence that speaking up will not jeopardize one's economic and personal security.

14. *Individual personality*: Every individual should be independent, responsible, and self-respecting. The group should not take precedence over the individual.
    Alternatives: Individualism promotes a form of aggression and competition that undermines the responsibility and self-respect of others; independence denies the social, cultural, racial, and economic realities that favor certain members of certain groups over others; sharing and humility are higher values than ownership and self-promotion; self-respect is not separable from respect for others, for community, and for that which is greater than oneself.

15. *Racism and related group superiority*: This theme represents the chief value conflict in the culture of the United States, because it emphasizes differential evaluation of racial, religious, and ethnic groups.
    Alternatives: Because racism combines prejudice with power and is personal, institutional, and cultural, we must acknowledge its existence, teach and learn about power, and collaboratively and proactively develop policy and practices that value pluralism and promote equity.

When we clarify our own cultural values and biases, we are better able to consider how they might subtly but profoundly influence the degree to which learners in our classrooms feel included, respected, at ease, and generally motivated to learn.

The range of considerations found in Williams's cultural themes can be helpful as we think of questions to ask ourselves about our own assumptions, and as we construct reflective questions that can enhance the learning experiences we are creating with our students. We offer the following examples, with related ideas:

1. Are classroom norms clear, so that if they are different from what students are used to at home or in their communities, they are able to understand and negotiate alternative ways of being? (It may be important to model behavior, provide visible examples of expectations, and elicit information about clarity through student polls or written responses to such questions as, Do I prefer to work in a cooperative group? individually? Some students are embarrassed about identifying what they do not understand. The anonymity of writing, or conferencing with peers and then sharing the information with an instructor, can facilitate communication.)

2. Have I examined the values embedded in my discipline that may confuse or disturb some students? (Ask questions that encourage students to represent alternative perspectives; with students, construct panels that can discuss key issues from diverse perspectives.)

3. Are the examples I use to illustrate key points meaningful and sensitive to my students? (Give one example from your own experience and then ask students to create their own examples to illustrate different points, providing an opportunity for group discussion; acknowledge the experiences of people from different backgrounds; be aware of nonverbal language.)

4. Do I have creative and effective ways to learn about my students' lives and interests? You might want to incorporate a photo board, artistic representations, occasional potlucks, regularly scheduled discussion topics (including current events), acknowledgment of birthdays and cultural holidays, open sharing about yourself, a coffee urn at the back of the classroom as a site for informal discussion, and other similar devices.

Peggy McIntosh (1989) has poignantly written: "As a white person I had been taught about racism as something which puts others at a disadvantage, but had been taught not to see one of

its corollary aspects, white privilege, which puts me at an advantage . . . I was taught to see racism only in individual acts of mean-
ness, not in invisible systems conferring dominance on my group
(p. 10).

Many of us have been socialized, regardless of racial-group membership, to think of the United States as a just society. It is hard to
imagine that each of us is responsible for everyday actions that can
render people as impotent as overt and intentional acts of racism.
The learning environment provides a meaningful context for
addressing and redressing the ways in which bias occurs. Learning
about who we are culturally, as individuals and as educators, can
create a consciousness that is personally, professionally, and socially
empowering.

Culturally Responsive Teaching and the Challenges of Cultural Pluralism

Amid great challenge, the United States is moving from the philosophy of an assimilationist melting pot to the philosophy of cultural pluralism, to a society in which members of diverse cultural,
social, racial, or religious groups are free to maintain their own identity and yet simultaneously share a larger common political organization, economic system, and social structure (Ovando and Collier,
1985). This implies the peaceful coexistence of diverse lifestyles,
language patterns, religious practices, and family structures. This
system of thought is most often aligned by educational scholars with
the philosophical position of multiculturalism, which assumes that
the gender makeup and ethnic, racial, and cultural diversity of a
pluralistic society should be reflected in the structures of educational
institutions, including staff, norms, values, and the curriculum
(Banks and Banks, 1993). Therefore, teaching that is culturally
responsive occurs when there is equal respect for the backgrounds
and contemporary circumstances of all learners, regardless of individual status and power, and when there is a design of learning

processes that embraces the range of needs, interests, and orientations to be found among them. For the pedagogy of the educational system of a society espousing cultural pluralism, *the challenge is to create learning experiences that allow the integrity of every learner to be sustained while each person attains relevant educational success and mobility.* Meeting this challenge is transformative as well as integral to a major purpose of higher education: the intellectual empowerment of all learners to achieve equity and social justice in a pluralistic democratic society (Weaver, 1991; Hill, 1991; Marable, 1992).

The whole activity of education is ethical and political in nature. Questions about the consequences of learning to the individual can always be asked in reference to society as a whole (Merriam and Caffarella, 1991). Whether or not teachers and learners acknowledge the pervasiveness of politics in their work, politics is inherent in the teacher-learner relationship (authoritarian or democratic), in the readings chosen for the syllabus (those left in and those left out), and in selecting course content (a shared decision or only the teacher's prerogative). Ethics and politics also reside in the discourse of learning (which questions get asked and answered, and how deeply are they probed), in the imposition of standardized tests, in grading and tracking policies, and in the physical conditions of classrooms and buildings, which send messages to learners and teachers about their worth and place in society (Shor, 1993). Politics certainly can be found in the attitude toward nonstandard English reflected in the curriculum, and in the way schools are unequally funded depending on the economic class of students served. Most important, as Shor has written, "Education is politics because it is one place where individuals and society are constructed. Because human beings and society are developed in one direction or another through education, the learning process cannot avoid being political" (p. 28).

A pedagogy respectful of multiculturalism and ethics begins not with test scores but with questions. What kinds of citizens do we hope to create through postsecondary education? What kind of society do we want, and how can we reconcile the notions of difference and equality with the imperatives of freedom and justice (Giroux, 1992)? Ethics relates to the educator's sense of social responsibility. We live at a time when geographic, cultural, and ethnic borders are giving way to shifting configurations of power and community. It is unconscionable not to connect our teaching to broader social concerns that deeply affect how people live, work, and survive. If there is anything our experience has taught us, which research also strongly supports (Ogbu, 1987; Courtney, 1991), it is that motivation to learn among people is vitally released by a vision of a hopeful future.

From an educational perspective, achieving a pluralistic democratic society that meets its ideal of equity and social justice is inextricably linked to the pedagogical practices of its educational institutions. An approach to teaching that meets the challenge of cultural pluralism and can contribute to the fulfillment of the purpose of higher education has to *respect diversity; engage the motivation of all learners; create a safe, inclusive, and respectful learning environment; derive teaching practices from principles that cross disciplines and cultures; and promote justice and equity in society.*

These are the *essentials* of culturally responsive teaching. They foster effective learning for all students with attention to the collective good of society, so that systems of oppression, whether they are conceptual or institutional, do not continue to proliferate. This is teaching guided by a vision of justice, a pedagogy that seeks to transform as well as inform. How to arrive at the essentials of this pedagogy and put them into practice is the narrative of the rest of this book.

Understanding a Motivational Perspective That Supports Culturally Responsive Teaching

The distinguishing features of culturally responsive teaching are generally based on theories of intrinsic motivation, a view of

motivation that is historically well documented but not widely practiced in college teaching. Theories of intrinsic motivation have
been broadly applied, researched, and advocated within a number of areas including cross-cultural studies (Csikszentmihalyi and
Csikszentmihalyi, 1988), education (McCombs and others, 1993),
bilingual education (Cummins, 1986), adult education (Wlodkowski, 1985), and work and sports (Deci and Ryan, 1985).

An analysis of the procedural and structural components of college teaching reveals that they largely follow an extrinsic rein-
forcement model. Teach-and-test practices, competitive assessment
procedures, grades, grade-point averages, and eligibility for select
vocations and graduate schools are aspects of a system of interrelated elements most students experience in their pursuit of a college education. This system is based on the assumption that human
beings will strive to learn and to achieve when they are externally
rewarded for such behavior. Strongly supportive of this network of
incentives is the implied value that individual accomplishment
merits academic and social rewards.

Three major issues cause us to question whether an extrinsic
motivation model should prevail in college teaching. The first is
the well-documented fact that colleges retain and successfully educate a disproportionately low number of low-income and ethnic
minority students. Since motivation strongly influences learning,
it may be that an extrinsically based approach to teaching is not
effective for many students and across many cultures.

The second issue is that because we as college teachers govern
the system of structured external rewards, we are unlikely to change
our teaching practices. Consequently, it is very difficult for colleges
to shift from monocultural education, an education largely reflective of one reality and usually biased toward the dominant group,
to an education responsive to cultural diversity (Nieto, 1992). From
the tendency to reward those who think like ourselves, to the intuitive recourse to rely on our own background and education for
determining subject matter, to our desire for the comfort of the

controlled, the familiar, and the predictable in our classes, we have little reason to change these habits when we specify the content, process, and assessment of what we teach and hold the educational rewards for students in our own hands. Student evaluations seem impotent as catalysts for change, and few of us are directly evaluated based on the actual learning of our students (Astin, 1993b).

The third issue is that using extrinsic rewards to enhance learning among students often undermines interest in and value for what is being learned (Ryan, Mims, and Koestner, 1983). The negative effects of such extrinsic motivators as grades have been documented with students of different ages and from different cultures (Kohn, 1993). There is research that shows that when a learning activity such as problem solving is undertaken explicitly to attain some extrinsic reward, people respond by seeking the least demanding and perfunctory way of ensuring the reward. From this perspective a system of external rewards may contribute to inferior learning among students. Cramming for tests is one of many examples that easily come to mind. Studies consistently suggest that the most destructive effects of extrinsic rewards are in activities that require creativity or higher-order thinking. A shift to a pedagogy based on theories of intrinsic motivation should enhance the learning of *all* students.

For reasons of this magnitude we have explored and used theories of intrinsic motivation, finding them to be much more informative alternatives for developing an approach to teaching that accommodates cultural diversity. These theories also stimulate and support the creation of teaching and assessment procedures that are open to the voices of students and enhance their learning and involvement.

We can more easily comprehend intrinsic motivation as a foundation for culturally responsive teaching by understanding the relationship of learning to motivation. William Blake believed that thought without affection separates love and wisdom as it separates body and soul. So it is with learning and motivation. They are inseparable. To discuss one without considering the other or to attempt to force them apart ruptures any intelligent discourse and leads to a fragmented notion of what being human might actually mean. Learning is a naturally active and normally volitional process of constructing meaning from information and experience (McCombs and others, 1993). Motivation is the natural human capacity to direct energy in the pursuit of a goal. Although our lives are marked by a continuous flow of activity with an infinite variety of overt actions, we are purposeful. We constantly learn, and when we do we are usually motivated to learn. We are directing our energy through the processes of attention, concentration, imagination, and passion, to name only a few, to make sense of our world.

In education, psychology dominates the literature about motivation. Yet why people do what they do—the focus of any motivational query—is well within the realm of anthropology, religion, philosophy, physics, and every person's common sense. We emphasize this because too often psychology and its practitioners—using mostly Eurocentric assumptions and values—have become the final arbiters and major decision makers regarding how to teach and, unfortunately, how to label those who have difficulty in the educational system (Wlodkowski and Ginsberg, 1993). One of us is a psychologist, and we both know the literature documenting that the field of modern psychology is only beginning to open itself to consideration of alternative values and to accept its own incomplete understanding of the many cultures that populate this country (Pedersen, 1994). For example, motivation is governed to a large extent by emotion. A person working at a task feels frustrated and stops. Another person working at a task feels joy and continues. But what may bring forth the reactions of frustration or joy may differ across cultures, because cultures differ in their definitions of novelty, hazard, opportunity, gratification, and appropriate responses. In fact, it is quite possible for another person with a different set of cultural beliefs to feel frustrated at a task and to continue with further determination. Depending on the culture to which one belongs, illness, for example, may be seen as caused by germs, God, anxiety, chance, or one's moral failure, and a person's emotional response to illness will reflect these beliefs. Cultures vary in their beliefs about the meaning of emotional experiences, expressions, and behaviors (Kitayama and Markus, 1994). Since the socialization of emotions is so culturally influenced, the motivational response a student has to a learning activity reflects this influence and its associated complexity. Psychology has only an incomplete understanding of this remarkable intricacy.

Since there is no science of human behavior with underlying, consistent, unifying principles that leads to predictable results, we advocate that teachers, at the very least, accept that each learner best represents her or his own reality, especially when it comes to what that individual finds motivating. This form of constructivism does not preclude the existence of an external reality, it merely claims that each of us constructs our own reality through interpreting perceptual experiences of the external world based on our unique set of experiences with the world and our beliefs about them (Jonassen, 1992). Since culture is an influential part of anyone's world, it is rare, perhaps even impossible, for any human being to behave without responding to some aspect of culture (Segall, Dasen, Berry, and Poortinga, 1990). Motivation is culturally fused and embedded. Generic motivational goals such as success or achievement and more personal traits such as ambition or initiative may not only have different meanings to different people but also be undesirable for cultural reasons. In this light, influences such as religion, myth, ethnicity, and regional and peer group norms have powerful motivational force.

In general, the internal logic as to why a person does something may not agree with ours, but it is there nonetheless. Being an effective teacher requires the willingness to understand that perspective and to co-create with the learner a motivating educational experience. Rather than knowing what to do to the learner we interpret and deepen the meaning we *share* together. Motivationally effective teaching has to be culturally responsive teaching.

With this orientation we are less likely to intervene, establish, or determine the learner's motivation to learn and more likely to elicit, affirm, or encourage the learner's natural capacity to make meaning from experience. From this perspective, motivation is seen as *intrinsic* rather than *extrinsic*. People are naturally curious and enjoy learning. To be active, to originate behavior, to be effective at what we value is part of human nature (Deci and Ryan, 1991). When one's actions are endorsed by oneself with a sense of integrity and cohesion, authenticity blends into self-determination, and intrinsic motivation occurs. It is when people are feeling insecure, worrying about failure, and fearing punishment, ridicule, or shame that intrinsic motivation recedes and coercion and extrinsic rewards such as money may seem more effective as motivational influences. From such intimidating circumstances comes the popular "carrot and stick" metaphor for motivational manipulation. When people are powerless; when they need jobs, promotions, and money; when they are merely surviving, holding on, stopping a downward spiral, or making themselves less expendable, they may seem less intrinsically motivated to learn. Yet even in such a grim existence, when people can relax their minds and become less self-conscious, humor, insight, and creativity emerge (Mills, 1991). Beyond survival, other primary sources of motivation—meaning, being effective at what one values, the intrinsic tendency to integrate oneself within, with others, and with the world—are available in all people almost all of the time.

How to elicit intrinsic motivation will be discussed intensively in the chapters ahead. At this time, however, it is important to deal with some of the language that surrounds motivation. The carrot and stick metaphor is a terrible one, a metaphor of control. It objectifies people and reduces their humanity. It also contributes to the idea of people "motivating" other people. In our opinion, the question, "How do I motivate these people?" implies that "these people" are in an inferior position, somehow less able and certainly less powerful than ourselves. This kind of thinking not only diminishes our acceptance of their perspective but also takes away their ownership of being intrinsically motivated. The attitude of such a "motivator" violates their self-determination and tends to keep them "less than"—dependent and in need of further help from a more powerful other.

Replacing the carrot and stick metaphor with the words *understand* and *elicit* changes the idea of motivation from one of manipulation and control to one of communication and respect. In the latter case we may certainly influence the motivation of people, but it happens through coming to know their perspective and inviting or drawing forth what they naturally and culturally possess. In this way they are seen as self-determined, unique, and potentially active. As teachers we may affirm, support, or encourage their motivation, but it is they who are in charge of themselves, and through sharing our resources with theirs we can together create greater energy for learning. Such a learning environment is neither teacher-centered nor learner-centered but more community-centered, with the teacher serving the agreed-upon leadership role.

Since motivation and learning are inseparable it stands to reason that those who are motivated to learn will learn more. When Uguroglu and Walberg (1979) analyzed 232 correlations of motivation and academic learning, they found that 98 percent of the correlations were positive. Although the sample included only students from the first through the twelfth grade, the researchers found that the relationship between motivation and learning increased along with the age of the students, with the highest correlations occurring in the twelfth grade. Motivation is not only the energy within learning but also the feeling that mediates learning and the attitude that is a consequence of learning. People work longer and more intensely when they are motivated than when they are not motivated. They are also more cooperative and open to what they are experiencing. Time spent actively involved in learning is definitely related to achievement (Levin and Long, 1981). Since motivation plays such a key role in learning, those teaching methods and educational environments that motivationally favor particular learners to the exclusion of others are unfair and diminish the chances of success for those excised learners. For example, a teacher who grades students on the basis of participation during discussions and calls mainly on voluntary respondents may unwittingly, yet blatantly, favor those students who are socialized to request personal attention and to offer opinions in front of groups of relative strangers.

Any educational or training system that ignores the history and perspective of its learners or does not attempt to adjust its teaching practices to benefit all its learners is contributing to inequality of opportunity. When we understand motivation to learn as a developing trait that influences lifelong learning we see how insidious such bias in teaching can be. People who eventually find reading, writing, calculating, and expanding their store of information interesting and satisfying are usually considered lifelong learners. The tendency to find such processes meaningful and worthwhile is considered to be the *trait* of motivation to learn, a propensity for learning, often narrowly conceived as "academic," that gradually develops over time. McCombs (1991), based on her survey of the research, believes this trait is an internal, naturally occurring capacity of human beings that is enhanced and nurtured by quality supportive relationships, opportunities to exert personal choice and take responsibility for learning, and personally relevant and meaningful learning activities. Deci and Ryan (1991), who have spent over twenty-five years studying the phenomenon of intrinsic motivation, offer the opinion that the key to acquiring such a value is feeling free enough to accept it as one's own. Such insights suggest that traditional teach-and-test methods and training programs based on the assumption that people can be motivated by external events (Keller, 1992) are unlikely to work with large segments of our population. Such practices may also deny many people the satisfaction of a life in which learning is a compelling joy and the means for a better future.

A Motivational Framework for Culturally Responsive Teaching

A motivational framework for culturally responsive teaching has to have enough breadth to accommodate the range of diversity found in most postsecondary educational settings. It also has to integrate the variety of assumptions from different disciplines found in this book. But most of all it has to explain how to create compelling learning experiences through which learners are able to maintain their integrity as they attain relevant educational success. In this respect the framework is inseparable from the broader issue of how to construct a world in which democratic ideals are a reality for all.

The framework we offer here is a holistic and systemic representation of four intersecting motivational goals or conditions (as in states of being):

1. Establishing inclusion

2. Developing attitude

3. Enhancing meaning

4. Engendering competence

Establishing inclusion refers to the norms, procedures, and structures that are woven together to form a learning context in which all learners and teachers feel respected by and connected to one another.

Developing attitude refers to the norms, procedures, and structures that create through relevance and choice a favorable disposition among learners and teachers toward the learning experience or learning goal.

Enhancing meaning refers to those norms, procedures, and structures that expand, refine, or increase the complexity of what is learned in a way that matters to learners, includes their values and purposes, and contributes to a critical consciousness.

Engendering competence refers to those norms, procedures, and structures that create an understanding for learners of how they are or can be effective in learning something of personal value.

In the chapters ahead each of these four motivational goals will be explained and exemplified in great detail. Each of these motivational conditions contains an initial verb as a way of emphasizing its dynamic and continuous state of existence. The goals are interrelated. They are simultaneously reciprocal. All affect one another. As shown in Figure 1.1 they work in concert as they influence the learner and happen in a moment as well as over a period of time.

People experience motivational influences polyrhythmicly— that is, as a simultaneous integration of intersecting realities on both a conscious and subconscious level. We meet a friend we have not seen for many years. Tears swell in our eyes as we embrace our comrade. In that moment our perceptions of our friend intersect with a history of past events recalled within our minds, with the possibility of a number of feelings arising from this dynamic network. One could give a score of reasons why one loves a companion. How many of them affect us at any given moment? No one really knows.

From Buddha to Bateson, life has been envisioned as multidetermined. It is also simultaneously and instantly multidetermined. Much of the time we experience life as a jazz musician might experience music improvising with a band, hearing many different sounds at the same time and blending in with our voice, reciprocal and distinct. Elsa Barkley Brown (1990) describes the polyrythmic way of understanding through the practice of *gumbo ya ya* (a Creole term for "everybody talks at once"), a conversation in which everyone is listening to everyone else while they themselves are speaking—symmetry through diversity. A growing number of researchers view cognition as a social activity that integrates the mind, the body, the process of the activity, and the ingredients of the setting in a complex interactive and recursive manner (Rogoff and Lave, 1984; Lave, 1988).

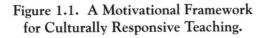

Figure 1.1. A Motivational Framework
for Culturally Responsive Teaching.

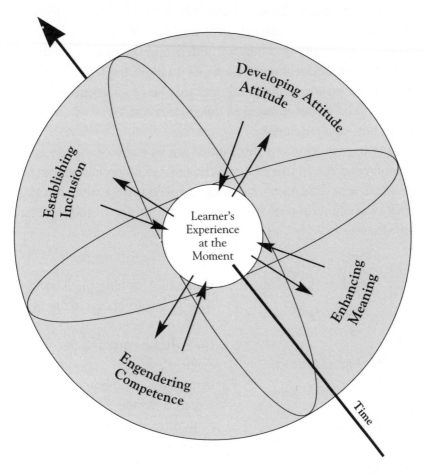

Scholars in the field of situated cognition understand human beings to frequently coordinate their interactions without deliberation, with perception and action arising together, each co-constructing the other through some form of immediate dialectic (Bredo, 1994). Much of the time we compose our lives in the moment. The conventional psychological model of perceiving, thinking, acting is a linear process that may occur far less often than previous theorists have imagined. There is evidence that in matters as profound as perspective transformation and cultural identity, most people change through immediate action in response to inter-cultural challenges, with little deep rational reflection and planned action (Taylor, 1994). Thus, we understand the four motivational conditions found in Figure 1.1 to be an evolving family of inter-secting dimensions that simultaneously and reciprocally interact with and as a part of learning to influence our motivation and learn-ing at any given moment.

Let us take a look at this framework in terms of the teaching/learning process. In this example the teacher is conducting the first two-hour session of a semester-long introductory course in research. It is a diverse group of students ranging in age from twenty to fifty-five.

Motivational Goal	*Process/Structure*
Establishing inclusion	Randomly forming small groups in which learners exchange con-cerns, experiences, and expecta-tions they have about research
Developing attitude	Asking learners to choose some-thing they could immediately research among themselves
Enhancing meaning	Assigning research partners to devise a set of questions to ask volunteers in order to make a prediction about them.
Engendering competence	After the predictions have been verified, asking learners to create their own statements about what they learned about research from this process.

This scenario might go like this: After the teacher has handed out the syllabus and had a dialogue with the learners about its contents, she explains that much research is conducted on a collaborative basis and it is important to get to know each other better in order to create such teams as the course continues. For a beginning activity she randomly assigns learners to small groups and encourages them to discuss any experiences they may have previously had in doing research as well as their expectations and concerns for the course (establishing inclusion). At the end of this activity, each group has a volunteer report a summary of its experiences, hopes, and concerns. In this manner, learners are beginning to establish rapport and trust with one another.

The teacher relates her belief that most people are researchers much of the time and asks the group what they would like to research among themselves at this very moment (developing attitude). After a lively and humorous discussion, the consensus is to investigate and predict the amount of sleep some members of the class had last night.

Five people volunteer to serve as subjects, and research partnerships form among the rest of the learners. Each team has to devise a set of observations and a set of questions to ask the volunteers, but no one can ask them how many hours of sleep they had the night before (enhancing meaning). After the questions have been asked, the teams rank the five volunteers from the most to the least amount of sleep. When the volunteers reveal the amount of time they have slept, it is found that no research team was correct in ranking more than two people among the five volunteers. The volunteers then tell the researchers questions they could have asked to increase their accuracy, such as, "How much coffee did you drink before you came to class?"

After further discussion each learner is asked to write a series of statements about what this process has taught him or her about research (engendering competence). In small, randomly assigned groups, learners exchange these insights, which include such comments as, "Thus far, I enjoy research more than I thought I might," and "Research is more a method than an answer."

One can see from this scenario how the four motivational conditions constantly influence and interact with one another. Without the establishment of inclusion (small groups to discuss concerns, experiences, and so on) and the development of a positive attitude (learners choosing something to research), the enhancement of meaning (research teams devising a set of questions for volunteers) may not have occurred with equal ease and energy, and the self-assessment to engender competence (what students learned from their experience) may have had a dismal outcome. Also, the future patterns of inclusion (future research teams) have been prepared for, because learners now have a positive common history.

This learning experience, like all learning experiences, is holistic as well as systemic. It can be imagined that removing any one of the four motivational conditions would have affected the entire experience and each condition's link to the rest of the course. In fact, from this viewpoint, once a course has started there is not really a beginning or an end to learner motivation. Rather there is a set of experiences connected through time in which teachers and learners can enhance or reduce the motivational conditions for eliciting intrinsic motivation and for improving learning for everyone.

Criteria, Norms, Procedures, and Structures for Using the Motivational Framework

Because it is possible to create conditions that suppress motivation and inhibit learning, one can see that with something as dynamic as motivation, care, planning, and sensitivity are extremely important. While there are no formulas for using this framework, there are heuristics. We can offer questions, criteria, norms, procedures, and structures that can suggest and stimulate. With reflection, teachers can use these to redesign their courses and create better ways of learning for their students.

Again, using the metaphor of a compass we offer a set of *two criteria* for each motivational goal or condition so that teachers and learners can be reasonably sure they are moving in the direction they desire. By using criteria rather than rules we allow for a more multidisciplinary and interpretive approach to creating the appropriate motivational conditions. For example, for establishing inclusion the criteria are *respect* and *connectedness*. People generally believe they are included in a group when they feel respected by and connected to the group. How inclusion is established may vary greatly, but the teacher realizes that the students' awareness of respect and connectedness is the distinctive feature that determines whether inclusion has actually occurred within the class.

This framework focuses more on the relationship between teachers and learners and less on either of them as individuals. Learning and teaching are understood as reciprocal and co-creative acts. Four questions that emerge from the framework and are essential to beginning and sustaining culturally responsive teaching are

What do we need to do to feel respected by and connected to one another? (Establishing inclusion)

How can we use relevance and choice to create a favorable disposition toward learning? (Developing attitude)

What are active ways to increase the complexity of what we are learning so that it matters to us and contributes to a pluralistic democracy? (Enhancing meaning)

How can we create an understanding that we are becoming effective in learning we value? (Engendering competence)

These questions carry the essential meaning of each of the four motivational goals. In most conventional postsecondary teaching situations their answers will be considered more the responsibility of teachers than of learners and teachers together. For each question and its related motivational goal there is an integrated set of norms, procedures, and structures that provide a holistic means to make the motivational goal a reality in a teaching situation.

Norms are the explicit assumptions, values, and purposes that are espoused by a learning group. An example of a norm is, Everyone has a right to speak from her or his own experience and perspective about what is being learned. Norms work in two fundamental ways. One is that they provide an atmosphere and a shared understanding that elicits intrinsic motivation among learners; secondly, they are the core constructs held in common that act to build community among learners. Norms not only support certain behaviors but also create expectations for behaviors.

Procedures are the teaching and learning strategies used by the teacher and learning group to work together in order to accomplish the desired learning objectives. Unlike norms and structures, they are less explicitly codified and are used relative to the topical material at hand to accommodate the varied capacities, knowledge, skills, and experiences within the learning group. They are not prescriptive. Rather, they are a variety of approaches, each of which has a theoretical, ethical, and frequently research-supported history of being an exceptionally useful means to accomplish the identified motivational goal. The motivational goal serves as a broad, thematic category in which to organize procedures to meet its essential criteria. Each procedure is a form of deliberate action. By reflecting on it, teachers and/or learners can think of specific activities that lead to learning as well as to the intended motivational goal. For example, to establish inclusion, the learning group may use the procedure of cooperative learning. A procedure may be used for a small fraction of a course or for the majority of the learning experiences in combination with other procedures. By knowing a variety of relevant procedures, teachers and learners have greater flexibility to accommodate differences among themselves and the topics to be studied.

Structures are formal patterns of organization, rules of operation, and other arrangements that determine such matters as how the learning group functions, how learning goals are achieved and assessed, and the binding expectations for individual learners. Although they may be determined by teachers or teachers and learners, they are often codified as part of the course syllabus or school bulletin. Common examples of postsecondary educational structures are course prerequisites and requirements, assessment and grading policies, and rules for attendance. Although not always self-evident, structures not only encourage particular values, they also sanction and validate specific behaviors. For example, grading along a normal curve nurtures a competitive orientation to learning and fosters highly individualized approaches to learning. By making certain structures fundamental to courses, teachers and learners can legitimize actions and outcomes conducive to enhancing motivation and equitable learning.

A congruent set of norms, procedures, and structures creates the symmetry that enables culturally responsive teaching to have its impact and evoke student motivation. Because each system supports the other—for example, norms support procedures, and structures support norms and procedures—all students have a better chance to learn. Whether you are a novice or experienced college teacher, by following the general example found below, you can peruse the norms, procedures, and structures found in this book to ascertain their potential application to your teaching.

A teacher in an urban university begins to plan for an upcoming course. The teacher knows from previous experience that the diversity in the class will approximate a group of students coming from low- to middle-income families, representing a variety of ethnicities of whom 40 percent will probably be people of color. Age is likely to range from twenty-one to fifty-five. About half the students will be women. There will be a few students with physical disabilities.

Reflecting on the rich diversity among these students and on the question for *establishing inclusion* the teacher studies the criteria, norms, procedures, and structures found in Exhibit 1.1 and decides to:

- Make collaboration an expected way of proceeding through-out the course (a norm to build a sense of community among such a diverse group)

- Create a number of learning activities using cooperative learn-ing groups (a procedure consistent with the above norm and effective as a method for enhancing motivation and learning)

- Establish ground rules with the students for the discussion of sensitive and controversial material (a structure to maintain safety and respect while engaged in dialogue)

Exhibit 1.1. Criteria, Norms, Procedures, and Structures for the Motivational Goal of Establishing Inclusion.

Question: What do we need to do to feel respected by and connected to one another?

Criteria: Respect and connectedness

Norms:

1. Coursework emphasizes the human purpose of what is being learned and its relationship to the learners' personal experiences and contemporary situations.

2. Teachers share the ownership of knowing with all learners.

3. Collaboration and cooperation are the expected ways of proceeding and learning.

4. Course perspectives assume a non-blameful and realistically hopeful view of people and their capacity to change.

5. There is equitable treatment of all learners with an invitation to point out behaviors, practices, and policies that discriminate.

Procedures:

1. Collaborative learning

2. Cooperative learning

3. Writing groups

4. Peer teaching

5. Opportunities for multidimensional sharing

6. Focus groups

7. Reframing

Structures:

1. Ground rules

2. Learning communities

3. Cooperative base groups

Thinking about the question for *developing attitude* the teacher examines the criteria, norms, procedures, and structures found in Exhibit 1.2 and decides to

- Conduct the course in ways that encourage learners to make choices about class topics and assignments based on their experiences, values, needs, and strengths (a norm to increase the relevance of the course for such a diverse group of learners)
- Use problem-solving goals and learning contracts (procedures to accommodate student choices and to respect their voice in determining topics and assignments)
- Create some learning activities suited to different profiles of multiple intelligences (a procedure to more equitably match learning experiences to the wealth of diverse intellectual strengths surely to be found among this multicultural group of students)

Exhibit 1.2. Criteria, Norms, Procedures, and Structures for the Motivational Goal of Developing Attitude.

Question: How can we use relevance and choice to create a favorable disposition toward learning?

Criteria: Relevance and self-determination

Norms:

1. Teaching and learning activities are contextualized in the learners' experience or previous knowledge and are accessible through their current thinking and ways of knowing.

2. The entire academic process of learning, from content selection to accomplishment and assessment of competencies, encourages learners to make real choices based on their experiences, values, needs, and strengths.

Procedures:

1. Learning-goal procedures

    a. Clearly defined goals

    b. Problem-solving goals

    c. Expressive outcomes

Exhibit 1.2. Criteria, Norms, Procedures, and Structures for the Motivational Goal of Developing Attitude, Cont'd.

2. Fair and clear criteria of evaluation

3. Relevant learning models

4. Goal setting

5. Learning contracts *

6. Approaches based on multiple intelligences theory

7. Sensitivity and pedagogical flexibility based on the concept of style

8. Experiential learning—the Kolb model

Structure:

1. Culturally responsive teacher-learner conferences

Continuing with a similarly reflective approach based on the question of how to *enhance meaning,* the teacher studies the criteria, norms, procedures, and structures found in Exhibit 1.3 and decides to

- Make challenging experiences that critically address relevant, real-world issues essential to learning throughout the course (a norm likely to engage the involvement of such a diverse group of students and to benefit from their backgrounds and experiences)

- Use critical questioning, posing problems, authentic research, and case studies for classwork and assignments (procedures that allow learners to construct and delve into real world issues and to utilize their strengths, experiences, and values to deepen understanding)

- Suggest projects as the main way for students to acquire course credit (a structure with the flexibility and range to accommodate in-depth learning experiences with real-world issues)

Exhibit 1.3. Criteria, Norms, Procedures and Structures for the Motivational Goal of Enhancing Meaning.

Question: What are active ways to increase the complexity of what we are learning so that it matters to us and contributes to a pluralistic democracy?

Criteria: Engagement and Challenge

Norms:

1. Learners participate in challenging learning experiences involving higher-order thinking and critical inquiry that address relevant, real-world issues in an action-oriented manner.

2. Learner expression and language are joined with teacher expression and language to form a "third idiom" that enables the perspectives of all learners to be readily shared and included in the process of learning.

Procedures:

1. Critical questioning and guided reciprocal peer questioning

2. Posing problems

3. Decision making

4. Authentic research

    a. Definitional investigation

    b. Historical investigation

    c. Projective investigation

    d. Experimental inquiry

5. Invention and artistry

6. Simulations

7. Case-study method

Structures:

1. Projects

2. The problem-posing model

Finally, with the consideration of assessment and the question related to *engendering competence*, the teacher peruses the criteria, norms, procedures, and structures found in Exhibit 1.4 and decides to:

- Make self-assessment a part of the overall assessment process (a norm for understanding the acquisition of competence through the unique and informative perspective of the learner)

- Use documentation of learning based on emerging and completed projects (a procedure that accommodates opportunities to integrate formative feedback and opportunities for students to apply their unique profiles of intelligences)

- Use contracts for grading (a structure that can reconcile the many interests, strengths, and needs of this diverse group of students with a fair assessment of their competence)

Exhibit 1.4. Criteria, Norms, Procedures, and Structures for the Motivational Goal of Engendering Competence.

Question: How can we create an understanding that we are becoming effective in learning we value?

Criteria: Authenticity and effectiveness

Norms:

1. The assessment process is connected to the learner's world, frames of reference, and values.

2. Demonstration of learning includes multiple ways to represent knowledge and skills and allows for attainment of outcomes at different points in time.

3. Self-assessment is essential to the overall assessment process.

Procedures:

1. Feedback

2. Alternatives to pencil-and-paper tests: contextualized assessment

    a. Comparing personal assessment values with actual assessment practice

    b. Generating creative alternatives to tests

    c. Documenting learning in ways that support variety in preferred approaches, developmental orientations, interests, and intelligences

3. Well-constructed paper-and-pencil tests

4. Self-assessment

Structures:

1. Overview of perspectives and approaches

2. Alternatives to conventional grading systems

    a. Narrative evaluations

    b. Credit and no credit

    c. Contracts for grades

With the use of these exhibits, the teacher now has an integrated set of norms, procedures, and structures for creating an overall approach to teaching that is more responsive to the diversity of the expected group of students. In the chapters ahead we will take each motivational goal and illuminate its social and academic value as we illustrate how to accomplish it with various subjects and in different learning situations. These chapters will include discussions of the criteria for the motivational goals and their relationship to diversity and intrinsic motivation. We will explain and exemplify the norms, procedures, and structures that contribute to meeting each of the motivational goals. This will give you a comprehensive overview of a motivation-based approach to culturally responsive teaching.

Fear, Conflict, and Resistance

Although the motivational framework we offer is comprehensive and explicitly detailed, we know from experience and the literature that not all of the ambiguities, conflicts, and dilemmas that emerge during culturally responsive teaching can be completely resolved. This is as true from the perspective of the student as it is from the view of the teacher. Yet these challenging realities are often more understandable than we might imagine. In the rest of this section we present insights and cite references that offer pragmatic ways of reckoning with many of the issues that may result from addressing diversity in the classroom.

Knowing that teacher and student resistance is predictable and often legitimate can reduce our feelings of discomfort and help us to remain effectively engaged and less reactive in challenging situations. By finding concepts useful for understanding our own as well as our students' reactions we can be less personally threatened and more open to learning. Let us begin with fear of conflict.

You are teaching a literature course in a large university. You have been careful to include in your syllabus authors from underrepresented racial and ethnic groups. At the moment a lively discussion is taking place in your class. You make a remark about the irony contained in a particular author's novel. After your comment a student who is of the same ethnicity as the author responds, "You don't know what you're talking about. That's a white middle-class interpretation." You look up, surprised, but before you can comment another student shouts out to the student who has just spoken, "That's rude! You have no right to tell anybody what they know or don't know. Just because you're a minority you think you can get away with that crap." Immediately, about four other students begin talking and yelling.

The scenario above illustrates just a few of the reactions that a culturally responsive teacher may encounter when learners are dealing with situations that touch their lives. Anxiety among teachers about such potential conflict can seem overwhelming. Gerald Weinstein and Kathy Obear (1992) speak for many of us when they say,

> Our socialization has taught us how important it is to be in control. Our worst fantasy is that the whole situation will go up in flames. There have been a number of times . . . when I have felt totally helpless in dealing with certain interactions. A participant may say something that stimulates great tension and anxiety, and a dense silence overtakes the group. The instructor becomes upset and somewhat paralyzed. All eyes are upon us, waiting to see what we will do, expecting us to take care of the situation. I cannot think of any helpful intervention. We are too upset to think clearly. It's a fearsome moment, one that we may anticipate with dread [p. 47].

The intrapersonal emotional dynamics of teachers who deal with bias and conflict are rarely described in pedagogical writing but are common, expected, and shared—in other words, normal. Those of us willing to assume some of these risks can support one another, teach one another, and reduce some of the misconceptions.

Paradoxically, we may realize the hope that often emerges following an honest discussion about collective moments of despair.

After asking a group of twenty-five university faculty from different disciplines to anonymously respond to the question, What makes you nervous about raising issues of racism in your classroom? Weinstein and Obear (1992, pp. 41–42) grouped their findings along with those found by others (Katz, 1983; Noonan, 1988; Cones, Janha, and Noonan, 1983) who had raised similar questions, under the following headings:

1. Confronting my own social and cultural identity conflicts:

    Having to become more aware of my own attitudes regarding my group memberships and identifications

    Feeling guilty, ashamed, or embarrassed for behaviors and attitudes of members of my own group

2. Having to confront or being confronted with my own bias:

    Being labeled racist, sexist, and so on

    Finding prejudice within myself

    Romanticizing the targeted group

    Having to question my own assumptions

    Having to be corrected by members of the targeted group

    Having to face my own fears of the targeted group

3. Responding to biased comments:

    Responding to biased comments from the targeted group

    Hearing biased comments from dominant members while targeted members are present

    Responding to biased remarks from members of my own social group

4. Doubts and ambivalence about my own competency:

Having to expose my own struggles with the issue

Not knowing the latest "politically correct" language

Feeling uncertain about what I am saying

Feeling that I will never unravel the complexities of the issue

Being told by a student that I don't know what I'm talking about

Making a mistake

5. Need for learner approval:

Making students frustrated, frightened, or angry

Leaving my students shaken and confused and not being able to fix it

6. Handling intense emotions; losing control:

Not knowing how to respond to angry comments

Having discussion blow up

Having anger directed at me

Being overwhelmed by strong emotions engendered by the discussion

Feeling strong emotions being stimulated in myself

Responses to Biased Expressions

In the chapter that lists these findings, Gerald Weinstein reflects on his personal experience with teaching fears and offers suggestions he and his colleagues have found useful in coping with them. His first-person description provides a humane and reassuring illustration of the apprehensions that can surface, and it offers some concrete skills and methods that can prevent and diffuse uncomfortable situations. The following narrative addresses one way of responding to biased expressions (Weinstein and Obear, 1992, pp. 43–45):

> Targeted group members usually have a long history of developing sensitivity to certain negative cues. They have been subjected to them, suffered from them, discussed and thought about them throughout the course of their lives. Therefore, most are very sensitive to such signals. Typically, members of nontargeted groups have been so effectively and monoculturally socialized that they consider their languaging "natural." They are usually unaware of whom they are cueing and are shocked when someone takes offense. We call these cues and signals *triggers*.
>
> Triggers are recurring phenomena in our workshops and classes. These are certain words, phrases, or concepts usually communicated by members of the nontargeted group about a targeted group or individual that signal an oppressive attitude toward that group. Some are blatantly obvious: "a woman's place is in the home"; "Blacks seem to want to stick together"; "the Jewish media"; "homosexuals are abnormal." Others are more subtle: "I don't see people as black, brown, red, yellow, or white. To me they're just people"; "I always hear Jews making fun of themselves"; "They aren't the only ones who suffered"; "they're just not as qualified."
>
> Triggers may immediately stimulate the defenses of the person whose group is being commented on, or an ally of that group, and can elicit intense emotional reactions. Responses to triggers can be especially volatile in a mixed setting of targeted and nontargeted groups. What often occurs is that one person makes the statement that triggers another student to respond in a confrontational or defensive style. The original "trigger giver" often will argue for the truth of what was said, or state that it was never his or her intention to give offense and that the respondent seems to be "overly sensi-

tive." This comment in turn may become another trigger. The exchange typically continues with a painful and unproductive debate of increasing intensity. It can sometimes lead to the shutdown of group discussion in stifling silence and barely controlled frustration. It is a fearful situation for the instructor, and one that is very difficult to manage.

An alternative is to raise the general issue of triggers at the outset and describe what they are and how they are experienced differently by members of the dominant and targeted groups.

It is important to handle the discussion of triggers so that the members of both dominant and targeted groups are validated as individuals. Targeted members have a right to ask that others be sensitive to their own language. Trigger givers need to understand that they came by their socialization innocently. They did not ask to be raised in racist, sexist, classist, homophobic, anti-Semitic society. They do not need to be assisted in castigating themselves but encouraged to learn how they have been socialized and how to gain control over their thoughts and feelings. One measure of success may be the extent to which individuals can self-monitor potential triggers for different groups.

. . . plan anticipated responses in part by establishing *ground rules*. That principle is demonstrated by initially introducing the concept of triggers and having learners supply their own examples before any arise spontaneously. A useful ground rule might be: "Anytime someone feels triggered, including myself, we can say 'trigger' or 'there is one for me' and we post the trigger on newsprint. Later in our session we can review them." By not having to deal with the trigger at that moment we create some distance between the person who gave the trigger and analysis of the trigger itself. The focus can then be on understanding the concept rather than dealing with the defenses of individuals.

Let us return to the literature class scenario that introduces this section. Without knowing the people or the immediate history of the course we can say that the teacher at the very least can: (1) give everyone a brief time out, (2) have people record their own immediate responses in their notebooks, (3) allow each member of the class to share responses with one other person, and (4) ask for any suggestions or ideas from the group concerning what just happened (Weinstein and Obear, 1992). Such a procedure might lead to setting new ground rules for further discussion and a host of other possibilities for enhancing communication and cohesion, material that we will cover in the next chapter.

Stages of Racial Identity Development

Concerning matters of race, a possible way of understanding tension and conflict in the classroom is that it results from the collision of developmental processes that are necessary for the racial identity development of the individuals involved (Tatum, 1992). Although space allows for only the summarization of one theory of racial identity development theory, there are a number of models that have been specifically formulated for black, white, Asian, Latina/o, or American Indian students (Cross, 1991; Helms, 1990; and Phinney, 1990). Each assumes that a positive sense of one's self as a member of one's group (which is not predicated on any assumed superiority) is vital to psychological well-being. Also, in a society where racial group membership is emphasized, the development of a racial identity will occur in some form for everyone. Most of these theories are *stage* theories, which means they describe states of consciousness or world views that are developmental in nature and that change over time in response to experience and knowledge to become more complex and adequate for examining and understanding one's own beliefs, values, and behaviors. People usually move from one stage to another when they recognize that their current world view is illogical or contradicted by new experience and information, detrimental to their well-being, or no longer serving some important self-interest. Using this paradigm, Hardiman and

Jackson (1992) have created a synthesis from their evolving work on the development of racial identity in black and white Americans. They use racial/color designators rather than ethnic terms such as African American to highlight the discrimination aspect of the interactions implied by the model. The following discussion (pp. 24–34) summarizes their developmental framework:

Stage One —Naive

The naive stage of consciousness describes the consciousness of race in childhood when there is little or no social awareness of race per se. Members of both dominant and target groups are vulnerable to the logic system and world view of their socializing agent such as parents, teachers, and so forth.

Stage Two—Acceptance

In the transition from naive to acceptance children begin to learn the ideology about their own racial groups as well as other racial groups. They begin to learn there are formal and informal rules that permit some behaviors and prohibit others in terms of how the races relate to each other.

The stage of acceptance represents the absorption, whether conscious or unconscious, of an ideology of racial dominance and subordination which touches upon all facets of personal and public life. A person at this stage has accepted the messages about racial group membership, the superiority of the dominant group members and the dominant culture, and the inferiority of target group people and cultures.

Stage Three—Resistance

The transition from acceptance to resistance marks a period that can be confusing and often painful for both targets (Blacks) and dominants (Whites). The transition generally evolves over time and usually results from a number of events that have a cumulative effect. People begin to be aware of experiences that contradict the acceptance world view. The contradictions that initiate the transition period can arise from interactions with people, social events, information presented in classes, stories in the media, or responses to so-called racial incidents on campus.

The initial questioning that begins during the exit phase of acceptance continues with greater intensity during the third stage, resistance. The world view that people adopt at resistance is dramatically different from that of acceptance. At this stage members of both target and dominant groups begin to understand and recognize racism in many of its complex and multiple manifestations—at the individual and institutional, conscious and unconscious, intentional and unintentional, attitudinal, behavioral, and policy levels. Individuals become painfully aware of the numerous ways in which covert as well as overt racism affect them daily as members of racial identity groups.

Resistance can manifest itself as active or passive. For example, for Whites, active resistance may show itself as indiscriminately challenging racism in many spheres and distancing themselves from White culture and people, and simultaneously "adopting" or borrowing the traditions and cultural expressions of communities of color. An example for Blacks of active resistance might be challenging and confronting Whites, especially those in positions of authority, and challenging or writing off Black faculty and administrators who are seen as not Black enough or as colluding with the White system. Passive resistance appears more unlikely for Blacks than for Whites and usually manifests itself as some form of withdrawal or "dropping out." Among traditional college-age students both White students and Black students are more likely to enter college at the acceptance stage and experience primarily the resistance stage during their college years.

Stage Four—Redefinition

The transition from resistance to redefinition occurs when members of both racial groups realize that they do not really know who they are, racially speaking, or what their racial group membership means to them. At resistance, they recognized that their sense of themselves as Whites or as Blacks has been defined for them in a White racist environment, and they actively sought to question it or reject aspects of it. Now they are no longer actively consumed by rejection, but the loss of prior self-definition of Blackness or Whiteness leaves them with a void.

Whites during the redefinition stage often redirect their energy in order to define Whiteness in a way that is not dependent on racism or on the existence of perceived deficiencies in other groups. There is a recognition that all cultures and racial groups have unique and different traits that enrich the human experience, that no race or culture is superior to another. They are all unique, different, and adaptive.

The redefinition stage is the point in the development process at which the Black person is concerned with defining himself or herself in terms that are independent of the perceived strengths or weaknesses of Whites and the dominant White culture. It is here that Black people shift their attention and energy toward a concern for primary contact and interaction with other Blacks at the same stage of consciousness. They find that many elements of Black culture that have been handed down through the generations still affect their lives, and the uniqueness of their group becomes clearer. They come to understand that they are more than victims of racism, more than just people who are not the same as the dominant group—in ways that engender pride.

Stage Five—Internalization

The transition from the redefinition stage to the internalization stage occurs when an individual begins to integrate some of their newly defined values, beliefs, and behaviors in all aspects of life. When the redefined sense of racial identity is fully integrated, the new values or beliefs occur naturally and are internalized as part of the person.

Indicators of internalization for Blacks include: recognition that their Black identity is a critical part of them, but not the only significant aspect of their identity; and the ability to consider other identity issues and other issues of oppression. Indicators of internalization for Whites include: a clear sense of their own self-interest as members of the White group in ending racism; acting on that self-interest; and not seeing others as "culturally different" and Whites as normal, but rather understanding how White European-American culture is different as well.

Racial identity development models can be viewed as roughly outlined maps of a journey from an identity in which racism and domination are internalized to an identity that is affirming and liberated from racism. We strongly agree with Hardiman and Jackson (1992) when they caution against using this model simplistically to label or stereotype students or others. Most people are in several stages simultaneously, holding different perspectives on the complex range of issues that relate to their racial identity. Such models can assist us in recognizing our own racial identity issues and how they may influence our teaching and reaction to students. They also help us to be less surprised or threatened by the strength and variety of student attitudes as well as their heightened emotions as they react to cultural issues. By appreciating these developmental processes, we are more likely to learn ways to avoid prematurely stifling, artificially hastening, or unfairly condemning the behavior of students as they grapple with topics and themes that confront their differences.

For courses that address multicultural issues, sharing models of racial identity development with students gives them a useful framework for understanding each others' reactions. This can normalize their experience and reduce their fears, resistance, and potential resentment. As Beverly Daniel Tatum (1992) writes:

In a course on the psychology of racism, it is easy to build in the pro-
vision of this information as part of the course content. For instructors teaching courses with race-related content in other fields, it may
seem less natural to do so. However, the inclusion of articles on
racial identity development and/or class discussion of these issues in
conjunction with other strategies . . . can improve student receptivity to the course content in important ways, making it a very useful investment of class time. Because the stages describe kinds of
behavior that many people have commonly observed in themselves,
as well as in their own intraracial and interracial interactions, my
experience has been that most students grasp the basic conceptual
framework fairly easily, even if they do not have a background in
psychology [p. 20].

Returning to the classroom incident that introduced this section, if a racial identity development framework were understood
by the teacher and students, this altercation might have been less
likely to occur. And if it did happen as stated, the teacher would
have been more likely to recognize the aggressive accusation as part
of a pattern of active resistance by the student, been less surprised
by it, and been more able to effectively respond to it. In addition,
the student who shouted, "That's rude!" might not have done so in
the first place, making the entire interaction less inflammatory.
There is no guarantee this revision would occur, but an understanding of racial identity development theory does lessen the lack
of awareness that can so easily lead to blame and anger.

Different Ways of Knowing

Conflict can also occur because of the different ways in which people construct what they know. Based on their interviews of students
as they moved through their undergraduate years at Harvard,
William Perry and his colleagues (1970) documented a scheme of
intellectual development that described how students give mean-

ing to their experience and understand themselves as knowers. Perry traced a progression from an initial position he called *basic dualism*, where the students view the world in polarities of right/ wrong, we/they, and good/bad. The final stage of this hierarchical sequence is position nine, *full relativism*, when the student comprehends that truth is relative, that the meaning of an event depends on the context in which the event occurs and on the framework that the knower uses to understand the event. Students are also able to see that relativism pervades all aspects of life, including and beyond the academic world. Students at the lower positions are understood to be more likely to view teachers as authority figures who dispense knowledge. These students tend to understand their role as filtering out the right answers from the material presented. Those at the higher end of the hierarchy are more likely to see their teachers as experts who guide them through a search for the relationships among ideas and information. Educators have used the Perry scheme as a developmental framework to guide educational practice.

Building on Perry's scheme but realizing the limitations of its perspective—interviews with a relatively homogeneous group of men in an elite university—Belenky, Clinchy, Goldberger, and Tarule (1986) studied the ways of knowing of women of widely different ages, life circumstances, and backgrounds. From their in-depth interviews with 135 women they found that the developmental stages outlined by Perry are far less obvious. They grouped women's perspectives on knowing into the following five major categories. These groupings (1986, p. 15) are not fixed, exhaustive, or universal, and similar categories can be found in men's thinking.

> *Silence*, a position in which women experience themselves as mindless and voiceless and subject to the whims of external authority. They have little awareness of their intellectual capabilities and believe people such as experts and teachers know the truth.

Received knowledge, a perspective from which women experience themselves as capable of receiving, even reproducing,
knowledge from the all-knowing external authorities but
not capable of creating knowledge on their own. Other
voices and external truths prevail, and the sense of self is
often embedded in sex-role stereotypes or in identification
with an institution. Their perception of the world tends to
be literal and concrete, good or bad.

Subjective knowledge, a perspective from which truth and
knowledge are conceived as personal, private, and subjectively known or intuited. For women, this often means a
turning away from external authority with the locus of truth
shifting to the self. There is a tendency to value intuition
over logic and abstraction. It is here women begin to gain a
voice.

Procedural knowledge, a position in which women are invested
in learning and applying objective procedures for obtaining
and communicating knowledge. Women often feel a greater
sense of control and seek real-life opportunities for exercis-
ing their own authority.

Constructed knowledge, a position in which women view all
knowledge as contextual, experience themselves as creators
of knowledge, and value both subjective and objective
strategies for knowing. In this stage there is the integration
of personal knowing with knowledge learned from others as
well as the development of an authentic voice.

As they conducted their study of women's ways of knowing,
Belenky and her colleagues documented two distinctive forms of
procedural knowledge. Referring to the work of Gilligan (1982) and
Lyons (1983) they called these orientations *separate knowing* and
connected knowing. Separate knowing is based on impersonal procedures for establishing truth, such as the scientific method. It is an

orientation where critical thinking, doubt, and rational argument are essential procedures. In connected knowing, truth emerges through care. It is a perspective based on the conviction that the most trustworthy knowledge comes from personal experience. Knowing comes from empathy and reception when people "open up" to receive another's experience into their own minds. In connected knowing, people understand other people's ideas in the other people's terms rather than in their own terms. These researchers believe that connected knowing comes more easily to many women than does separate knowing.

Frequently, as teachers we assert our intellectual authority by referring to research. "The research says . . ." and "A study has found . . ." are expressions as natural to us as saying hello. Often, for some of our students, what the "research says" is questionable based on their personal experience (connected knowing). When these learners offer their conflicting perspective, a question can emerge within the class as to which position exerts greater authority. Because of different ways of knowing, debate will not usually settle this issue. Also, in a contentious atmosphere questions from the teacher such as, "Do you have any research to support that opinion?" often only frustrate or silence rather than enlighten the discussion. To avoid discounting our students' voices and to encourage constructed knowledge and dialogue, we can request learners to use their experience to inform our opinions and research-based generalizations as we present them. This approach is likely to lead to a more balanced and perhaps more truthful understanding for all of us.

Different Belief Systems

Societies throughout the world differ in their belief systems. Social roles, codes of behavior, and what is considered to be true can vary remarkably among a group of diverse learners, often more so when international students are present. The status of teachers may be much higher in one society than in another. Some students may see important and knowledgeable remarks as forthcoming only from the teacher and not from other students. The roles of men and women may be rigidly defined. Even with such a short list of possibilities, one can see how questioning the intellectual authority of the teacher or a procedure like cooperative learning could lead to tension, resistance, or conflict for some students. By studying patterns of values based on belief systems, Geert Hofstede (1986) has found characteristic dimensions that are more strongly present in some countries as compared to other countries. For example, *uncertainty avoidance* is the extent to which people within a culture are made nervous by situations that they perceive as unstructured, unclear, or unpredictable. These cultures are often characterized by strict codes of behavior and belief systems anchored in absolute truths. To illustrate, on Hofstede's continuum, Japan is considerably stronger in uncertainty avoidance than is Hong Kong.

Although the unit of analysis to arrive at these characteristic dimensions has been a country, theoretically they might apply to any number of specific populations including religious or occupational configurations. Different people see and react to the same thing differently for many reasons that are beyond their immediate awareness or control. When we consider racial identity development processes, different ways of knowing, and different belief systems, we see how profound the influences of culture are and how legitimate the sources of conflict within a class of diverse students may be. This is why students must learn to succeed in classes that appreciate diversity. Cultural diversity is central to their future, and they must *learn to learn and work* with knowledge and skills that accommodate its rich complexity.

The assumptions we bring as teachers about how people know and how to know are crucial in determining the atmosphere and discourse of learning in our courses. Most interpersonal conflict is caused by different perceptions or understandings of an event, a person, or an idea. When arguments are based on culturally different assumptions such as religious beliefs, two or more persons may disagree without one being right and the other being wrong (Pedersen, 1994). The issues of controversy can range from the morality of capital punishment to the value of particular scientific inventions.

Truth in a multicultural world is not entirely indeterminate. There are facts. Nurturing freedom of expression in a learning environment does not have to be confused with an obligation to facilitate every point of view. But purpose plays a pivotal role. If the goal of a learning group is to deepen its understanding of *what the truth may be*, rather than to find out *who knows the truth*, then a real dialogue, a "thinking together," is more likely to occur. Under such circumstances the group has a much better chance to discover insights not attainable individually (Senge, 1990).

No single strategy works best in all situations of conflict, especially when that conflict is multicultural. There are numerous models for confronting, mediating, and resolving conflict. Most have to do with helping the parties involved find common ground among their purposes and expectations. We have found the work of Pedersen and Ivey (1993) to be very informative. Our experience and the literature (Amir, 1969) strongly support the understanding that a well-planned approach and a proactive stance in matters of cultural relations prevent dysfunctional conflict, conflict that threatens to erode the consensus that brings a group together. This is one of the main reasons why our approach to culturally responsive teaching is organized within an integrated set of norms, procedures, and structures. They form a symmetry that respects diversity while establishing and maintaining a common classroom culture that all students can relate to with integrity.

Resistance

In addition to a complex variety of beliefs there are many apprehensions toward issues of diversity and culturally responsive teaching that can lead to resistance. The resistance may be a reaction to a particular topic, but it also may be a response to methods of teaching, assignments, and other aspects of pedagogical practice.

From her teaching in predominantly European-American college classrooms, Tatum (1992) documents that frequently students consider race a taboo topic for discussion, especially in racially mixed settings. She also finds that many students, regardless of racial group membership, are uncomfortable with an understanding of racism as a system of advantage for European Americans over people of color because it contradicts their socialization to think of the United States as a just society where rewards are based on one's merit. Gale Auletta and Terry Jones (1994) have found that some students and faculty believe that acts of racial bias must be mean-spirited and/or conscious to signify racism. They offer the insight that some portion of the racial uneasiness that is felt in many college classrooms may be due to differences in perception about what constitutes racism.

In addition to reasons such as these, students and teachers may remain silent or unresponsive to issues of diversity because of justifications that can include fear of being misunderstood, anxiety about disclosing too much and becoming too vulnerable, memories of former bad experiences of speaking out, fear of creating anger the group cannot manage, confusion about level of trust, and resentment for having to prove one is not "the enemy." Based on her experience as a college teacher with such issues of disclosure and controversial matters of diversity (her course occurred during a campuswide crisis over visible acts of racism), Elizabeth Ellsworth (1989) does not believe that dialogue as a pedagogical strategy can surmount the power relations in class or the personal, fragmentary, and unstable nature of knowledge. In her opinion, the belief that rational agreement based on universal moral principles can be attained in controversial matters may more often mislead students than liberate them. We agree there are times when history, context, the issues at hand, and the orientations of the people present reveal the inadequacy of a reasoned perspective. At issue here is not the rejection of reason but the notion that reason is not the total way to know something. Art, insight, creativity, humor, intuition, and the spiritual may not be rational but they may approach a greater wisdom. In certain matters, heeding resistance, putting analysis and the quest for solution aside, and moving on to other ways of knowing and learning may approach a profoundness not otherwise available.

Seeing resistance from a number of perspectives helps us to realize that as a human process it has many forms, that it can be self-protective and personally and socially restrictive, but also that it can reflect perceptiveness and socially beneficial strivings. Most resistance appears to stem from apprehensions about vulnerabiliity or control. Although the advocacy of this book is clearly to change conventional teaching practices, we realize things hardly ever go easily during change efforts. Most college students have gone through secondary schools where teaching methods still mimic those used in universities. They may not be thrilled about how they were taught, but they adapted, were generally successful by the standards applied, and have formed habits and expectations that may run counter to some of the suggested teaching approaches found in this book. To label their fearfulness, reluctance to buy in, complacency, or failure to recognize the need for change as resistance is usually ineffectual. It can divert attention from such real concerns as inadequate teaching skills, dubious assessment practices, or the need for more clarity regarding learning goals. Such labeling tends to be blameful, places more of the responsibility for the solution on the students, and leads to thinking that immobilizes our creativity.

We prefer an understanding of resistance as a concern about facing difficult realities that is expressed indirectly. For example, if some students maintain that there is not enough time to discuss a controversial topic when the time is actually available, they are probably being resistant. However, if there really is not enough time for an adequate discussion, they are judiciously expressing a realistic concern.

We do not have a formulaic set of guidelines for dealing with resistance. We have found it to be so contextually determined (who, where, when, what, and so forth) that a recommended series of steps flies in the face of the complexity and variation inherent in this reaction. We have found that focusing on the positive meanings and functions of resistance is vastly more informative to our teaching than focusing on the negative. For example, the perception "Indirectly, we are being told to proceed more slowly and cautiously, to make the situation safer, to provide concrete results" is more constructive than "They only want to avoid; they are cynical; they don't want to do the work." Respectfully listening and soliciting information about the nature of learner concerns usually provides insights. We often ask for examples and evidence of the problem as well as suggestions for other courses of action. One communication technique we have frequently found helpful is to use "suppose" or words to that effect to introduce ideas, to probe a comment, or to keep a conversation more open: "Suppose we . . ."

In general, gradually shifting toward a more culturally responsive pedagogy involves new and flexible approaches to teaching and intense personal learning. Both teachers and students need to assess such change for its genuine possibilities and to comprehend its effect on their self-interest. Initially, there may be little certainty about the kinds of processes or outcomes that may ensue and less assurance that they will be any better than the status quo. These are legitimate issues that deserve careful attention. The chapters that follow are written with mindful respect for this inevitable and salubrious scrutiny.

Chapter Two

Establishing Inclusion

Education can never be merely for the sake of
  individual self-enhancement.
It pulls us into the common world or it fails
  altogether.

—Robert Bellah

Anyone who sincerely seeks to be culturally responsive as a teacher simultaneously embraces two challenges: to create with learners a genuine community and to promote justice and equity in the society at large. As we will see in this chapter, the impetus for innovations such as collaborative learning and learning communities lies as much in their capacity to help us learn how to make a more cooperative world as it does in their instructional effectiveness for the individual learner. Feelings of cultural isolation often deteriorate student motivation to learn. In a classroom a sense of community with which all students can identify establishes the foundation for inclusion.

Our ability to create community is prompted and supported by natural human traits and qualities. We are community-forming beings. Our capacity to create and recreate social coherence is always there, enduring and irrepressible (Gardner, 1991). It is in communities that we find security, identity, shared values, and people who care about us and whom we care about. This is where our

ideals of justice and compassion are nurtured. We do not live ethical lives by following the precepts of intellectual philosophies. Our
worlds are built from experience up, not from abstractions down
(Wolfe, 1993). The practices that ensure our freedom, whether
they be an individual act of kindness or a free press, are learned
and constructed where the connection among people is felt as living and real.

The word community has its roots in two Latin words: *commu-
nitas*, the association of people on mutually equal and friendly
terms, and *communis*, belonging to all. A visual image of community as well as its root meaning set the context for how the motivational goal of *establishing inclusion* can be accomplished in a
learning environment. In such a setting, learners and teachers know
they are included because they are *respected by and connected to one
another*. In other words, in real communities there are most likely
to be the norms and experiences present that allow people to feel
respected and connected. To hear a person genuinely say, "I feel a
sense of community in that class," is a compliment of the highest
order to every member of that group. Let us now take a look at why
the criteria of respect and connectedness are so important to the
intrinsic motivation of all learners.

Respect, Connectedness, and Intrinsic Motivation

Often it is mentioned that classes should be conducted in an
"atmosphere of mutual respect." What does that really mean? We
understand respect in a learning environment to mean that the
integrity of each person is valued in ways that welcome the worth
and expression of one's true self without fear of threat or blame. In
such an atmosphere, people know they are respected because they
feel safe, capable, and accepted.

In a climate of respect, intrinsic motivation can emerge because
people can be authentic and spontaneous and can accept full
responsibility for their actions. These are the qualities of self-deter-

mination, which is a hallmark of intrinsic motivation; they are qualities fear and alienation quickly suppress.

Connectedness in a learning group is a sense of belonging for each individual and a felt awareness that one is cared for and one cares for others. There is a shared foundational purpose to support each other's well-being. In such an environment, people feel trust, some degree of community, and emotional bonds with others; because of this, there exists a spirit of tolerance and loyalty that allows for a measure of uncertainty and dissent.

Feeling connected elicits intrinsic motivation in people not only because their basic social needs are being met but also because they are in groups in which their authentic selves are endorsed. They can freely enter into meaningful discussions and relevant action. When we are in a group in which we do not feel included we are far more likely to guard our resources, strengths, and weaknesses to protect ourselves from others. Feeling related to others helps us to recognize individual concerns as collective issues rather than strictly problems for those directly experiencing them. Not accidentally, we are much more likely to feel connected to those who respect us.

Inclusion is at the core of genuine empowerment and agency. True agency means more than knowing how and being able to attain learning outcomes; it means feeling free enough to make authentic and relevant choices with respect to those outcomes (Deci and Ryan, 1991). We seldom do this unless we are learning in groups in which we feel included, where some degree of harmony and community exists. Even the approximation to such unity is a powerful force for engendering learning and motivation.

Norms for Establishing Inclusion

For each of the motivational goals presented in this book we offer a set of norms. Norms provide an atmosphere and a shared understanding that elicits intrinsic motivation among learners. They are the core constructs held in common that act to build community among learners. Norms not only support certain behaviors but also create expectations for behaviors. For the specific motivational goal of inclusion and for the broader purpose of culturally responsive teaching, these conditions are essential. To respect cultural differences among learners and to integrate diversity into the study of any subject matter means possibly addressing controversy and conflict. Norms can provide the kind of atmosphere and understanding that allow highly charged feelings and responses to be buffered as well as acknowledged and considered by the learning group. Thus motivation, learning, and teaching are greatly enhanced. Based on our experience and study we offer the following norms to foster inclusion in any learning setting.

1. *Coursework emphasizes the human purpose of what is being learned and its relationship to the learners' personal experiences and contemporary situations.* People can feel a part of something that is relevant to them. They adhere to a group because it somehow meets their personal needs. A human goal is a goal every learner can potentially share, care deeply about, and work in common to achieve. A relevant academic goal is a goal that is authentically connected to the learner's world and frames of reference. A learning goal with salient relevancy and human purpose has the potential to become a shared vision among class members. It is capable of inspiring participation, responsibility, and action.

Anything that is taught somehow bears a relationship to a human need or interest. Otherwise, why would we teach it? For us as teachers, the question is, what are the human ramifications of what we are helping learners to know or do? Once we have an answer to this question, the relevance to our learners of what we teach will be clearer, especially if we can find a way with them to relate it to all of our daily lives. For example, learning about health care is one thing. But learning about health care to improve the quality of our daily lives or the lives of members of our immediate community is quite another kind of task. In the same vein, studying a set of health topics in order to assist others in our own families makes this learning of obvious value.

Whenever we and our students understand that our learning is connected to real-world issues it becomes more apparent that different perspectives lead to different viewpoints and the diversity in the learning group has value for perceiving the complexity and depth of these issues. When our topics lie more in the realm of physical and natural sciences such as biology, chemistry, physics, and geology, showing how these courses of study and their knowledge relate to understanding challenges faced by humanity or how they can make life more sane and peaceful for everyone helps to bond learners in a common cause. Using human problems to learn and practice skills from disciplines as divergent as math to medicine can help to create teamwork and a sense of solidarity among learners.

McMaster University in Ontario, Canada, has developed a problem-based program in medical education that allows learners to focus on real-life issues and challenges. This program has fundamentally altered this frequently competitive arena into a cooperative venture, a teaching practice now implemented in numerous other universities (Aspy, Aspy, and Quinby, 1993). In the Freirean approach (McLaren and Leonard, 1993) a student-centered dialogue occurs in the first hour of class around problems posed from everyday life as well as topical issues from society and the academic subject matter. Students have equal speaking rights in the dialogue as well as the right to negotiate the curriculum. Taking a critical attitude toward discrimination and inequality, the students co-develop a process to inquire into the problems posed and seek an action outcome whenever feasible. As teachers, the closer we bring the purpose of our course to the humanity we hold in common with our learners, the more we can share a hope for a better world. Ultimately, it is the hope that binds us in a peaceful search for understanding, wisdom, and skill.

2. *Teachers share the ownership of knowing with all learners.* This is a value that establishes the dynamic to encourage all learners'

understanding of their own construction of meaning and the integrity of their own thinking (Oldfather, 1992). It undergirds a deeply shared responsiveness to each class member's oral, written and artistic self-expression. According to this norm, the thoughts, feelings, interests, and needs of every learner in the community are invited, listened and responded to, acted upon, and honored. This condition embraces the notion of *voice*, which in the view of feminists and critical theorists expresses our innermost knowing and feeling (Gilligan, 1982; Lather, 1991; Apple, 1982; Freire, 1970).

From this perspective, truth is a process of construction in which the knower participates (Belenky, Clinchy, Goldberger, and Tarule, 1986). To trust one's own thinking, to gain epistemological confidence, is essential for intrinsic motivation to occur. How many times have we heard, "Those students just don't like to think"? Well, if it isn't our own thinking, if we don't agree and we cannot say we see things differently without fear of rejection or threat, then thinking is not very appealing.

Telling and hearing our stories is essential to human nature. It is personal. It is the way we make sense of things. It is compelling. To know we are using our own powers of mind to transcend what we know, to play with ideas, and to realize clearly what was once vastly incommunicable is a kind of ecstasy.

Perry (1970) found in a study of predominantly male students that those who moved from a view of knowledge as absolute to a view of knowledge as mutable and as subject to multiple perspectives were able to affirm their own personal identities. Belenky, Clinchy, Goldberger, and Tarule (1986) found the personal construction of knowledge to be a salient feature in some women's motivation to learn. When learners know that the having and sharing of ideas, assumptions, and hypotheses is a sincerely respected way of being in a learning environment, they will be more likely to expose their thinking. In fact, it is one of the few ways they can come to realize that there are multiple viewpoints on any issue and to appreciate how others also use the process of construction for their own learning and grasp of knowledge and truth.

3. *Collaboration and cooperation are upheld as the expected ways of proceeding and learning.* People often work together. People can help each other. People are concerned that everyone makes relevant progress in learning. The fundamental orientation of the group is to get along. People are encouraged to see themselves as a "community of learners."

The West African proverb "I am because we are and we are because I am" helps us understand the mistaken perception that there is an inherent conflict between autonomy and community. People are usually autonomously interdependent: willing to depend on others and wanting to authentically provide care for them, realizing that by having their emotional needs met they have the emotional freedom to meet the needs of others. It is through relationships and support that most people meet their individual hopes, and it is often through freedom of individual expression that many groups find ways to remain cohesive and strong.

When learners work within a competitive framework, communication is often more difficult and more easily misleading. Helping may be viewed as cheating, and there is frequently an aura of suspicion (Johnson, Johnson, and Smith, 1991). Competitive and individualistic learning environments minimize sharing the ownership of knowing and usually detract from seeing learning goals as having a common human purpose. In such situations many learners, especially those from supportive and interdependent ethnic minority communities, tend to feel isolated (Cuseo, 1993). There is extensive research at the postsecondary level indicating that higher individual achievement, intrinsic motivation, and more positive interpersonal relationships result from cooperative than from competitive or individualistic learning (Johnson and Johnson, 1993; Astin, 1993b).

Cooperative learning also tends to promote greater cognitive and affective perspective taking, the ability to understand how a

situation appears to another person and how that person is reacting to the situation (Johnson and Johnson, 1989). We as well as
our learners live in a complex, interconnected world in which
many different ethnic and cultural groups continuously interact
and where dependencies limit the flexibility of individuals and
nations. We need to learn the constructive competencies involved
in managing interdependence and making shared meaning from
conflicts. Skills as well as caring relationships come from mutual
accomplishment and the bonding that results from joint efforts.
Willingness to listen and to influence and be influenced by others is a consistent finding in cooperative learning situations (Johnson and Johnson, 1991).

Never before in the history of postsecondary education has
there been a more diverse body of learners (Levine, 1989). Part-
time students make up almost one-half of the students at public
four-year colleges and two-thirds of the population at public two-
year colleges. In 1989, an estimated 69 percent of all entering fresh-
men were commuters. The dramatic increase of adult learners has
raised the average age of today's college student to twenty-six. Pro-
jecting from such demographic trends informs us that only about
20 percent of the total college population is made up of traditional
full-time, residential students whose ages are from eighteen to
twenty-two (Levine, 1989).

With more and more learners sandwiching their education
between work and family, the curriculum and the forum in which
learning occurs may provide critical opportunities to experience
community and a sense of belonging. Diversity within such a tran-
sient and demanding milieu is likely to be more overwhelming for
everyone. Short-term exposure of underrepresented ethnic minorities to a system dominated and bureaucratically administered by
middle-class European Americans may exacerbate historical mistrust and personal experiences of alienation. Mere contact with
those different from ourselves does little to enhance interracial or

intercultural appreciation. Mutual respect and appreciation evolve from the nature of the contact. Most human beings—European Americans, people of color, women, international students—favor learning experiences that are collaborative and participatory. It simply makes sense to set a tone in which learners can come together in friendly, caring, and supportive ways (Cuseo, 1993).

Without a set of cooperative values firmly embedded in the learning environment there is little chance for diversity to become a pedagogical asset and for the occurrence of the kinds of cross-cultural dialogue and learning experiences that reduce bias and transform higher education from a privileged system to an institution that is a living conduit for justice, equity, and global peace. Alexander Astin's remarks (1993a, p. 5) underscore this perspective:

> I am convinced the only hope for the future is a cooperative world view. I believe that all significant human progress has come as a result of cooperation . . . And if we really believe that cooperative endeavor is the best solution to the human dilemma, then we have to exemplify that belief in the way we run our institutions.
>
> That is why I believe that higher education has great power to change the world for the better. We can multiply our effectiveness by exemplifying in everything that we do the values we feel represent the most noble side of human nature. What I am saying is that we are not powerless; we all have the freedom to decide—even in our daily work on a campus— which world view we will see prevail.

4. *Course perspectives assume a non-blameful and realistically hopeful view of people and their capacity to change.* Justice and equity inhabit a hopeful consciousness. They do not reside in those places where cynicism and accusation reign. The fate and faith of multiculturalism lie in a belief in a better and more peaceful world where different human beings have found essential common bonds. Unless education in the classroom, at its most fundamental level, reflects

this perspective, the developmental experience of learners will be contrary to this ideal. Students, unfortunately, will learn to ridicule rather than to embrace such a dream.

People are not only selfish and narcissistic but also decent and concerned about the pain of others. It is as "natural" to help as it is to hurt (Kohn, 1990). In teaching, a realistically hopeful view of human nature respects this possibility and affirms learners' assets and strengths, recognizing that it is the action founded on this belief that will lead to ethical and relevant accomplishments. This is not "positive thinking" nor the superficial mentality of clichés on buttons and bumper stickers. A realistically hopeful view of people is not a mask or an analgesic to smother problems and difficulties in phony feel-good affirmations. Human suffering is not ignored. This is a way of thinking that pays attention to opportunity, gives the benefit of doubt, expects learners to do well, and finds joy in the process of working toward the solution of human problems.

From this point of view a learning environment is a place (filled with people) in which multiple worlds of experience exist. Individuals will change their behavior when changes in the interactions in this system allow them to perceive different behaviors as appropriate and possible (Molnar and Lindquist, 1989). Therefore, something such as a cultural misunderstanding between people is seen as an opportunity for learning rather than as a basis of estrangement.

While this norm acknowledges how compelling the need to blame is, it does not condone the act of blaming. In our experience, of all human propensities, blame is among the most damaging to relationships among people, especially culturally different people. Blame frequently provokes and sanctions our inhumanity to one another. Once blame occurs, a cycle of attitudes and actions can emerge whose reciprocal destruction is often only surpassed by the mutual incomprehension of those involved.

Yet we must acknowledge how extremely powerful the grip of blame is for most of us. The act of blaming releases three highly desirable states of consciousness. The first is a sense of control over whatever the situation is. Life is less chaotic. We can find fault. We can, at the very least, accuse. The second is the reduction of guilt. Our misery is not of our own making. It's not me, it's them. The third is the arrogant belief we do not have to change. "They" (usually the *other* person, racial or ethnic group, gender, and so on) have to change. In a single thought, blame can relax us or set off the nuclear fission of our righteous indignation. It is an insidious and explosive tonic.

The blame cycle in Figure 2.1 graphically represents the series of outcomes that seem to emerge automatically and then recur, with devastating impact on the relationship of the people involved. In this instance the cycle occurs in the relationship between a teacher and a student.

Let us say that in this case there is a difference in perspective between the teacher and the student regarding required assignments. It could be a series of papers or small projects. At the top of the cycle the teacher wants to help because the student appears to

Figure 2.1. The Blame Cycle.

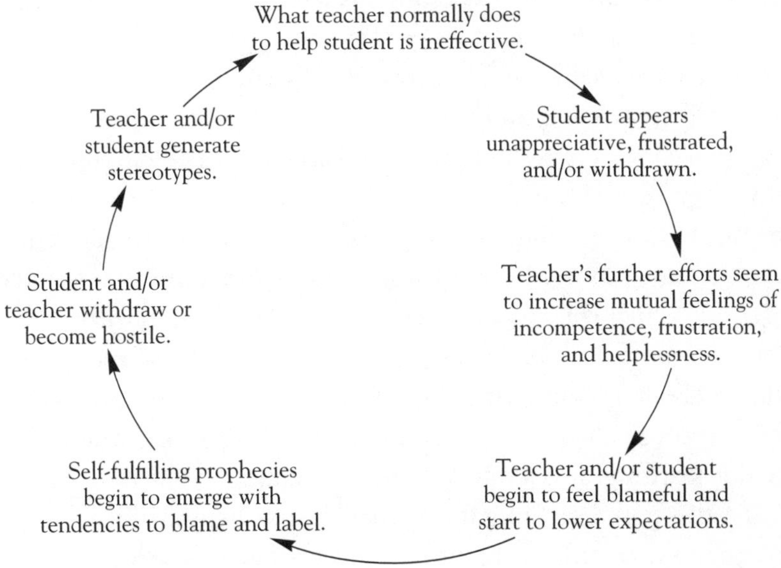

What teacher normally does to help student is ineffective.

Teacher and/or student generate stereotypes.

Student appears unappreciative, frustrated, and/or withdrawn.

Student and/or teacher withdraw or become hostile.

Teacher's further efforts seem to increase mutual feelings of incompetence, frustration, and helplessness.

Self-fulfilling prophecies begin to emerge with tendencies to blame and label.

Teacher and/or student begin to feel blameful and start to lower expectations.

be struggling with attaining a competent performance on the assignments. The teacher's normal procedure is to encourage persistence, greater effort, and a series of study habits that might include reviewing notes, outlining chapters, and making revisions. The student sees the issue as the irrelevance of the tasks. The assignments seem contrived, unnecessarily analytical, and unrelated to the reasons the student took the course. As they talk, the teacher acknowledges the student's comments with little empathy or validation. The teacher continues to emphasize previous advice, giving more detail and explanations as to why it should help. Upon departure, the student's frustration is noticeable.

When the student's performance on the next assignment has not improved, the teacher does what many of us do in circumstances where we feel responsible and see our actions fail: the teacher gives a variation of former advice, telling the student to join a study group to see how other students are preparing their assignments. As performance still does not significantly improve, both the teacher and the student feel more incompetent and frustrated. Now, each feels justified in blaming the other. Once this occurs, the rest of the cycle comes quickly, and the deterioration of their relationship is hastened as the student's continued poor performance on the assignments confirms their lowered expectations of each other.

Both the teacher and the student are now in a frame of mind to search for labels— "unfair," "insensitive," "lazy," "unprepared," and so on. As hostility, withdrawal, and stereotyping are likely to emerge, both will feel more compelled not to change, to maintain a sense of not having been intimidated or not having lost their integrity. Until they can leave each other, this cycle will tend to maintain itself, with blame as its frequent catalyst. Listen to faculty talking about students who don't learn in their classes and to students in those classes who talk about the faculty with whom they are not learning. It is a mirror image of blame.

At this point, one might ask what the teacher or student should have done to avoid falling into this cycle of events. Although that is an appropriate question, the purpose of this example is not to offer an intervention. The point of this illustration is to emphasize how quickly and devastatingly blame can emerge. Our experience is that in difficult matters between people who do not know one another, blame often occurs after only one negative encounter. A norm that prevents blaming is much more effective than interventions that are applied after its corrosion has begun.

Blame is a classic trap, something that uses our normal behavior or instincts to entangle or disable us. Although it is a symptom of such deeper issues as dominance or prejudice in a relationship, it can sabotage efforts toward positive change when new behaviors and attitudes feel awkward and trust is beginning to develop. This is one of the primary reasons why some school improvement programs, such as the one pioneered by James Comer (1993), have a "no-fault" approach. Meeting time is not used to blame others. The focus is on solving problems and taking advantage of opportunities first. A similar approach is used by Beverly Daniel Tatum (1992) in the teaching of her course, The Psychology of Racism. She is explicit with her students in providing the working assumption that because prejudice and racism were inherent in our environments when we were children, we cannot be blamed for learning what we were taught intentionally or unintentionally. She points out that we all have a responsibility to interrupt the cycle of oppression and that understanding and unlearning prejudice and racism is a lifelong process. She acknowledges that each of us may not be at the same point in the process and should have mutual respect for each other, regardless of where we perceive each other to be.

Ridding a learning environment of blame does not mean giving up our critical reasoning or confronting that which may seem unethical or contradictory. Since many things cannot be changed until they are faced, telling the truth and living with some degree of confrontation is essential to promoting collaboration in a learning community. This means knowing that the general purpose of the disagreement or other viewpoint is to be honest and provide information that leads to shared understanding, the resolution of a mutual problem, and a clearer path for communication and community; that even though I may see it differently from you, I do not withdraw my support from you as a person. This form of confrontation is the expression of a differing opinion with the consideration of the other person's welfare. Procedures for establishing the context and means to accomplish such communication are considered in the next section.

5. *There is equitable treatment of all learners with an invitation to point out behaviors, practices, and policies that discriminate.* Even in classes where establishing inclusion is an explicitly stated motivational goal, the attitudes and dispositions developed by people in informal settings may carry over to the learning environment and must be considered within interactive learning groups. Women are often silenced or placed in traditional gender-stereotyped roles by men in these groups. Sadker and Sadker (1990) found men are twice as likely to monopolize class discussions, and women are twice as likely to be silent, with minority males also remaining much more quiet than white males in postsecondary classrooms. Hall and Sandler (1982) report that in their investigations, professors give males more nonverbal attention, wait longer for them to answer, make more eye contact with them, and are more likely to remember their names. Consider this classroom scene drawn from the research files of Sadker and Sadker (1994, pp. 168–170), which illustrates how subtle sexism can permeate classroom dialogue:

> The course on the U.S. Constitution is required for graduation, and more than fifty students, approximately half male and half female, file in. The professor begins by asking if there are questions on next week's midterm. Several hands go up.
>
> *Bernie:* Do we have to memorize names and dates in the book? Or will the test be more general?

Professor: You do have to know those critical dates and
people. Not every one but the important ones. If I were
you, Bernie, I would spend time learning them. Ellen?

Ellen: Will we have the whole class time?

Professor: Yes, we'll have the whole class time. Anyone else?

Ben (calling out): Will there be an extra-credit question?

Professor: I hadn't planned on it. What do you think?

Ben: I really like them. They take some of the pressure off.
You can also see who is doing extra work.

Professor: I'll take it under advisement. Charles?

Charles: How much of our final grade is this?

Professor: The midterm is 25 percent. But remember, class
participation counts as well. Why don't we begin?

The professor lectures on the Constitution for twenty minutes
before he asks a question about the electoral college. The electoral
college is not as hot a topic as the midterm, so only four hands are
raised. The professor calls on Ben.

Ben: The electoral college was created because there was a
lack of faith in the people. Rather than have them vote
for the president, they voted for the electors.

Professor: I like the way you think. (*He smiles at Ben, and Ben
smiles back.*) Who could vote? (*Five hands go up, five out of
fifty.*) Angie?

Angie: I don't know if this is right, but I thought only men
could vote.

Ben (calling out): That was a great idea. We began going down-
hill when we let women vote. (*Angie looks surprised but
says nothing. Some of the students laugh, and so does the
professor. He calls on Barbara.*)

Barbara: I think you had to be pretty wealthy, own property—

Josh (not waiting for Barbara to finish, calls out): That's right.
There was a distrust of the poor, who could upset the

democracy. But if you had property, if you had something at stake, you could be trusted not to do something wild. Only property owners could be trusted.

Professor: Nice job, Josh. But why do we still have electors today? Mike?

Mike: Tradition, I guess.

Professor: Do you think it's tradition? If you walked down the street and asked people their views of the electoral college, what would they say?

Mike: Probably they'd be clueless. Maybe they would think that it elects the Pope. People don't know how it works.

Professor: Good, Mike. Judy, do you want to say something? (*Judy's hand is at "half-mast," raised but just barely. When the professor calls her name, she looks a bit startled.*)

Judy (speaking very softly): Maybe we would need a whole new constitutional convention to change it. And once they get together to change that, they could change anything. That frightens people, doesn't it? (*As Judy speaks, a number of students fidget, pass notes, and leaf through their books; a few even begin to whisper.*)

Notice in this scene Mike was challenged to improve his answer and then rewarded for the correction. The professor praised three male students: Ben, Josh, and Mike. Women's comments never received the professor's approval. They were acknowledged at best, in addition to being interrupted or ridiculed. The men in this class received more attention and better attention. Also, Judy speaks in a tentative manner, reflecting how self-doubt is often a part of women's public voice (Tannen, 1991). Based on their research and years of study in the area of sexist behavior in educational settings, Sadker and Sadker (1994) believe this bias is most pronounced in postsecondary settings. Yet, most teachers, regardless of gender, race, or ethnicity, report that they are completely unaware of these inequitable interaction patterns. When shown videotapes of their

discussions or when a colleague comes into a class and systematically records interaction, they are usually surprised to see these problems of bias emerge (Sadker and Sadker, 1992). Although less
documented, racial, ethnic, classist, heterosexist, and ability bias
during classroom interaction can be as subtley prevalent in postsecondary settings as sexist behaviors are.

One might begin to establish the norm of equitable treatment
by disseminating copies of this section of the book, having everyone read the professor-student scenario, and openly discussing this
kind of discrimination and how it relates to other types—and the
lack of awareness of them—so prevalent in everyday learning interactions. The tone of such a dialogue would be friendly rather than
accusatory, with the goal of being alert to these matters to inform
one another and to further equality, rather than to catch wrong-
doers. If we as teachers approach this norm with a calm and sincere
attitude, without being overbearing or self-righteous, we invite our
own as well as our students' growth in matters of equitable treatment while learning. In Resource A (see numbers 2, 7, 8, 9, 10, 11,
13, 15, 17, and 19) we offer some specific strategies for promoting
participation during discussion and learning activities.

One particular idea we have adopted from Sadker and Sadker
(1992) and found pleasantly helpful in both small and large interactive groups is to, at times, distribute three poker chips or markers
to each learner in the group with the idea that in order to talk, a
learner has to deposit a chip in the center of the group. Before the
activity or class has ended learners are expected to spend all of their
chips, but learners are not allowed to talk after their chips are spent.
This encourages the more garrulous learners to think about their
comments and to filter the more significant from the more trivial.
On the other hand, quieter learners are prompted by this process to
think of something relevant to say. We have found this to be an
enjoyable way to increase the involvement of all learners.

We have also found, as Sadker and Sadker (1992) report, that
when learners are allowed to form seating clusters that consistently

reflect gender, ethnic, or racial segregation, there are several negative consequences. Perspectives are frequently narrowed; teachers are often drawn to the white and/or male areas of the class, and females and minority males are less likely to receive teacher attention. There are a variety of ways to intervene, from seating according to a chart, to openly discussing why those seating patterns may occur and their potential negative impact, to integrating by forming cooperative learning groups.

It is important to note that these researchers have also found that when teachers become aware of their inequitable interactions with learners, the teachers want to change. They are sensitive to the irony of enhancing bias against others while in the pursuit of knowledge.

When multicultural content is fused into any course or learning situation, and when diverse learners are present, there is a dire need for a climate and a community, short-lived though it may be, that provides the respect and connectedness needed to engage everyone in learning and to deal with the social and personal contradictions at hand. These norms and their shared expectations build the cohesiveness that allows people to feel validated and confirmed as they learn and, sometimes, struggle beyond their doubts and discomforts.

There are several ways norms can be implemented in a group. One is to clearly communicate them in the beginning of the course along with information about attendance, assignments, and assessment procedures. It may be wise to write them down and distribute them so they can be reviewed and emphasized as needed and as time together progresses.

When ground rules (discussed in the next section) are established, one may wish to make these norms explicit and part of this procedure. Some teachers prefer to incorporate norms in a consensual decision-making process in order to increase learners' sense of self-determination and ownership. Certainly, they should be discussed and clearly understood. The degree to which they are modeled by the teacher, both in tone and in practice, formally and informally, goes a long way toward establishing their credibility. The procedures and structures of the course must reflect the norms and support them. In general, the more clearly the learners see how these norms lead to the accomplishment of salient goals to which they are committed, the more readily they will accept and internalize them.

Procedures for Establishing Inclusion

For each of the motivational goals presented in this book, we offer a set of procedures. These are the motivation/learning strategies and processes used by the teacher and learning group as they work together to accomplish the agreed-upon learning goals. The procedures associated with the motivational goal of inclusion are those that foster its essential criteria, respect, and connectedness. Since motivation and learning are imbued with culture, the most effective procedures can vary for different learners. We invite you to consider the following procedures as possible extensions of your teaching practice.

Collaborative Learning

In their comprehensive overview of collaborative learning, Smith and MacGregor (1992) define collaborative learning as an umbrella term for a variety of educational approaches involving joint intellectual efforts by students, or students and teachers together. In these situations, learners are working in groups of two or more, mutually constructing understanding, solutions, meanings, applications, or products. Although there is a wide variability in collaborative activities, most emphasize the learners' exploration and interpretation of the course material to an equal or greater extent than the teacher's explication of it. As everyone participates, working as partners or in small groups, questions and challenges to create something energize group activity.

Teachers who use collaborative learning procedures tend to think of themselves less as authoritarian, singular transmitters of knowledge and more as mutual learners, acting as creative designers and empathic leaders who, by working in cooperation with their students, help to compose compelling learning experiences for all. This orientation invites active learner participation. Such involvement in learning, with other learners and with faculty, are factors that make an overwhelming difference in student retention and success in college (Tinto, 1987). As Astin (1993a) has pointed out, many postsecondary educational reform efforts are unsuccessful because they fail to address the implicit values of ravenous individualism and the relentless competition in higher education. Collaborative learning represents another value system, one that holds cooperation and community to be as important as academic achievement. This approach invites learners to offer their perspectives and to sensitively listen to the voices of others, to deliberate and to build consensus, and to find in academic learning a model of an equitable means to civic life.

Cooperative Learning

Among the many collaborative learning possibilities, cooperative learning represents the most carefully organized and researched approach. Over one-third of all studies comparing cooperative, competitive, and individualistic learning have been conducted with college and adult learners. Having recently completed an analysis of 120 of these investigations, David and Roger Johnson (1993), pioneers and advocates of this teaching practice, have found that cooperative learning significantly promotes greater individual achievement than do competitive or individualistic efforts. In addition, when students learn cooperatively, positive and supportive relationships tend to develop across different ethnic, language, social class, and gender groups.

Through the stimulation that comes from different perspectives (Vygotsky, 1962) and the social support of group members, cooperative learning simultaneously promotes intrinsic motivation, new learning, and interpersonal cohesion. According to Johnson and Johnson (1993), cooperative learning groups provide a setting in which learners can

1. Construct and extend conceptual understanding of what is being learned through explanation and discussion

2. Use the shared mental models learned in flexible ways to solve problems jointly

3. Receive interpersonal feedback as to how well procedures are performed

4. Receive social support and encouragement to take risks in increasing one's competencies

5. Be held accountable by peers to practice and learn procedures and skills

6. Acquire new attitudes

7. Establish a shared identity with other group members

8. Find effective peers to emulate

While these opportunities are not guaranteed in every cooperative learning group, the likelihood of their occurrence in competitive and individualistic learning situations is remote.

As its supporters and practitioners strenuously emphasize, cooperative learning is more than placing learners in groups and telling them to work together (Goodsell, Maher, and Tinto, 1992; Johnson, Johnson, and Smith, 1991). Positive interdependence and individual accountability are fundamental components of effective cooperative learning (Cooper and Mueck, 1992). Groups lacking either of these two features are more properly identified as a form of collaborative learning, but not cooperative learning. According to Johnson and Johnson (1993), to organize lessons so learners do work cooperatively requires an understanding of five components—positive interdependence, individual accountability, promotive interaction, social skills, and group processing—and their rigorous implementation in the group and in the lesson.

Positive Interdependence. When learners perceive that they are linked with group mates in such a way that they cannot succeed unless their group mates do (and vice versa) and/or they must coordinate their efforts with the efforts of their partners to complete a task (Johnson, Johnson, and Smith, 1991), they are positively interdependent. They "sink or swim together." Each group member has a unique contribution to make to the group because of her or his resources, role, and/or responsibilities. For example, in the popular "jigsaw" procedure (see Exhibit 2.1), a reading assignment is divided among the group, with each member responsible for comprehending a separate part and explaining or teaching that part to all other members of the group until the entire group has a coherent understanding of the total reading assignment. The following three approaches are additional ways to create positive interdependence within a cooperative learning group.

1. *Positive goal interdependence:* The group is united around a common goal, a concrete reason for being. It could be to create a single product, report, or answer, or it could be general improvement on a task so that all members do better this week than they did last week. Outcomes might include a skill demonstration, a media product, an evaluation summary, a problem solution, an action plan, or just about anything that leads to greater learning and that a group can produce and hold each other responsible for.

2. *Positive resource interdependence:* Each group member has only a portion of the resources, information, or materials necessary for the task to be accomplished, and the members' resources have to be combined in order for the group to achieve its goals. The metaphor for this approach is a puzzle, for which each group member has a unique and necessary piece to contribute to reach its solution. For example, for an upcoming exam each member of a group is respon-

sible for a different study question; when the group convenes, that member shares her or his knowledge of the question and checks to make sure all group mates have satisfactorily comprehended this knowledge.

3. *Positive role interdependence:* Each member of the group selects a particular role that is complementary, interconnected, and essential to the roles of the other group members. For example, consider the learning goal as the development of some form of skill, such as interviewing. One person is the skill practicer (the interviewer), another person is the recipient of the skill (the interviewee), and a third person is the observer/evaluator. In this manner, each person has an essential contribution to make in terms of either skill practice or feedback. Roles can easily be rotated as well.

In all cooperative learning groups it is extremely important that the learners are very clear about the assignment, goal, and/or role involved. Especially with diverse groups of learners, checking for this kind of understanding can make the difference between a satisfying or a confusing learning experience. Positive interdependence works best when all group members realize each person has a part to do, all members are counting on them, and all members want to help them to do better.

Individual Accountability. This is present when the learning of each individual in the learning group is assessed, the results are shared with the learner, and the learner is responsible to group mates for contributing a fair share to the group's success. One of the main purposes of cooperative learning is to support each member as a vital, competent individual in his or her own right. Individual accountability is the key to ensuring that all group members are strengthened by learning cooperatively and that they have a good chance to effectively transfer what they have learned to situations in which they may be without group support.

Sometimes texts emphasize individual accountability as a means to prevent "hitchhiking," the situation in which a learner contributes little of worth to the total success of a group's learning experience and overly benefits from the contributions of other group members. Our experience is that this seldom occurs when cooperative norms are well in place and competitive norm-referenced grading procedures are eliminated. (We will say more about this in Chapter Five.) In our opinion, it is a lack of appropriate norms and a powerful extrinsic reward or grading framework that systemically undermines cooperative learning groups and encourages individuals to seek the greatest amount of external gain for the least amount of effort (Wlodkowski, 1985).

Specific ways to enhance individual accountability include the following:

1. Keep the size of the group small. Keep the role of each learner distinct. Typical size is two to four members.

2. Assess learners individually as well as collectively.

3. Observe groups while they are working.

4. Randomly request individuals to present what they are learning to you or another group.

5. Request periodic self-assessments and outlines of responsibilities from individual group members.

6. Randomly or systematically ask learners to teach someone else or yourself what they have learned.

A simple and positive way to support individual accountability and prevent related conflict among group members is to brainstorm with the learning groups and ask the question, How would we like to find out if someone in our cooperative learning group thought we were not doing enough to contribute to the total group's benefit? What are some acceptable ways of letting us know? Then write the possible actions on the chalkboard and discuss them. Such a procedure can go a long way to avoid unnecessary suspicion or shame.

Promotive Interaction. When cooperative group members, in face-to-face contact, encourage and assist each other with information, insight, emotional support, and challenges as well as deliberations to reach relevant goals, they are engaged in promotive interaction. A moderate level of intensity and some degree of mutual care should permeate such interaction (Johnson, Johnson, and Smith, 1991). This is when group members can act on their interpersonal accountability—for example, when someone in a cooperative writing group hears another member read her or his own words and offers suggestions to improve a subsequent draft of the manuscript. Interaction of this sort is when different perspectives and commitments take hold. It is of paramount importance that a significant amount of cooperative learning takes place within the learning environment to permit monitoring by the teacher and to allow groups to initially establish themselves while they can receive any needed support.

Social Skills. Cooperative work depends on communication proficiencies that enable groups to reach goals, get to know and trust each other, communicate accurately, accept and support each other, and resolve conflicts constructively (Johnson, Johnson, and Smith, 1991). Even though people want to cooperate they may not be able to do so effectively if they lack interpersonal skills.

Our experience with diverse groups of learners is that when the five norms (cited earlier in this chapter) are present and the ground rules (discussed in the next section) are established, there is far less need for direct training in conventional social skills such as "active listening," which often feel contrived and alien to many people and especially to people who do not strongly identify with the dominant culture. It is appropriate for a teacher to intervene in a group, when necessary, to suggest more effective procedures for working together. Yet we agree with Johnson, Johnson, and Smith (1991) that teachers should not intervene in a group any more than is absolutely necessary. We often find that with a little patience, cooperative groups work their way through their own problems and construct not only timely solutions but also methods for solving similar problems in the future. Sometimes, simply asking a group to set aside their task, describe the problem as they see it, and come up with a few solutions and then a decision as to which one to try first is enough to get things moving along satisfactorily.

Group Processing. Cooperative learning benefits from group processing—reflecting on a group experience or series of events to describe members' actions that were helpful and unhelpful and to make decisions about what actions to pursue or to change (Johnson, Johnson, and Smith, 1991). When dealing with diversity and diverse groups of learners, discussing group functioning is essential (Adams and Marchesani, 1992). Learners need time to have a dialogue about the quality of their cooperation, to reflect on it, and to learn from how they work together. This "processing time" gives learners a chance to receive feedback on their participation, understand how their actions may be more effective and cohesive, plan for more helpful and skillful interaction for the next group session, and celebrate mutual success. As teachers we need to allow enough time in the learning environment for this activity to take place and to provide some basic structure for it—for example, suggesting the group discuss a few things it is doing well and one thing it could improve. We should also clearly communicate the purposes of such an activity and at appropriate intervals conduct whole-group processing to better understand how the entire learning group is working together.

In general, the more heterogeneous the groups, the better. Most experienced practitioners find that grouping learners works best with attention to such characteristics as age, gender, and ethnicity. However, sometimes practical reasons may override heterogeneity as the best approach. Interest in a specific topic, accessibility for meetings outside of class, very limited skills, or language acquisition issues might predicate more homogeneous groups. Diversity, however, should be encouraged to the extent possible.

Once the cooperative learning groups start working, the role of the teacher is one of co-learner, observer, adviser, and consultant. Without being obtrusive, it helps to watch cooperative groups, especially as they *begin* their tasks. Sometimes we can see that certain groups need clarification or guidance. Otherwise we remain available, always keeping in mind that it is the learners themselves who are the major resources for support and assistance to one another. In Exhibit 2.1 we have adapted the "jigsaw" procedure from the informative text *Active Learning* (Johnson, Johnson, and Smith, 1991) to provide a descriptive example for conducting cooperative groups. A Cooperative Lesson Worksheet is provided in Resource B to use as a possible model for planning cooperative learning activities. A continuing resource is the *Cooperative Learning and College Teaching* newsletter available through New Forums Press in Stillwater, Oklahoma.

Exhibit 2.1. Jigsaw Procedure

When you have information you need to communicate to students, an alternative to lecturing or assigning the same reading to every student is a procedure for structuring cooperative learning groups called *jigsaw* (Aronson and others, 1978).

First, think of a reading assignment you will give in the near future. Next, proceed through the following steps for structuring a "jigsaw" lesson:

1. *Cooperative groups:* Distribute a set of reading materials to each group. The set needs to be divisible into the number of members of the group (two, three, or four parts). Give each member one part of the set of materials. This activity assumes at least four groups.

2. *Preparation pairs:* Assign students the cooperative task of meeting with someone else in the class who is a member of another cooperative group and who has the same section of the material. They are to complete two tasks: (a) learning and becoming an expert on their material, and

Exhibit 2.1. Jigsaw Procedure, Cont'd.

(b) planning how to teach the material to the other members of their groups.

3. *Practice pairs:* Assign the pair of students the cooperative task of meeting with another pair who have learned the same material and share ideas as to how the material may best be taught. These "practice pairs" review what and how each plans to teach her or his group. The best ideas of both pairs are incorporated into each student's presentation.

4. *Cooperative groups:* Assign students the cooperative tasks of (a) teaching their area of expertise to the other group members, and (b) learning the material being taught by the other members.

5. *Evaluation:* Assess the students' degree of understanding of all the material.

Source: Adapted from Johnson, Johnson, and Smith, 1991, p. 4:17.

Writing Groups

Whether explicitly organized as cooperative learning groups or arranged less formally as peer response groups or helping circles, writing groups have a long history in postsecondary education (Gere, 1987). This format may involve learners working in small groups at every stage of the writing process. With their peers they can formulate ideas, clarify positions, test arguments, focus theses, or probe the authenticity of their characters before or while they are in the process of writing. Collaboration allows learners to exchange written drafts and to receive feedback from their peers; to read, listen, and communicate with insight and helpful suggestions; and to experience firsthand the rich and creative force that diversity can be.

Writing groups make the process of composing and revising less lonely and alienating (Spear, 1988). In a supportive milieu, people who have different perspectives and values can use dialogue with their peers to safely explore their visions and reflections.

The quality of thinking exhibited in the compositions of those in peer writing groups exceeds the quality of thinking of those in more conventional writing formats (Hillocks, 1984). Since 1982 the Behavioral Science Graduate Program at California State University, Dominguez Hills, has offered students in two of its three master's degree programs the option of a team thesis. Approximately 80 percent of the eligible students select this option. Over 250 students have made this choice since 1982, succeeding at a 98 percent completion rate compared to the 55 percent success rate among students in the program attempting the traditional thesis (Churchman, 1992).

Marcia Curtis and Anne Herrington (1992) eloquently describe the evolution of a basic writing course at the University of Massachusetts, Amherst, in which peer writing groups and multiculturalism are common denominators. With 20 to 60 percent of their students being recent graduates from the University's second language English (SLE) program and nearly equal percentages of Cambodians, Central and South Americans, Chinese, Japanese, Puerto Ricans, Soviets, and Taiwanese, they use interstudent exchanges of drafts and completed papers to foster self-reflection during the composing process and to simultaneously extend the students' sense of audience beyond the teacher alone. In this way, they help their students as well as other educators to see that "writing is a social process constituted by myriad worlds that we, alongside our students, set out to explore anew each term" (p. 83).

Peer Teaching

One of the oldest forms of collaborative learning is peer teaching, the process of learners teaching learners (Smith and MacGregor, 1992). Peer teaching approaches have expanded in postsecondary education, under many names and structures. We present two of the most successful and widely adapted models of this genre, both of which depart from those forms that focus on a remediation or rescue orientation toward learners.

The *supplemental instruction* approach was developed by Deanna Martin at the University of Missouri, Kansas City, and has been adopted at hundreds of colleges in the United States and abroad. Beginning in the health sciences and later in general arts and science classes the emphasis was not on the "at-risk student" but on the "at-risk class" where more than 30 percent of the students were either withdrawing or failing (Blanc, DeBuhr, and Martin, 1983). The university invited those undergraduates who had done well in those classes to become "SI leaders." These students were paid to attend the class and to convene supplemental instruction sessions at least three times a week at hours convenient to students in the class. *All* the students in the class were welcome to attend the SI sessions.

In this model the course teacher works closely with the SI student leaders to develop ways to help students master the content of the class. The SI leader is presented as a student of the subject, not an expert on the subject—an approach meant to reduce perceptions of hierarchical status. Evaluations of this approach have shown that if students attend the SI sessions consistently, their grades and their persistence in college are significantly higher regardless of whether they are perceived as strong or weak academically (Center for Academic Development, 1991).

The second peer teaching approach is the *intensive mathematics workshops* program developed by Uri Treisman (1985) at the University of California at Berkeley. This program assumes the orientation of an honors program rather than a remedial program. By emphasizing the development of strength rather than the remediation of weakness, and peer collaboration rather than solo competition, Treisman completely reversed the prevailing patterns of failure in calculus classes by Latino and African-American students.

Bonsangue (1993) conducted a longitudinal study of the effects of participation in this workshop model upon the persistence and achievement of underrepresented minority students enrolled in mathematics, science, and engineering (MSE) majors at California State Polytechnic University, Pomona. Meeting in small groups twice a week for two-hour sessions to work collaboratively on calculus problems, the students are facilitated mainly by upper-division ethnic minority undergraduate MSE students. These facilitators meet weekly with the course instructors, who conduct the regular lecture and discussion sections to ensure the relevance of the material presented in workshop sessions and to discuss specific academic issues related to individual students. Among the 320 students studied, 85 percent were Hispanic and other Latino, and the rest were African American and American Indian, with approximately 25 percent of the total population being women.

Bonsangue found that within three years after entering school, 40 percent of the non-workshop students had withdrawn or been academically dismissed from the institution compared to fewer than 5 percent of the workshop students. Moreover, 91 percent of the workshop students still enrolled in MSE after three years had completed their mathematics requirement, compared to only 58 percent of the non-workshop students. Persistence and mathematics completion were highest among women participating in the workshop, all of whom remained in the university. Bonsangue concluded:

> This research has demonstrated that an intervention program such as the calculus workshop, which promotes academic excellence and peer interaction, can significantly improve student performance in technical majors, and particularly, the performance of women independent of precollege academic measures. Achievement in mathematics, science, and engineering disciplines among underrepresented minority students may therefore be less associated with precollege ability than with in-college academic experiences and expectations [1993, p. 20].

After conducting an extensive review of peer teaching in higher education, Whitman (1988) concluded that providing students with opportunities to teach each other may be one of the most important educational services a teacher can render. In addition to a collaborative, small group learning process, both of these programs employed "near-peers," peer teachers who are slightly more advanced than the main body of learners. This provides not only a linguistic advantage—language and exemplification relevant to the learner's own understanding and perspective—but also connectedness and a vicarious sense of competence, the awareness by the learners that similar others perform successfully and that therefore they, too, possess capabilities to meet comparable challenges. Whitman suggests that faculty and student involvement in the recruitment, selection, and training of peer teachers is a key to program success.

Although problem-centered instruction and learning communities are often categorized as forms of collaborative learning, we will discuss them later in this book under a heading that is more appropriate for our purposes. By structure and tone, collaborative learning invites us as teachers to be co-learners, to establish procedures that authentically model what it means to question, to learn, and to understand in concert with others. Let us now consider a basic procedure that, although it is often not directly subject-matter related, does much to establish inclusion and a sense of common humanity in a learning group, the feeling that creates a spirit of unity among learners. This useful process is the opportunity for multidimensional sharing.

Opportunities for Multidimensional Sharing

Opportunities for multidimensional sharing are those occasions, from introduction exercises to personal anecdotes to classroom celebrations, when people have a better chance to see one another as complete and evolving human beings who have mutual needs, emotions, and experiences. These opportunities give a human face to a class, break down biases and stereotypes, and support the identification of the self in the realm of another person's world.

There are many ways to provide opportunities for multidimensional sharing, depending, of course, on the history, makeup, and purpose of the group. If there is a caution we have, it is to be more gentle than intrusive. Especially to students from backgrounds that value modesty, such activities may seem contrived and psychologically invasive: "Let's all share about one person who loves us," or "What is the gift from our heart that we bring to this group?" are examples of what not to ask.

Meals and extracurricular activities usually offer people ways to be themselves and to reduce self-consciousness. Potluck meals, recreational activities, drinks after class, and picnics are still popular ways for learners and teachers to relax and get to know one another. Anything that helps people to learn each other's names and laugh together deserves our serious attention as a possible activity. For teachers, a little self-deprecating humor, not taking ourselves too seriously, reveals our humanity and suggests that we have some perspective on life, that the way we teach will allow for the vitality of other feelings and views. The following are three introductory activities that we have used successfully. They range in the directness with which they consider cultural difference. They are conducted in a relaxed, trustful and enjoyable manner.

1. This first activity can be a small or large group process. Each person (a) introduces herself or himself; (b) names one, and up to five, of the places he or she has lived; (c) offers one expectation, concern, or hope he or she has for this course.

2. Learners usually need some time to think before they begin this activity. This can be a small or large group process. Each person introduces himself or herself and recommends: (a) one thing they have read (such as an article, story, or book) *or* (b) one thing they have seen (such as a TV program, film, or real-life experience) *or* (c) one thing they have heard (such as a speech, record album, or song) that has had a strong and positive influence on them; the student states the reason for recommendation.

3. This activity is conducted in triads with a Venn diagram (Figure 2.2).

Figure 2.2. Venn Diagram.

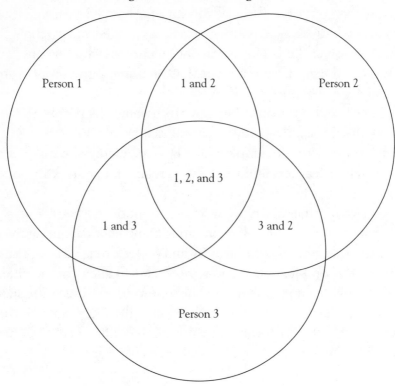

The teacher begins the activity by asking the entire group of learners to consider the concept of culture and the qualities, characteristics, and experiences that might influence their cultural identity. People will normally suggest such possibilities as gender, socioeconomic class, ethnicity, or regionality. Some will mention jobs they have had, the number of members in their family, and so forth. The idea here is to create an orientation toward examining our unique identities, rather than a comprehensive list. We emphasize that culture is a complex concept that cannot be reduced to a simple list of nouns and adjectives.

After the teacher has solicited about five to ten examples and contributed a few to stimulate thinking, the teacher shows the

Venn diagram and asks the group to break into triads. Then each triad draws a Venn diagram with each person selecting one of the circles to represent himself or herself. Participants now work together to locate and write on the Venn diagram the words that identify how they understand themselves culturally.

As they do this, they will observe that all three of them have some things in common—perhaps gender or occupation. These are entered in the center of the diagram where the space is intersected by all three circles.

Some characteristics or experiences will be shared by only two of them, and in different pairs—for example, marital status for persons one and two and perhaps region of birth for numbers two and three. These are entered in the space intersected by the two circles belonging to the two people who share the particular characteristic.

And finally, there will be qualities unique to each member of the triad, such as ethnicity or languages spoken. These are entered in the portion of each circle that does not overlap. The teacher's primary goal is to make the process clear but to leave the learners as much discretion as possible as to what they enter into each section of the diagram. They should be encouraged to share what they are comfortable sharing, to get to know each other, and to enjoy themselves. After about fifteen to twenty minutes, a short time is taken for each person to reflect on what can be understood as a consequence of this activity. Some participants prefer to discuss this collaboratively. The teacher then conducts a whole group discussion and records the generalizations. Some generalizations occur more frequently than others—"We realized we had more characteristics and experiences in common than we would have predicted"—but there is no limit to what might be said. As appropriate, the teacher can probe for emotional reactions as well, asking, for example, "Did any particular feelings emerge as you discussed these topics?"

We originally developed this activity as a means of introducing cultural aspects of ourselves and students from a safe perspective.

We found that this exercise encourages respect for cultural differences. Pedagogically, it models sharing the ownership of knowing, since learners select that which is personally meaningful and develop their own processes for revealing and charting cultural influences. Often, learners remark on the value of commonality or connectedness. We frequently discuss how common it is to simultaneously find similarity and diversity among a group of learners, and we note the value of retaining each of these dimensions within the learning setting. Our experience is that the drawing of the diagram tends to focus people, encourages greater participation, and lessens self-consciousness.

In general, as with many other practitioners, we believe introductions are most inclusive and motivating when they help people learn each other's names, validate the unique experiences of the individuals involved, relieve the normal tension that most new groups feel in the beginning of a workshop or class, and establish a sense of affiliation with the teacher and other learners. Learning about each other is a continuous process. The more natural and appropriate such opportunities feel, the more likely a genuine sense of community can evolve. In the beginning of a course, these activities can contribute to the initiation of sustainable relationships for personal and academic growth.

Focus Groups

Focus groups are meetings of learners and teachers assembled as representatives of a larger group and organized for the purpose of obtaining information, generating ideas, and assessing course materials, activities, assignments, and social climate. A focus group can serve as a vehicle for collecting sensitive feedback about a class as well as offer a means for creating and improving how a given course evolves (Cross and Angelo, 1988). Focus groups provide not only a way to acknowledge the range of diversity in a learning group, but a direct means of enhancing the inclusion, adjustment, and refinement that differences among learners may require for a culturally responsive learning experience. For large classes where learners frequently feel anonymous and distant, focus groups can be especially useful.

Because postsecondary courses vary so dramatically, focus groups can range from informal to formal contexts for addressing something as narrowly defined as classroom participation to something as broadly encompassing as the entire operation of a course, including required texts and student assessment. In all cases, planning is essential. We have found it helpful to decide early on about how frequently and regularly the group will meet. This will influence who can participate and how dependable that participation can be. It is important that the group represent the diversity within the class. Four to eight members usually make adequate discussion possible. When appropriate and desirable, each focus group member can meet with a designated number of learners from the entire class to elicit their reactions and exchange information.

A carefully considered agenda with learner input and with guidelines on how to work effectively together (the "ground rules" discussed in the next section) makes an immeasurable difference in how successfully a focus group operates. We strongly suggest making clear to the members which aspects of the course they can expect to influence. If there are areas of the course that are not open to discussion, directly explain this. By encouraging all learners in the course to seek out focus group members and to offer suggestions, appreciations, and questions, teachers further enhance what is discussed at the focus group meetings. In addition, such an invitation creates an opportunity for participation from learners who might feel vulnerable directly expressing feelings, ideas, or concerns. Allowing class time for members to report to the class can help to validate the focus group and increase cohesiveness within the class. The questions that follow are some that we have found helpful in eliciting culturally sensitive information in a focus group:

1. How do the learning experiences and assignments build on what learners know and value? What avenues have been overlooked? What should we emphasize more?

2. How do the learning experiences, materials, and assignments allow all learners to use their talents and preferred ways of learning? How do they inhibit?

3. Do all learners in our course believe they can successfully accomplish what is required? If not, why? If so, what is being done that helps?

4. How are we progressing as a community of learners where there is mutual respect and a sense of connection for everyone? What more could be done?

We have sometimes found that learners need to "warm up" before they can address questions as complex as the ones we propose. Often, we begin by asking participants to think about and discuss a course they really enjoyed and where they felt valued and challenged. Beyond this, we agree with Cross and Angelo (1988) that any teacher who uses this process must commit to taking learner suggestions seriously.

Reframing

The last procedure we recommend for the motivational goal of establishing inclusion is directly intended for teachers. We know only too well how we can remain in a blameful and problematic relationship with a learner where whatever we do seems of no avail. Reframing has helped us and other teachers, and therefore other learners, in such circumstances. This technique is based on the ecosystemic view that human behavior can be legitimately interpreted in a variety of ways and that people tend to view their behavior as appropriate to the situation as they perceive it (Molnar and Lindquist, 1989).

Consider a simple example. A teacher regards a learner as too pushy and aggressive and sees the learner's repeated blurting out of comments and answers in class as proof of this estimation. The learner considers it necessary to blurt out answers because he believes the teacher tends to ignore him. Their perceptions are mutually reinforced when the learner suddenly raises his voice to get the teacher's attention and the teacher rigidly ignores the learner in an attempt to discourage his behavior. And on it goes, with the likelihood of consequent labeling and stereotyping from both parties.

One powerful way of promoting change in such problematic patterns of behavior is to formulate a *positive* alternative interpretation of the behavior and to begin acting in ways that are consistent with this new interpretation. This technique is called *reframing*.

For a teacher, reframing means finding a new perceptual "frame" for what is considered to be the problem behavior, one that is positive, fits the facts of the situation, and is plausible to the individual personalities and congruent with the cultures of the people involved. The process of reframing will also suggest how to act differently in the situation when it reoccurs. If the teacher in our example were able to interpret the learner's blurting out answers as impassioned involvement in the learning experience instead of a hostile act to gain attention, then responses other than ignoring the learner would suggest themselves, along with a change in voice, demeanor, and perhaps even a chance for some disarming humor.

Reframing is not meant to be a trick or a manipulation. It is realizing people hold multiple ideas about the world they experience. Often these are different than ours. With this in mind we can view the behavior of others positively and then sincerely act toward them accordingly. In our work, we have found that those teachers who are familiar with and can embody the norms found in this chapter have the most ease in using reframing with integrity. If you are not clear about these norms, you may want to review them before proceeding. This procedure is not meant to eliminate talking to someone about a sensitive matter (see the discussion of culturally responsive teacher-learner conferences in Chapter Three). Reframing is a creative alternative.

Elements in the process of reframing are as follows (Molnar and Lindquist, 1989, p. 61):

1. Awareness of your current interpretation of what you consider to be the problem behavior

2. Creation of positive alternative interpretations of the behavior

3. Selection of a plausible positive interpretation

4. Formulation of a sentence or two that describes the new positive interpretation

5. Action that sincerely reflects this new interpretation

We have found using these elements to reflect on problematic student behaviors to be an excellent process for the generation of creative and effective solutions.

Structures for Establishing Inclusion

For the motivational goals presented in this book we suggest structures for the learning environment. These are formal patterns of organization, rules of operation, and other arrangements that determine such matters as how the learning group functions, how learning goals are achieved and assessed, and the binding expectations for individual learners—for example, course prerequisites, requirements, and grading policies. They are often codified as part of the course syllabus or school bulletin.

The motivational goal helps identify those structures that promote perspectives and behaviors necessary to realize its essential criteria. In this case the motivational goal is *inclusion*, and the criteria are *respect* and *connectedness*. By making certain structures fundamental to their courses, teachers and learners can legitimize actions and outcomes that enhance motivation and learning. This understanding becomes immediately obvious as we explore our first structural consideration: ground rules.

Ground Rules

Ground rules are the specific guidelines and explicit assumptions that govern the operation of the class. By clearly identifying the kinds of interactions that will be encouraged and discouraged, the teacher and learners can create a climate of safety and reassure everyone that they will be respected.

The first class meeting is the appropriate time to convey the guiding perspective of the course and to request cooperation in implementing its ground rules. Ground rules can be entirely constructed in a collaborative manner with learners. However, those courses whose primary purpose is to diminish social injustices such as racism and sexism usually report greater chances for mutual respect among learners and teachers when ground rules and assumptions are directly conveyed by the teacher (Cherrin, 1993). For example, if the course holds a *committed perspective* that learners will be using as they study, such as a feminist viewpoint or a value system that favors change toward equality in society, this should be clearly communicated. Therefore, the idea of striving for equality is not up for debate, although what equality means and how best to achieve it are issues that require further thought and discussion. Such clarity about operating assumptions helps learners to know what to expect and how it will be framed, reducing the emergence of unnecessary conflict. As an example, see the context and working assumptions employed by Beverly Daniel Tatum (1992) in her course, The Psychology of Racism.

Using a consensus decision-making process, where everyone has to agree, we have found the following rules to be acceptable as well as extremely beneficial to establishing inclusion (Adams and Marchesani, 1992; Tatum, 1992).

1. No put downs, even for comic relief.

2. Respect the confidentiality of the group.

3. Speak from one's own experience, to say, for example, "I think . . ." or "In my experience I have found . . ." rather than to generalize our experience to others, as in "People say . . ." or "We believe . . ."

4. No blame.

5. Carefully listen.

6. Offer honest expressions and opinions.

Although we do not use a specific conflict negotiation model, when a serious disagreement emerges, a method that we have found effective is to request that before one can state an opposing opinion, the individual must be able to state the position of the other person in a way that will satisfy that person. This usually helps to defuse careless arguing.

While the above list is sometimes longer, most learners easily accept and generate these rules because they reduce feelings of awkwardness, embarrassment, shame, and being threatened. They also provide the framework for critical discourse, an essential component of challenging learning and an equitable society. Leaving ground rules open to further additions and referring to them as necessary keeps the boundaries of the class clear and dynamic.

Learning Communities

To establish inclusion we have encouraged the idea of building a sense of community among learners. *Learning communities,* as the term is used here, refers to the intentional restructuring of a postsecondary curriculum to link together courses or different disciplines around a common theme so that students find greater coherence in what they are learning and increased interaction with faculty and peers (Gabelnick, MacGregor, Matthews, and Smith, 1990). Thus, learning communities are facilitating structures for the practice of collaborative learning.

Thirty colleges in Washington and dozens of additional colleges in the United States and Canada have launched a wide variety of learning community programs. On two- and four-year campuses interest in the approach continues to grow. Although they vary widely from campus to campus, learning communities appear to serve two common purposes: (1) they attempt to provide intellectual coherence for students by linking classes together and building relationships between subject matter, or by teaching a skill such as writing in the context of a discipline; and (2) they strive to build both academic and social community for learners by enrolling them as a cohort group in a large block of course work (Smith and MacGregor, 1992).

Learning communities directly address many of the issues that concern postsecondary education, such as isolation of learners, lack of intellectual connection between courses, and the dire need for greater interaction among learners and faculty, especially on large campuses and in commuter schools. Initial research indicates these programs are generally successful, resulting in higher rates of student retention, increased student achievement, and more complex intellectual development (MacGregor, 1991).

An example of a particular learning community is one of the Coordinated Studies Programs (CSP), Our Ways of Knowing: The African-American Experience and Social Change, at Seattle Central Community College. The school serves a diverse population of students, most of whom work while attending college. Students enroll for eighteen credits within the subjects of sociology, art, political science, and English. They attend class Monday through Thursday from nine to one-thirty. On Wednesday from twelve to one-thirty the class of about eighty to ninety students breaks up into seminars, with each of four instructors meeting with about twenty students. This course is not completely devoid of lectures and writing papers. However, the key elements of cross-disciplinary topics, team teaching, continuous class meeting times, and a focus on collaborative learning provide a distinctly different learning experience for most students.

A study of the Coordinated Studies Programs (Tinto, Goodsell-Love, and Russo, 1994) found student persistence (reenrollment) was greater among CSP students than among students in the traditional class settings. In addition, CSP students were more socially and academically involved. As the researchers point out, rather than focus on student behaviors and student obligations alone, postsecondary institutions should more carefully consider the character of their own obligations to construct the sorts of educational settings in which all students, not just some, will want to become involved.

For a comprehensive discussion of learning communities that addresses their conception, implementation, and learning processes, read *Learning Communities: Creating Connections Among Students, Faculty, and Disciplines* (Gabelnick, MacGregor, Matthews, and Smith, 1990).

Cooperative Base Groups

Another possible structural means to enhance inclusion are cooperative base groups. These are heterogeneous, cooperative learning groups that last for the duration of a course, have a stable membership, and whose primary responsibilities are to provide support, encouragement, and assistance in completing assignments and to hold each other accountable for striving to learn (Johnson, Johnson, and Smith, 1991). The larger the class and/or the more complex the subject matter the more base groups can provide a sense of connectedness and reduce feelings of alienation and anomie. Such groups also increase the probability that diverse perspectives will be shared, increasing the richness and intrinsic value of the learning experience.

In order to effectively establish base groups we suggest the following guidelines and goals adapted from the work of Johnson, Johnson, and Smith (1991):

1. Use cooperative learning groups from the very beginning of the course for class activities and instructional purposes until the five essential components (see the section on cooperative learning in this chapter) are understood and some expertise in using cooperative learning is evident among the learners before assigning base groups.

2. Have a reasonable awareness of your students and wait for class membership to stabilize before assigning base groups.

3. Set base groups at four to five members to allow for more diversity and lessen the pressure of initial interdependence.

4. Schedule frequent meetings of the base groups during class time (at the beginning and/or ending of class often works best).

5. Make sure the purposes of the base groups are well understood.

The following are suggested goals for base groups; they can be modified according to your course and learners' profile.

1. To give assistance, support, and encouragement for mastering course content and skills and to provide feedback on how well the content and skills are being learned.

2. To give assistance, support, and encouragement for thinking critically about course content, understanding what one learns, engaging in intellectual controversy, getting work done on time, and applying what is learned to one's own life as well as to the broader world.

3. To provide comradeship throughout the course and a means for trying out collaborative learning procedures and skills.

4. To provide a structure for managing course procedures, such as homework, attendance, and assessment.

5. To enjoy one's success and to help other groups to be successful until all members of the class are successful. This is a means to share the rewards of the members' talents and experiences.

It often helps to provide an agenda for base group meetings, especially in their beginning phase. Such an agenda could include:

1. Checking in, using such questions as, How are people doing and are we all prepared for this class period? Has everyone read the assignment? Has everyone done the problems?

2. Focusing on academic support by checking what assignments each member has and what help he or she may need to understand or complete them, preparing for tests and reviewing them afterwards, and sharing expertise and helping each other to practice skills (during or outside of class).

3. Summarizing, reviewing, or critiquing what they have read and sharing resources they have found regarding course content and assignments.

4. Getting to know each other better by asking such questions as, What's the best thing that has happened to you this week? What's a problem you'd like to solve?

Some base groups will face relationship challenges. Some take longer to cohere. Teacher patience and the suggestions offered in the earlier discussion of group processing apply to base groups as well. Periodically assessing how base groups are functioning (with a short survey) as well as being available to meet with them to enhance relationships are typical ways to ensure the success of this structure from the beginning to the end of a course. For information about college base groups (those lasting from a year to four years) and advisee base groups, see *Active Learning: Cooperation in the College Classroom* (Johnson, Johnson, and Smith, 1991).

This chapter has discussed the three organizational constructs of norms, procedures, and structures as a way of conceptualizing and creating a learning environment with attendant experiences and consequences that foster a critical motivational condition—in this case, inclusion. These elements work in concert. Therefore, a norm such as *sharing the ownership of knowing* makes a procedure like *cooperative learning* more effective and attractive, especially as conducted within the structure of a *learning community*. Each specific organizational construct we have proposed acts as an integrative force in support and facilitation of the others. A procedure like peer teaching is worthwhile in a classroom where the norm is cooperation. Otherwise, in a classroom where competition is the norm, such an approach might be considered a waste of time.

What we believe and how we act are inextricably bound. Until we espouse norms and provide fundamental structures with consistent, appropriate procedures, there will be little chance for genuine transformation in postsecondary teaching. Nowhere is this more true than in the area of inclusion as it supports diversity. People need to know they are respected in order to risk being who they are. A mere teaching technique does not instill such a faith. It is the result of a determined symmetry of explicit ideals, practices, and structures.

Chapter Three

Developing Attitude

"I sure did live in this world."

"Really? What have you got to show for it?"

"Show? To who? Girl, I got my mind. And what goes
on in it. Which is to say, I got me."

"Lonely, ain't it?"

"Yes. But my lonely is *mine*. Now your lonely is
somebody else's. Made by somebody else and
handed to you. Ain't that something?
A secondhand lonely."

—*Toni Morrison, Sula*

Even though she has been getting above-average test scores, Maria
Sanchez is thinking about dropping the geology course taught by
Beverly Kubiak. Ms. Sanchez still ruminates over why her opinion
about this class has changed, remembering how it began and
seemed to get off to such a good start. Ms. Kubiak's enthusiasm
and sincerity were compelling. She said no one should fail the
course, all assignments would be clear, and she would be available
to help anyone who needed it. These are promises she has kept, as
Ms. Sanchez's classmates reminded her when she first spoke of feeling dissatisfied.

Although she finds it difficult to explain, Ms. Sanchez knows
what bothers her most: she's finishing, not learning. The course is

laid out like a map. Read chapter six, do experiments three and four, make appropriate notes in your journal, pass the quiz on Friday, and it will be all right. When she suggested to Ms. Kubiak that she'd like to substitute a couple of different experiments for the ones assigned and that she'd prefer to do the semester's project on geological formations native to the region where she grew up, Ms. Kubiak said she had good reasons why Ms. Sanchez could not do this. The course had specific standards of performance, and there was a related sequence of skill and knowledge acquisition. To alter the assigned pattern would interrupt these objectives and unfairly increase Ms. Kubiak's work load. With a smile, case closed.

Some of Ms. Sanchez's friends think she's foolish to be upset.

"You got an attitude."

"Just do it."

"Get the grade and move on. You won't even think of this course two weeks after it's done."

"She's not so bad."

Ms. Sanchez resists. She feels as if she's stepped onto a train and she doesn't like where it's going. She knows Ms. Kubiak's course is better than a few others she's already passed. Yet, somehow, in it, she feels more trapped than successful.

In the scenario just depicted, Ms. Sanchez might be considered by some to have a bad attitude. She's in a course that is thoroughly organized, with a teacher who wants her to do well and is willing to help her. The road to success is clear. Yet from Ms. Sanchez's perspective, there is a catch. You have to do the course exactly the way the teacher has designed it. No exceptions. Learners who find the assignments interesting, who are highly motivated to receive a high grade, who are at ease with benevolent authoritarian teachers, or who possess cultural values that accept and prepare them for this routine would probably find Ms. Kubiak's requirements to be acceptable, if not typical. For Ms. Sanchez, completing the course may be at the very least a minor surrender and possibly, in a deeper sense, a further step along the path to cultural suicide.

Yet, from Ms. Kubiak's perspective, the rationale she has given Ms. Sanchez is probably legitimate. Her work load may be overwhelming. She may think Ms. Sanchez does not like the assignment because its similarity to the procedures other students must follow forces a comparison between the quality of her work and theirs. Ms. Kubiak may also fear that making an exception for Ms. Sanchez is unfair to the other students, possibly requiring her to individualize assignments for many other learners. From each of their viewpoints, Ms. Sanchez and Ms. Kubiak have arguments to support their behavior. However, by allowing so little flexibility in the procedures of learning and topical choice, Ms. Kubiak has eliminated opportunities to make learning relevant to the social identities of *all* her students and inadvertently denied the influence that cultural interaction styles and profiles of intelligences have on the learning and motivation of people.

Many students of color, especially students whose families and communities continue to experience racial, class, and gender disparities that are centuries old, may distrust the larger European-American society and its institutions, including postsecondary education (Sleeter, 1994; Ogbu, 1987; Gibson, 1987). Historically, the very notion of human nature has been addressed in terms of an implicit standard that is primarily white, primarily male, and primarily Western (Sampson, 1993). The possibility for marginalized and underrepresented learners to be heard in their own way and on their own terms, reflecting their own interests and ways of knowing and learning, is institutionally denied in most college classrooms. These conditions do not reflect mere chance but rather the ability of those in power to create the terms according to which social reality will be encountered.

To deny these political aspects of education is a serious mistake. It is also why, in part, the two most important criteria for developing a positive attitude among learners are relevance and self-determination. Because attitudes help people to make meaning of their world and give cues as to what behavior will be most helpful in dealing with that world, irrelevant learning can startle, annoy, and frighten us. Not only does such learning seem unimportant or strange, we implicitly know we are doing it because of someone else's domination or control. This triggers or develops a negative attitude. We are wasting our time or worse because of someone's power over us. In such instances, self-determination would act as a means of avoiding or altering irrelevant learning to better fit our perspectives and values. Without choice or voice our alienation is invited.

Relevance, Self-Determination, and Intrinsic Motivation

Personal relevance is not simply familiarity with a learning activity based on the learner's prior experience. Because of media inundation a person could be familiar with a particular television program or magazine and find it totally irrelevant. Personal relevance is the degree to which learners can identify their perspective and values in the course content, discussion, and methods of inquiry. In other words the learning processes are connected to who they are, what they care about, and how they perceive and know. In its most comprehensive dimensions, relevancy occurs when learning is contextualized and anchored in the personal, communal, and cultural meanings of the learner; allows the learner's voice to remain intact; and reflects the learner's construction of reality. In this process the teacher and the learner figuratively become co-authors, taking neither their own view nor the view of the other to be specially privileged but entering into a genuine dialogue, with each standpoint having its own integrity (Clifford, 1986).

Once learners can be this spontaneous and authentic, acting from their deepest and most vital selves, they naturally strive for coherence among the aspects of themselves and their world that are in their awareness (Deci and Ryan, 1991). Their natural curiosity emerges; they want to make sense of things and seek out those challenges that are within their range of capacities and values. All of this leads to what human beings experience as interest, the emotional nutrient for a positive attitude toward learning.

When we feel interested we begin to have to make choices about what to do to follow that interest, which leads to our need for self-determination, the second criterion for developing a positive attitude among learners. Self-determination is the need to be the origin of one's own behavior. Acting self-determined involves a sense of choice, a sense of feeling free in doing what one has chosen to do (de Charms, 1968; Deci and Ryan, 1991). For the process of learning—the thinking, the practicing, the reading, the revising, the studying, and other similar activities—to be desirable and within proximity to genuine enjoyment, learners must see themselves as personally endorsing their own learning. From the perspective of democracy, from the perspective of personal well-being, and from the perspective of academic achievement, global history and psychological research merge to support this observation: people consistently struggle against oppressive control and strive to determine their own lives as an expression of their true selves. For us as teachers, the question is not *should* we but *how can* we provide learners with choice and minimize pressure on them to perform in specified ways while encouraging their initiation of new learning with a respect for their perspectives, values, strengths, and needs? The consideration of the role of language as it relates to learners' attitudes can further deepen our understanding of how to approach some of the answers to this multifaceted question.

Language and Attitude

Integral to relevance and the development of a positive attitude toward learning is the learner's ability to identify with the values of the learning context and to negotiate inconsistencies for social, intellectual, emotional, creative, and spiritual growth. Because language manifests values and shapes reality, *words are deeds*

(Wetherell and Potter, 1992). Language is, perhaps, the strongest influence on whether or not a learner believes that what is happening in the classroom is relevant to his or her own beliefs, needs, and interests. Language leads to rapport when purposes, interests, values, and outlooks among people become mutually understandable and trusted. This is the "common ground" that supports the capacity to accept and negotiate differences between people. Although *multicultural communication skills* is too large and complex a topic to be adequately discussed in a book with our focus, we want at least to address the issues of (1) negotiating language with learners to remove inaccurate and demeaning labels and (2) understanding how language can be used to promote participation for non-native speakers of English. In general, anything teachers can do to respectfully communicate a sensitive awareness of the figures of speech, interests, and values of their diverse students should enhance their positive attitudes toward the teachers and the learning at hand.

Negotiating Language

In culturally diverse classrooms, because we and our students frequently originate from different communities, the language we use varies. Certain words or terms have connotations that make them acceptable or objectionable to different people. Literal definitions interact with connotations, and ultimately connotations may be the most significant reason why a word is accepted or rejected. In addition, words and terms change periodically with new rationales. For example, *American Indian* is a term that has been reclaimed by many native people. *Native American,* a term once preferred by many American Indian activists, is sometimes criticized for its non-specific reference to all native people—including native Hawaiians, several native Alaskan tribes, Aleuts, and Mexican people whose families originate from the part of the United States that was once Mexico. Although American Indian, which connotes residence on the United States mainland, is often preferred to the more generic term, Native American, many native people prefer reference to their specific tribal affiliation, when possible.

Another term that is commonly used but is criticized by some for subsuming vast numbers of distinct peoples under a single rubric is *Hispanic*. Consider that Hispanic people can originate from countries such as Cuba, Puerto Rico, Mexico, Spain, or Portugal and nations in Central or South America. Some people prefer *Latino*, which connotes an identification with Latin America. Some people prefer *Chicano*, a term that was reclaimed by people from Mexico to stress the strong and unique culture that is being developed in the United States. In that Latino and Chicano are masculine terms, many people encourage the use of *Latina* and *Chicana* in reference to women.

These are only two words from many possibilities that teachers and learners may wish to clarify. As other words arise in conversation, it may be necessary or desirable to ask for assistance and other perspectives. This can be easy and enjoyable — especially when, early on, students have had experience identifying potentially problematic words, considering alternatives, and selecting language that conveys the greatest degree of respect. Different classes may elect different words of which to be cognizant. There is not a perfect solution to words that seem outdated, inaccurate, or pejorative. Even if this were so, we do not want to be so self-conscious that we are paralyzed out of fear of making a mistake. The experience of openly learning together and appreciating that language strongly influences our ability to be heard and to be fair is foremost. We have known verbal purists who rarely make a mistake with language but who thwart rather than invite sincere dialogue. Our goal is greater appreciation for each other and the diversity of meaning we inadvertently convey.

The process of negotiating language can take many forms. Our preference has been, when appropriate, to initiate a dialogue early on with a class about terms or language that could jeopardize the ability to be heard and to hear others. We ask learners to think for a moment about words that cause self-consciousness when used or heard. We also ask learners to think of words that can cause anger. Learners pursue this process in concert with a partner, recording words and related concerns about them. Working with a partner enhances the involvement of all class members and creates a less reactive alternative to a large group discussion. We then ask partners to identify other words that may be more acceptable. Finally, we come together as a class to compose a list of problematic terms and expressions and to cooperatively identify our best ideas. Even if different preferences for certain terms are expressed within a group, the dialogue sets the stage for greater understanding and latitude later on when words might otherwise create obstacles.

Promoting Participation for Non-Native Speakers of English

The scholarship of Jim Cummins (1981) has greatly influenced methodology employed by teachers of learners acquiring English as a second language by distinguishing between language used for social and academic purposes. Kate Kinsella's consolidation (1993) of his theory completes this section and offers college teachers a number of useful insights.

Basic Interpersonal Communications Skills (BICS) is the social language that enables learners to participate in everyday, informal, conversational exchanges. They largely acquire BICS naturally in daily interaction at school, at work, and socializing with peers. Therefore, the more opportunities learners have to communicate in a variety of contexts in English both in and away from school, the faster they become fluent users of social English. Most of the common activities in college classes require not only a strong foundation in BICS but an equally high proficiency in Cognitive Academic Language Proficiency (CALP). CALP is the academic language that enables learners to deal with more cognitively demanding and context-reduced communicative situations and materials such as formal lectures, lengthy class discussions, standardized tests, mainstream textbooks, and educational films.

Research suggests that it takes English learners approximately two years to become proficient in BICS and five to seven years to acquire native-like competence in CALP. Academic language proficiency is largely developed through extensive reading in a variety of academic contexts and through years of repeated exposure to academic terminology during classes. However, many English learners enter the United States school system or advance to mainstream secondary and postsecondary content area classes with limited academic literacy in English. Even learners who speak social English with fluency may have surprisingly weak reading and listening skills in their academic English proficiency.

To further clarify the distinction between BICS and CALP, Cummins has proposed that language uses be located on a quadrant with two continua. The horizontal line in Figure 3.1 distinguishes between *context-embedded* communicative situations, which offer a variety of contextual clues to assist in the comprehension of language (for example, facial expressions, gestures, real objects, and feedback from the speaker/listener), and *context-reduced* communicative situations, which offer few clues (for example, a formal lecture, a textbook page, a calculus equation). The vertical line in Figure 3.1 extends from *cognitively undemanding* to *cognitively demanding* communicative situations. The distinction between these two terms may be explained as the difference between a more automatic subconscious control of the routines of everyday life (undemanding) and a conscious deliberate focus on comprehending new language, concepts, and material (demanding).

Most common academic activities within college classes are both cognitively demanding and context reduced, making comprehension and retention of material extremely challenging for learners who have not yet acquired full English language proficiency. Instructors across all disciplines can greatly enhance

Figure 3.1. Range of Contextual Support and Degree of Cognitive Involvement in Communicative Activities.

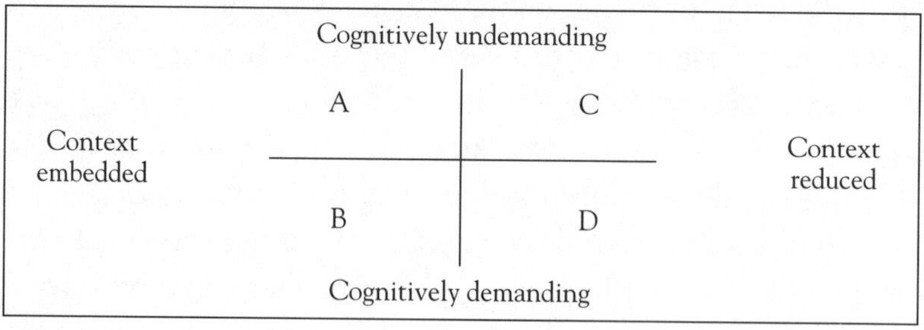

Source: Kinsella, 1993, p. 12. Used by permission.

learning and participation for non-native speakers of English by adding linguistic and contextual support to their lessons, thereby moving the cognitively demanding curriculum form quadrant D (context reduced) to quadrant B (context embedded). For example, students learning another language with the use of audio tapes (context reduced) would much prefer learning the same language in conversation with native speakers of the language in real-life settings (context embedded).

One can immediately see the advantages of collaborative, experiential, and active learning procedures that tend to be context embedded and rich with communication cues. In Resource A we have provided Kinsella's suggestions for increasing the effectiveness of lectures and discussions that involve non-native speakers of English.

Norms for Developing a Positive Attitude

In order to help learners to develop a positive attitude toward learning we offer two norms. These norms create an awareness and an expectation that within the educational community, learning will consistently be relevant and self-determined. To this end the first norm is: *In general, all teaching and learning activities are contextualized in the learners' experience or previous knowledge and are accessible through their current thinking and ways of knowing.* Principles and abstractions can be related to the everyday world of the learners (Tharp, 1989). Personal and community-based experiences can be drawn upon to provide a foundation for developing skills and knowledge (Wyatt, 1978–1979). As teachers we can display an open and accommodating sensitivity to the learners' knowledge, experience, values, and tastes. When application of learning is considered, it ought to be, where possible, related to the interests and cultural perspectives of the learners. When learners' previous circumstances and current knowledge have not allowed for a development of personal interest in the topics and concepts to be learned, experiences need to be constructed to allow the learners to appreciate the emerging relevance (see Chapter Four) such new learning activities afford. A pedagogical approach to fostering this norm is offering learner choice and teaching to a range of profiles of intelligences (Gardner, 1993) and learning styles. This helps us to identify and respect the learning preferences and differences that exist within a group of diverse people.

Pragmatically, the second norm, student self-determination, is what enables teachers to establish relevance in multicultural classrooms. From a purely functional standpoint we as teachers cannot possibly be aware of all the different experiences and backgrounds of our diverse students. We need ways to hear their voices, and unless there are meaningful choices for learners about how and what to learn, their voices have little chance to be genuinely expressed about academic matters. Also, the process of co-learning cannot take place without our acceptance of the learners' prerogative. The norm of self-determination means the educational community accepts and understand that *the entire academic process of learning, from content selection to accomplishment and assessment of competencies, encourages learners to make real choices based on their experience, values, needs, and strengths.* With an appreciation for the limitations of institutional requirements (for example, licensing and certification codes), time, and the rights and preferences of other learners, students can make academic decisions about *what, how, how well,* and *why they learn.*

Choosing what to learn is usually a fairly direct process. Choices include the actual topic, the types of materials dealing with the topic, the skills or questions of concern relative to the topic, and/or the types of assignments and learning goals based on the topic. How we frame topics and assignments usually determines the degree to which learners may be autonomous. Consider the wording, "After you have read the *assigned* story, select *one* of these *two* artists and exemplify how you imagine she would render an expression of the story's protagonist." Another possibility is "Select a story by one of your favorite authors and consider an artist whose work has passionately affected you. Then exemplify how that artist might render an expression of what you find most vital about the story." Each assignment offers choice, but the degree of potential choice and relevance vary considerably between the two possibilities.

Issues about how to learn relate to learner choice. Among them are whether to work alone, in small groups, or as an entire class. There is also the matter of where to learn: in class, in the community, on a class trip, and so on. If practice reflects theory, most postsecondary educators apparently believe that all students learn in similar ways. College classrooms continue to use the lecture and the textbook as their main staples of instruction. However, recent advances in our understanding of individual learning tell us that learners who are motivated to learn but whose own learning styles and profiles of intelligence are not in tune with prevailing instructional practice are frequently casualties of this system (Gardner, 1991). The norm for self-determination means schools and teachers make efforts to provide instruction and resources compatible with the variety of capabilities and preferred ways of learning among students. For example, some people may be better able to remember and understand a quantitative concept in biology if it is approached numerically and with deductive reasoning (abstract-quantitative, as in an analysis of reported research), while others may be more likely to excel by dealing directly with the materials that experientially embody or convey the concept and its numerical considerations (concrete-quantitative, as in a field study). Making these choices available to learners increases their chances of learning in an engaging way that is relevant to their characteristic learning modes.

Offering learners opportunities to decide how well they have learned something may be seen by conventional postsecondary teachers as the most radical set of academic choices to make available to learners, but it is probably the kind of decision making that gives them the greatest sense of control over their learning. Determining the criteria by which work will be judged and then playing a role in assessing work against those criteria makes one's personal sense of responsibility for learning self-evident, catalyzes one's inborn motivation to be autonomous and competent, and is a terrific learning experience in itself. Learners can derive immense intellectual benefits from considering what makes an essay well written, a problem solution creative, or an example conceptually clear. When learners help to decide what a test should include and how it should be given, determination of their own learning is evident. (We deal with this issue more thoroughly in Chapter Five.)

For learners, choosing why they are learning something gets at the philosophical heart of their own education. Cultural values are bound to enter into the creation of the purposes that direct learning. Consider, for example, that when learners believe in why they are solving a problem or developing a project their learning has a chance to attain deep personal significance as well as intellectual insight. Do we do a research study only to find an answer or also to elevate our minds with a more thorough understanding of an important phenomenon? Do we decide on an environmental project because it is a convenient way to complete a course or because it might offer an insight about something we believe ought to remain on this earth? When courses have the possibility of aligning their purposes with the deeply held beliefs of their learners, something quite powerful and lasting for learners and teachers is possible.

Resistance to the norm of self-determination is not uncommon. Schooling frequently socializes us to accept a posture of passivity. Schooling has also created conditions in which a mistrust of authorities who offer choice is a healthy reaction to histories of feeling manipulated or used for "experimental purposes." Further, some learners have found schooling to be so oppressive and difficult that they believe the locus of causality in learning is outside of themselves. Choice only increases their sense of apprehension. It is also important to respect the authoritarian and hierarchical orientation toward sustained learning held, for example, by some international students. These learners may find too much choice to be a disorienting and uncomfortable option. Therefore, we recommend that this norm be established as a flexible set of assumptions where learners still find among their choices some of the more conventional alternatives. Where those do not exist, we recommend the establishment of a support system to help learners evolve toward a more self-determined approach to learning. For example, a learner might prefer to take a test based on a standard textbook in order to convey her or his grasp of a set of concepts rather than to create a project in a collaborative learning group that offers a more robust display of similar knowledge. If such a preference can be accommodated without destroying the integrity of the course, this or a similar option should be made available. With each subsequent set of choices, learners can be encouraged to try other approaches. To continue to respect the voices of learners means relevance and self-determination are guided by their perspective and not our singular vision. At times this is, indeed, a tightrope we must carefully walk.

Procedures for Developing a Positive Attitude

The process of teaching and learning is complicated and, when done well, quite intricate and subtle. As we begin to discuss procedures for developing a positive attitude toward learning we see more clearly the shift from conventional instructional practices that emphasize discreet, competitive, "ability-based" academic goals to application-based goals where development of understanding and competence are of primary concern. If we desire to provide equitable motivational opportunities for diverse learners in post-secondary education we have to offer complex and meaningful academic experiences that present a variety of performance opportunities across multiple profiles of intelligences and styles and that allow for learner choice and responsibility. In this manner we can increase the possibilities for the motivated learning of all students, not simply of the high achievers. Table 3.1 offers a comparison of conventional teaching and culturally responsive teaching.

Learning-Goal Procedures

Self-determination among learners requires choice and minimizing teacher control. It also requires making available information that is needed for decision-making and for performing the agreed upon learning goal (Deci, Vallerand, Pelletier, and Ryan, 1991). As soon as people know the goals and procedures of a course, they begin to form a personal theory about the choices and competencies necessary for accomplishing those tasks (Paris and Byrnes, 1989). They ask themselves such questions as, What do I already know about this? Is this worthwhile? Where do I start? What can I do to do this well? Am I able to do this? Is the evaluation system used fair and reasonable? From this sort of reflection, people hypothesize how much control they can exert and how effective they will be while learning. The conclusions they reach very much influence their attitude toward learning.

Clearly Defined Goals. When specific skills or competencies are appropriate and meaningful, as in technical subject areas such as medicine and engineering, clearly defined goals can heighten learners' conscious awareness of control and competence. These goals

Table 3.1. Comparison of Conventional Teaching
and Culturally Responsive Teaching.

Key Elements	Conventional Teaching	Culturally Responsive Teaching
Source of knowledge and skills	Simple, one-way, from teacher to learners or textbook to learners. Perceived value is teacher-centered.	Complex, teacher-learner interactive, allowing individual search and reflection—frequently with integrated subject matter. Perceived value is amalgam of teacher and learner preferences.
Learning environment organization	Hierarchical and linear. Teacher directed. Competitive.	Complex. Thematic, integrative, cooperative, open, and individualized. Teacher-learner controlled.
Preferred outcomes	Specified and convergent. Emphasis on memorized vocabulary, concepts, and skills. Ability-based goals.	Complex. Emphasis on understanding and competence as well as reorganization of knowledge and skills in unique ways. Both predictable and unpredictable outcomes. Divergent/convergent thinking. Learning demonstrated in varied and relevant contexts. Authentic, application-based goals.

let learners know the skills they need to acquire, informing them about what is necessary to achieve them. Confusion is less likely, and learners more clearly understand and can discuss what is expected of them. For non-native speakers of English this may be critical. A medical technician is likely to appreciate knowing he or she is expected to learn to take a blood sample and obtain the blood type, hemoglobin content, and Rh factor using standard laboratory procedures (Gronlund, 1978). However, we should not feel compelled to abandon educational aims that cannot be reduced to measurable forms of predictable performance. Unnecessarily standardizing knowledge often devalues critical and intellectual work, trivializing the deeper meanings of relevance and choice.

Problem-Solving Goals. Much—perhaps most—of what we aspire to and cherish as human beings is not amenable to uniform and pre-specified description. Language is a substitute for experience. We try to say in words what we know in nonlinguistic ways. How could one convincingly define integrity or describe how water tastes? As Elliot Eisner (1985) has stated, "For much of our experience, discursive language performs rather well. But for the subtleties of human experience, for our knowledge of human feelings, for modes of conception and understanding that are qualitative, discourse falls far short . . . The point here is not an effort to inject the mystical into educational planning but rather to avoid reductionistic thinking that impoverishes our view of what is possible. To expect all of our educational aspirations to be either verbally describable or measurable is to expect too little" (p. 115).

The problem-solving goal differs in a significant way from the conventional instructional objective. In the problem-solving goal, the learners formulate or are given a problem to solve. In a social science course, for example, they might be asked how to reduce heterosexism on campus; or for an architecture course, how to design a paper structure that will hold two bricks sixteen inches above a table. In each of these examples the problem is posed and the goals that need to be achieved to resolve the problem can be made fairly clear. But the forms of its solution range from many to infinite (Eisner, 1985; Schön, 1987). Relative to heterosexism, some learners might design a conference, including topics, format, speakers, and interaction strategies; others might create a course, outlining its syllabus, readings, and learning activities; and another group might develop a survey, research the campus with it, and as a result of the data gathered submit a proposal that best reflects the opinions and suggestions of those interviewed.

The idea here is that the kinds of solutions and the forms they take are highly variable. Alternative solutions to problem-solving goals can be shared in class so that learners can appreciate the different perspectives and their related outcomes. This enhances relevance and self-determination and simultaneously affirms the value of multiple perspectives and ways of knowing.

Problem-solving goals are common in the design field, science laboratories, media arts and technology, and local and national politics. Designers, for example, are usually given a set of criteria or specifications and asked to generate a creation that will satisfy those criteria. Often they are asked to create several alternatives so that the client can decide which of these options best suits his or her needs.

With problem-solving goals the potential answers are not definite or known beforehand. The problem is a genuine one. The solution learners reach has the possibility of being a genuine surprise for them. Problem-solving objectives place a premium on intellectual exploration and the higher mental processes while supporting different cultural perspectives and values. Because this approach encourages ingenuity it breeds interest for students from a variety of cultures.

Expressive Outcomes. Another type of educational aim identified by Eisner (1985) focuses on expressive outcomes, learning goals that emerge as the result of an intentionally planned activity. In these instances, learning goals do not precede educational activity; they are formulated in the process of action itself. They are what we and the learner construct, intended or not, after some form of engagement. How many times have we read a book, or seen a film, the brilliance of which affords so many questions and inspirations that to limit a learner to our educational intention is a confinement of imagination? The encouragement of expressive outcomes allows us to reciprocally share with learners various media or experiences (that may derive from the learners themselves) and then to mutually decide what direction learning should take. Again, this approach supports the preeminence of learner self-determination and perspective in defining relevant learning goals. One of the authors once began a course in adolescent psychology by watching and discussing with his class five mutually chosen films in which adolescents were the main characters. After these viewings and through the dialogue that evolved, the learners participated in constructing the course topics, the selected reading list, and the projects they wanted to do to evidence their learning. The experience was so successful that it was expanded the next semester to include two seniors from a local high school as co-teachers.

Fair and Clear Criteria of Evaluation

Assessment is comprehensively discussed in Chapter Five. However, because learning goals and evaluation procedures go hand in hand in most postsecondary courses, we need to pay some attention to criteria of evaluation as an attitudinal issue at this stage of the text. The outcomes of assessment in the form of grades and quantitative scores powerfully influence self-determination, self-worth, and the access of learners to careers, further education, and financial aid (for example, scholarships and grants). Therefore, evaluation criteria are extremely relevant to developing or inhibiting a positive attitude toward learning. Whenever learning goals are formulated, evaluation procedures and criteria should be addressed simultaneously.

If the criteria of evaluation are clear and agreed to as fair by learners, they know which elements of performance and creativity are essential. They can more easily self-evaluate and self-determine their learning as they proceed. This should enhance learner motivation, because learners can anticipate the results of their learning and regulate their options (for example, studying, writing, practicing, and so on) with more certainty.

In general, we ought to demonstrate how we and/or our learners will go about assessing the quality of their learning: what is being looked for, how it is valued, and, how it will be indicated. This usually means clarifying terms, standards, and calibration of measurement so that we and our learners come to a common under-standing and agreement about how these are applied, scored, and integrated as indicators of learning.

The less mystery about evaluation criteria, the more learners are likely to self-evaluate and self-direct their learning. We recom-mend allowing for questions and suggestions about assessment. It is often very beneficial to make available examples of concrete learn-ing outcomes that have already been evaluated by the criteria to be used. Past tests, papers, projects, and media can give learners real-istic examples of how these criteria have been applied. Exemplary models of other learners' accomplishments often hold the power to inspire their peers (Wlodkowski, 1985).

Relevant Learning Models

Any time learners can witness people similar to themselves (in age, gender, ethnicity, class, and so on) competently performing the desired learning goal, their self-confidence is heightened, because they are prone to believe that they, too, possess the capabilities to master comparable activities (Bandura, 1982). People that learners can identify with also convey information more likely to be rele-vant to the perspectives and values of the learners themselves. This further increases the learners' trust in using the strategies being seen or suggested.

With film and video technology we have creative and eco-nomical ways to offer learners vicarious examples that are pertinent and realistic. Past students or graduates are an excellent source for live modeling sessions.

Goal Setting

As postsecondary pedagogy becomes more flexible and teaches for relevance across multiple perspectives and abilities, learning goals will more frequently take the form of projects and complex tasks.

The process of setting goals can help learners to consider present and future choices related to their learning goals and to become more aware of what is necessary to have an effective learning experience. This prevents learners from creating unrealistic expectations and gives them a chance to anticipate obstacles to learning. Learners realize more clearly that they can determine their own learning and, before ever beginning the learning task, have a chance to gauge their probability for accomplishment.

There are many different methods of goal setting. The one that follows is an eclectic adaptation of various models in the literature. If the learning goal is to have a good chance of being achieved and therefore initiated, the following criteria are to be considered with the learner. In order to take these criteria beyond abstract suggestions, we present an actual case from our experience to exemplify how the criteria can be applied.

Yolanda Scott-Machado, whose tribal affiliation is Makah, is a student in a research course. In order to learn more about a variety of skills and concepts including research design, validity, reliability, sampling procedures, statistical analysis, and operationalization, she wants to design, conduct, and report a research study in an area of personal interest. Yolanda has questions about the concept of learning styles, especially as it is applied to American Indians. She wants to carry out a study to determine if urban Indian high school students, when compared to urban European-American high school students, score significantly higher in the field-sensitive mode (a cognitive style in which patterns are perceived as wholes) as measured by the Witkin's Group Embedded Figures Test. This is an ambitious study for a new research student. We begin the goal-setting process by examining the criterion of achievability.

Achievability. Can the learner reach the learning goal with the skills and knowledge at hand? If not, is there any assistance available, and how dependable is that assistance?

Yolanda feels confident, and her competent completion of exercises in class substantiates that confidence. She is also a member of a class cooperative learning group and values her peers as knowledgeable resources. We work out a plan that includes a preliminary conference with peers to garner their support, and a follow-up call to me.

Is there enough time to reach the goal? If not, can more time be found, or should the goal be divided into smaller goals?

This is a bit tricky. Yolanda will need at least fifty students in each of her comparison groups. This will mean involving, at minimum, two high schools. Can she get the necessary permission? Who will do the testing and when? This could drag on and complicate the study.

Measurability. How will the learner specifically be able to gauge progress toward the goal and its achievement? In many circumstances this can be done quantatively, in terms of problems completed, pages read, or exercises finished. To respect different conceptualizations of how to accomplish long-range goals, scheduling intervals to talk about evolving experience is important.

We decide the most important next step is for Yolanda to write a research proposal and bring it in for a meeting with me. Then we might work out a schedule for her completion of the study.

Desirability. Why is the goal important? The learner may have to do it or should do it, but does the learner *want* to do it? If not, then the satisfaction level and sense of self-determination for the learner will be less. Goal setting can be used for required tasks, but this is best handled if we are clear about it and admit to the learner the reality of the situation to avoid any sense of manipulation.

Yolanda wants to do this study. She believes certain teaching practices derived from learning-styles research may not apply to some Northwest Indian tribes or urban Indians. Because these methods are so often advocated by educators for teaching Indians, she believes more caution about their use may be necessary.

Focus (optional). For some people, to avoid forgetting or procrastination, it is important to have a plan to keep the goal in the learner's awareness. For others, such an idea may seem oppressive. Possible reminders are outlines, chalkboard messages, and daily logs.

Yolanda found this option unnecessary.

Identify Resources and Learning Processes with the Learner.

Engaging the learner in a dialogue about how she or he would like to reach the learning goal can be a very creative process. This is the time to consider various talents and preferred ways of knowing. Will accomplishing the learning goal involve media, art, writing, or some other possibility? What form should it take—a story, a research project, or a personal multimedia presentation? Identifying outside resources such as library materials, local experts, exemplary models, or films, aid and sometimes inspire the entire learning process.

Yolanda decided to review the literature on learning styles, especially as it referred to American Indians and other native peoples. She also chose to interview a professor at another university and an Indian administrator at a local school district. She decided the format for reporting her study would be the conventional research thesis outline.

Commitment. A formal or informal gesture that indicates the learner's acceptance of the learning goal is a valuable part of the goal-setting process. It can range from a shared copy of notes taken at the meeting to a contract. This affirms the learner's self-determination and acknowledges the mutual agreement between the learner and the teacher, building trust, motivation, and cooperation for further work together.

Yolanda composed a contract that we agreed upon at our next meeting.

Arrange a Goal Review Schedule. Some time for contact between the learner and the teacher to maintain progress and refine learning procedures is usually necessary. Because of the way time varies in its meaning and feeling to different people, contact can be along regular or irregular intervals. The main idea is that trust and support continue.

We had three meetings at irregular intervals prior to Yolanda's completion of an excellent study. To find a large enough sample for her research, she eventually involved five high schools. Her research indicated that urban Indian high school students are more field-independent than European-American high school students, suggesting the possibility that previous research conducted on American Indian learning styles is far from conclusive across tribes and regions.

Learning Contracts

One of the fields most familiar with the use of learning contracts is adult education. Learning contracts are considered by practitioners in this field to be a significant means of fostering and providing for self-direction in learning (Knowles, 1986). They are an effective technique for helping learners pinpoint their learning interests, plan learning activities, identify resources that are relevant, and become skilled at self-assessment (Brookfield, 1986). The ability to write contracts is a learned skill, and teachers may have to spend considerable time guiding learners to focus on realistic and manageable activities. Our experience as teachers in undergraduate programs and graduate school support Brookfield's observation, "Particularly in institutions where other departments and program areas conform to a more traditional mode, learners will often find it unsettling, inconvenient, and annoying to be asked to work as self-directed learning partners in some kind of negotiated learning project. Notwithstanding the fact that learners may ultimately express satisfaction with this experience, initially, at least, there may be substantial resistance. It is crucial, then, that learners be eased into this mode . . . and faculty must make explicit from the outset the rationale behind the adoption of these techniques" (pp. 82–83).

Learning contracts are used to individualize the learning process and to provide maximum flexibility for content, pace, process, and outcome. They usually detail in writing what will be learned, how the learning will be accomplished, the period of time involved, and frequently the evaluation criteria to be used in assessing the learning. Learners can construct all, most, or part of the contract depending on the learner's and teacher's knowledge of the subject matter, resources available, restrictions of the program, and so on. For example, what is learned (objective) may not be negotiable, but how it is learned may be wide open to individual discretion.

The actual document is frequently divided into the categories found below (O'Donnell and Caffarella, 1990):

1. The learning goal or objective. (What are you going to learn?)
2. The choice of resources, strategies, and activities for learning. (How are you going to learn it?)
3. The target date for completion.
4. Evidence of accomplishment. (How are you going to demonstrate that you have learned it?)
5. Evaluation of the learning. (What are the criteria on which you will judge that learning, and who will be involved in that judging process?)

Exhibits 3.1 through 3.3 are different types of learning contracts. Exhibit 3.1 applies to a specific skill to be accomplished in a short period of time in an undergraduate communication skills course. Exhibit 3.2 applies to a very broad and comprehensive learning goal to be accomplished within a full semester in a graduate education program. Exhibit 3.3 is the contract submitted by Yolanda Scott-Machado.

Exhibit 3.1. Learning Contract for a Specific Skill.

Learning Goal: To apply paraphrasing skills to actual communication situations.

Learning Resources and Activities: View videotapes of paraphrasing scenarios. One hour of role-playing paraphrasing situations with peers.

Target Date: End of one week (date specified).

Evidence of Accomplishment: Participate in paraphrasing exercise under teacher's supervision.

Evaluation of Learning: Can contribute appropriate paraphrasing responses to 80 percent of the communicated messages. Validated by teacher.

Exhibit 3.2. Learning Contract for a Broad Goal.

Learning Goal: To learn about the effects of parent influence on student learning in school and to learn how to increase parent-school involvement in support of student learning activities.

Learning Resources and Activities: Go to the library and conduct a computer search for relevant research from the Educational Resources Information Center (ERIC). Read this literature and attend a workshop on parent partnerships sponsored by the National Association for Young Children. Request information from the National Black Child Development Project and the National Committee for Citizens in Education. Read books and articles by prominent parent involvement researchers and advocates, including Joyce Epstein, Dorothy Rich, James Comer, and Anne Henderson. Interview five parents, five teachers, and five school administrators on this topic.

Target Date: End of semester (date specified).

Evidence of Accomplishment: Create a parent-teacher handbook containing the following sections: The Role of Parents as Educators of Their Children; How to Develop School and Family Partnerships; Involving Parents in Student Learning; Communication Between Parents and School Personnel; and Suggestions for Successful Parent-Teacher Conferences. Make a two-hour presentation on the topic of "Parents and Schools: A Two-Way Commitment" to the local Parent Teacher Association, and videotape the program. Upon completion, present handbook, videotape, workshop participant evaluations, and self-evaluation.

Evaluation of Learning: Handbook will be clearly written for an audience of families, educators, and community members; will use examples

Exhibit 3.2. Learning Contract for a Broad Goal, Cont'd.

consistent with the experiences of the intended audience, and will contain recent research and references (validated by the teacher). Workshop evaluations will indicate the presentation was useful for learning new ways to create better teacher-parent collaboration. My self-evaluation will identify the value of what I learned from this entire process.

Exhibit 3.3. Learning Contract for a Research Study.

Learning Goal: To conduct a research study to determine if urban Indian high school students when compared to urban European-American high school students have a significant perceptual difference as measured by the Witkin's Group Embedded Figures Test.

Learning Resources and Activities: Conduct a review of the literature on learning styles, especially as this concept relates to American Indians. Interview a professor at the University of Washington who specializes in the relation of learning styles to people of color. Also, interview a local American Indian school administrator who has responsibility for a number of projects involving American Indian students. Carry out the research in communication with my cooperative learning group and our teacher.

Target Date: Two weeks before the end of the semester, to allow for revisions.

Evidence of Accomplishment: Completed research study according to the design agreed upon by myself and my teacher.

Evaluation of Learning: A self-evaluation indicating what I learned and why it was important to me. Validation by the teacher regarding the quality of my research design and analysis and the soundness of my discussion and conclusion as drawn from the research evidence.

Whether grades should be assigned to learning contracts is discussed in Chapter Five. O'Donnell and Caffarella (1990) have some helpful ideas about the use of learning contracts with learners who are inexperienced or unfamiliar with them:

- Enlist the aid of those learners more familiar with designing learning contracts to help those beginning this process.

- Give those with less experience more time to develop their plans.

- Allow the less experienced learners to first develop a mini-learning plan and then complete a more in-depth one.

- Give learners clear guidelines for developing contracts. Supply a number of diverse samples to encourage a variety of learning processes and outcomes.

In general, the use of learning contracts is often, like good writing, a process of revision and refinement. Using focus groups and requesting feedback from learners about contracts and their formats are two ways we know to ensure their effective use.

Approaches Based on Multiple Intelligences Theory

We subscribe to the definition of intelligence, offered by Howard Gardner (1993), as the ability to solve problems, or to fashion products, that are valued in one or more cultural or community settings. Problems may range from how to create an end to a mystical story to finding a physics equation that describes the interaction among subatomic particles. Products entail anything from making delicious bread to creating musical compositions to designing computer software. The range appears to be nearly infinite and highlights the realization that intelligence cannot be conceptualized apart from the context in which individuals live. Gardner describes seven intelligences (see Table 3.2) and understands there are probably more. Each, however, makes no sense as an abstraction, as a biological entity (like the stomach), or even as a psychological entity (such as emotion). There is always an interaction between biological proclivities and the opportunities for learning that exist in a culture (Kornhaber, Krechevsky, and Gardner, 1990). For example, a person might have the potential to be a great chess player, but if that person happened to be born in a culture without chess, that potential may never be realized. This individual's spatial or logical intelligence might distinguish this person eventually as a navigator or a scientist, but it is just as possible this person might not excel in any way.

According to Gardner's analysis (1991) all human beings are capable of at least seven different ways of knowing the world—through language, logical-mathematical analysis, spatial representation, musical thinking, the use of the body to solve problems or to make things, an understanding of other individuals, and an understanding of ourselves. Where people differ is in the strength of these intelligences—their *profile of intelligences*—and in the ways in which such intelligences are invoked and combined to complete different tasks, solve a variety of problems, and progress in diverse domains. Therefore, learners possess different kinds of minds and learn, remember, perform, and understand in different ways. All of these ways are inextricably bound to the interaction of a person's biological proclivities with the practices and assumptions of his or her culture.

There is considerable documentation that some people take a primarily linguistic approach to learning, while others favor a spatial or a quantitative tack. Some learners perform best when asked to manipulate symbols of various sorts, while others are better able to demonstrate their understanding through a hands-on process or through interaction with other individuals (Gardner, 1982; Shade, 1989). Another important implication of multiple intelligences theory is that the cultural tools, procedures, techniques, and social supports are part of one's intelligence as well as how one demonstrates intelligence. Without writing and its instruments how would we know the genius of people such as Alice Walker or Gabriel Garcia Marquez? The crucial question, then, is not How intelligent is one? but How is one intelligent?

Table 3.2. Gardner's Multiple Intelligences.

Intelligence	Example	Core Components
Linguistic	Novelist Journalist	Sensitivity to the sounds, rhythms, and meanings of words; sensitivity to the different functions of language, written and spoken
Logical-Mathematical	Scientist Accountant	Sensitivity to and capacity to discern logical and numerical patterns; ability to handle long chains of inductive and deductive reasoning
Musical	Composer Guitarist	Abilities to produce and appreciate rhythm, tone, pitch, and timbre; appreciation of the forms of musical expressiveness
Spatial	Designer Navigator	Capacities to perceive the visual-spatial world accurately and to perform transformations on one's initial perceptions and mental images
Bodily-Kinesthetic	Athlete Actor	Abilities to know and control one's body movements and to handle objects skillfully
Interpersonal	Therapist Politician	Capacities to discern and respond appropriately, to communicate the moods, temperaments, motivations, and desires of other people
Intrapersonal	Philosopher Spiritual leader	Access to one's own feelings and inner states of being with the ability to discriminate among them and draw upon them to guide behavior; knowledge of one's own strengths, weaknesses, desires, and intelligences

Source: Adapted from Gardner and Hatch, 1989.

These well-documented differences in intelligence and its actu-alization challenge a postsecondary educational system that in day-to-day operation largely assumes that everyone can learn the same materials in the same way and that uniform measures suffice to test learning. As currently constructed, this system is heavily biased toward linguistic—and, to a lesser degree, logical-quantitative—modes of instruction. Because people learn in ways that are identi-fiably distinctive, determined to a large extent by their profiles of intelligences and unique cultural persona, the broad spectrum of learners and society as a whole would be better served if learning could be offered in a number of ways and assessed through a vari-ety of means (Gardner, 1991).

The current postsecondary system produces many needless casu-alties, dropouts, and labeled academic failures because of its inflex-ibility and resistance to accommodating learners who might exhibit their understanding but cannot because the pathways of learning and teaching are restricted to verbal/written and logical/mathe-matical modes devoid of any context beyond a paper and pencil. For example, there is a significant student population that lacks facility with formal examinations but can display relevant compre-hension when problems arise in natural contexts. Teachers and medical educators bear witness to this phenomenon on a daily basis.

Culturally responsive teaching incorporates the theory of mul-tiple intelligences and integrates the notion of Gardner (1991) and others (Perkins, 1991) that for learning to be relevant and pro-found, teaching must be flexible and aimed at promoting deep understanding. This means avoiding educational formats that ask learners to merely spew back what they have been taught and replacing them with opportunities to use concepts and skills in meaningful contexts with their own words and analogies to actively solve problems and carry out fresh projects.

Gardner (1993) proposes that any concept worth teaching can be approached in at least five different ways that, roughly speaking, map onto the multiple intelligences and allow all learners relevant access. He advocates thinking of any topic as a room with at least five doors or entry points. Awareness of these entry points can help the teacher to introduce the topic with materials and formats that accommodate the wide range of cultural backgrounds and profiles of intelligences found among a diverse group of learners.

As Gardner (1993) suggests, let us look at these five entry points one by one, considering how each one might be used in approaching one topic or concept in the natural sciences (photosynthesis) and one in the social sciences (democracy).

In using a *narrational entry point*, one presents a story or narrative account about the concept in question. In the case of photosynthesis one might describe with appropriate vocabulary this process as it occurs among several plants or trees relevant to one's environment, describing differences as they are noted. In the case of democracy one could trace its beginnings in ancient history and draw comparisons and contrasts with the early development of constitutional government in a selected nation.

In using a *logical-quantitative entry point*, one approaches the concept by invoking numerical considerations or deductive and/or inductive reasoning processes. Photosynthesis could be approached by creating a time line of the steps of photosynthesis and a chemical analysis of the process. In the case of democracy, one could create a time line of presidential mandates, congressional bills, constitutional amendments, and Supreme Court decisions that broadened democratic principles among people in the United States, or one could analyze the arguments used for and against democracy by relevant political leaders throughout history.

A *foundational entry point* explores the philosophical and terminological facets of a concept. This approach is appropriate for people who like to pose fundamental questions, of the sort that one often associates with young children and with philosophers. A foundational corridor to photosynthesis might examine a transformative experience of oneself or a relevant individual, family, or institution and compare it with the actual process of photosynthesis assigning parallel roles as they fit (for example, source of energy, catalyst, and so on). A foundational means of access to democracy could ponder the root meaning of the word, the relationship of democracy to other relevant forms of decision making and government, and the reasons one might prefer or not prefer a democratic rather than a social political philosophy.

With an *esthetic entry point* the emphasis falls on sensory or surface features that will appeal to learners who favor an artistic approach to the experience of living. In the case of photosynthesis one could look for visual, musical, or literary transformations that imitate or parallel photosynthesis and represent them in artistic formats that might include painting, dance, mime, video, cartooning, or a dramatic sketch. With reference to democracy, one could experience and consider the variations of artistic performance that are characterized by group-oriented control versus individual control: a string quartet as compared to an orchestra, experimental modern dance compared to ballet; improvisational acting compared to a stage play; and so on.

The last entry point is an *experiential approach*. Some people learn best with a hands-on approach, dealing directly with the materials that embody or convey the concept. For photosynthesis such individuals might carry out a series of experiments involving photosynthesis. Those learners dealing with democracy might consider a recent relevant news issue and "enact" a democratic procedure, whether it be legislative, judicial, and/or executive; they might then enact another approach to the same issue, replicating a less democratic system from another country and finally comparing their experience of the two diverse processes.

A teacher can open a number of doors on the same concept. Rather than presenting photosynthesis only by example, or only in terms of quantitative considerations, the teacher makes available several entry points at the beginning or over time. In this way there is a good chance diverse learners with different ways of knowing and differing intelligence profiles will find a relevant and engaging way of learning. They may also suggest entry points of their own design. The use of technology such as films, microcomputers, and interactive video can further enhance these efforts. In Exhibit 3.4 we present another example of a concept with five entry points.

Multiple entry points are a powerful means for dealing with learner and teacher misconceptions, biases, and stereotypes. When only a single perspective is offered on a concept or problem, learners are forced to understand it in a most limited and rigid fashion (Gardner, 1991). By encouraging learners to develop multiple representations and having them relate these representations to one another, we can move away from the correct-answer tyranny of postsecondary education and arrive at a fuller understanding of our world. Most knowledgeable and innovative practitioners of any discipline are characterized precisely by their capacity to access critical concepts through a variety of routes and apply them to a diversity of situations. In addition, this overall approach makes us co-learners with our students and likely to take their views and ideas seriously, with all of us developing a more comprehensive understanding. Implementing this approach is an enormous challenge, but it is more than time, materials, or methods that may block progress toward teaching of this sort. These issues are manifestations of what we most value and believe. As Gardner (1991) states, "Whether we will choose to follow this route, to educate for understanding is a political issue rather than a scientific or pedagogical one" (p. 248).

Sensitivity and Pedagogical Flexibility Based on the Concept of Style

In the field of education, style, as a concept, fulminates considerable controversy. Scholars debate its definition, relevancy, and impact on learning (Hilliard, 1989; Shade, 1989; Tharp, 1989; King, 1994; Kleinfeld and Nelson, 1988; Anderson, 1988). Con-

Exhibit 3.4. Multiple Intelligences Learning Activities.

Concept and Related Principle

Concept: All living things are essentially related.

Principle: All human behaviors affect the earth's land, water, air.

Learning Entry Points

Narrational: Learners generate views of how they recognize the effects of human behavior taking place in other countries and from distant places. Identify behaviors according to whether they harm or benefit the planet. Based on interests generated, select relevant reading materials.

Logical-quantitative: Choose a harmful but controversial human systemic influence such as overpopulation. After finding data that quantify various (population) trends and the effects that result from this systemic influence, search for cultural, economic, and political factors (possibly from a country of interest) that inhibit or exacerbate this influence.

Foundational: Reflect on one's personal influence on the local environment. Consider those behaviors that improve the environment and those that pollute it. Examine the beliefs, assumptions, and values that appear critical to each set of these behaviors. Create a personal environmental philosophy. Sharing it in small groups is optional.

Esthetic: Create either a sketch, photo journal, video, or poem to depict relevant systemic relationships in one's own environment.

Experiential: Create mini-environments in local yards and/or terrariums. Experiment according to relevant influences (for example, temperature, water, pollutants, pets, traffic, and so forth). Observe and report effects on various life forms.

---

siderable intellectual agreement continues to grow (Hollins, King, and Hayman, 1994; McCombs and others, 1993) that for education to serve a more democratic, just, and culturally diverse society, teachers must have specific knowledge about the learner's varied ways of thinking, believing, learning, and communicating that are influenced by culture. Tharp (1989) and Jordan (1985) believe that such aspects of the natal culture as cognitive style should be used as guides in formulating educational programs. But which features are critical and how are they to be chosen? Kleinfeld and Nelson (1988) argue, for example, that virtually no research actually supports the popular view that Native American students will learn more when instruction is adapted to their supposedly "visual" and observational learning style. They conclude that this area of research is unlikely to prove fruitful as a source of knowledge about how to improve education for Native American learners. Our experience as teachers and our review of the literature have led us to believe that educator reactions to learner characteristics often attributed to style can be a critical influence on student attitudes and on the motivation of students to learn. We are also aware of how frequently the literature on teaching diverse learners refers to style (Anderson and Adams, 1992) and wish to clarify what may seem to many teachers to be an overwhelming myriad of educational imperatives.

Hilliard (1989) offers a simple and direct definition of style: "Consistency in the behavior of a person or of a group that tends to be habitual—the manifestation of a predisposition to approach things in a characteristic way" (p. 67). Most scholars would agree that style is learned through culture (Tharp, 1989). Because different ethnic or other cultural groups have different histories, adaptive approaches to reality, and socialization practices, they are likely to differ in style in at least three dimensions: cognitive, learning, and behavioral.

Cognitive styles are generally characterized as consistencies and preferences in information processing that develop in concert with underlying personality trends (Merriam and Caffarella, 1991; Shade, 1989). They are reflected in how people use "typical modes of perceiving, remembering, thinking, and problem solving" (Messick, 1976, p. 5). For example, some people tend to see and make sense of their world from a holistic perspective while others approach it more analytically. While the latter persons would want the specifics, facts, and figures first to understand something, the former would request the whole story or picture to comprehend a situation. Studies have identified ethnic differences on variables directly related to patterns of cognitive functioning.

Studies that compare holistic-visual versus verbal-analytic

thought are cited frequently in the literature (Phillips, 1983; Tharp, 1989; Shade, 1982, 1989). These studies report that American Indians and African Americans are frequently found to be more holistic-visual in their patterns of organizing learning and thought, while European Americans (more often males than females) are frequently found to be more verbal-analytic. Investigators attribute these differences to socialization practices such as learning by doing rather than conveying theory before practical application of ideas. In a similar vein, stylistic differences between males and females have been found dating from the classic work of Maccoby and Jacklin (1974) to more recent research on college men and women by Baxter Magolda (1989, 1990).

Although there is a great deal of research on cognitive styles, most of it has been done with children and it is unclear how or whether the findings translate to college students and adults (Bonham, 1988). Even the research with children has begun to cast doubt on the notion that styles are generally applicable (Gardner, 1993). A person who needs to see the big picture while painting may not be so inclined while doing math. Someone apparently spontaneous and impulsive in a musical realm may be quite reflective while working on a puzzle. Therefore, for any individual, style may vary according to content.

Because some authors use the terms interchangeably, the literature describing learning style and cognitive style is often confusing. *Learning* style discussions and investigations tend to emphasize the relationship of the learner to the learning situation versus the more general notion of how people perceive, organize, and process information (Hiemstra and Sisco, 1990). *Behavioral* style can include matters pertaining to dialect, language, questioning and narrative styles, participation patterns, expressiveness, and in general behaving consistently in certain ways (Hilliard, 1989; Hollins, King, and Hayman, 1994). Issues pertaining to both learning and behavioral styles overlap with issues of cultural congruence—the idea that students of diverse backgrounds often do poorly in school because of a mismatch between the culture of the school and the home culture of the learners (Au and Kawakami, 1994). All of these concepts support the proposition that culturally diverse learners will have better learning opportunities and higher motivation if teaching is compatible with the norms of behavior and values of their own cultures. This does not mean replicating home or community environments but finding educational practices and structures that accommodate and incorporate the learners' culturally influenced styles and practices.

Without reference to research we know there are considerable differences between cultures regarding how one appropriately interacts and communicates with other people; how one gets the floor in conversation or shows deference or respect; and how one indicates concurrence or disagreement and approval or disapproval. For teachers from the dominant culture, the norms of participation in class may seem obvious and their derivation from European-American norms of conduct unimportant, but to a learner from another culture such expectations may be alienating, exhausting (the relentless anxiety of determining how to behave appropriately), and unfair, especially if learners are directly called upon to recite and are graded for oral participation in class.

For those learners who have learned to directly experience reality and engage in concrete tasks before considering theoretical abstractions, courses that require the comprehension of theory to precede application or laboratory exercises may undermine their best chances to learn. As Anderson (1988) points out, the writing/speaking styles of Mexican Americans, African Americans, and Puerto Rican Americans are frequently viewed by teachers as too flowery, too subjective, involving an excessive use of metaphors, and utilizing the wrong tense of verbs. What had been a valuable and valid communication process in their own cultural domain is too often perceived as an example of linguistic deficiency in the postsecondary classroom.

Probably the area where the dominant perspective in education is in greatest conflict with other behavioral styles is that of language and dialect. When learners and teachers differ in language, teachers frequently use their own language as a normative reference (Hilliard, 1989). They consider "standard English" as language, instead of *a* language. As a result, learners who speak a different version of English are seen as language deficient. Rather than the issue being defined as an object for teaching in the area of "standard English" the learner is seen as impaired and using "inferior English." The most common result of this perspective and the one most disastrous to the attitude of the learner and the teacher is a lowered learning expectation on the part of the teacher for the student. There is clear and long-standing evidence that low expectations on the part of teachers lead to lower motivation and learning on the part of students (Good and Brophy, 1991).

These examples highlight the reasons why we believe there must be a sensitivity and pedagogical flexibility among teachers toward the ways diverse populations communicate, behave, and think. So then how do teachers of diverse learners adjust to and enjoy such a complex array? Let's begin by acknowledging that with the general exception of courses on art, music, and technology, most postsecondary courses still employ a verbal-analytic, emotionless approach to teaching. This usually means the learner does some outside reading, the teacher lectures and discusses topical material, and paper and pencil tests are given. This is the least compatible way of learning for most people outside of (and many people within) the majority culture. Therefore, having culturally responsive alternatives available would benefit learning and motivation. These would include but not be limited to a direct experience related to subject matter, a holistic perspective of course content, social contexts for learning experiences, and the appreciation of fantasy, humor, and emotion in the process of learning.

In general, we suggest avoiding practices that devalue dialect, rely too heavily on public classroom responding, and fail to accept variations in styles of narration and questioning. Because styles appear to be learned, they can be changed, and people can learn to use more than one style, switching when appropriate. Learners can become more balanced in their dispositions toward learning and, for certain vocations, will need to be capable of a variety of ways of communicating and processing information. Using a compatible style as a starting point or introduction to other styles is often an effective means to new learning as well as a positive attitude. For example, if highly verbal-analytic learners want to intensify the emotional quality of the way they process and perform their learning, they may need to be instructed verbally and analytically in how to accomplish their goal before they begin to practice achieving it.

On the whole, we recommend that teachers have an attitude that is open to alternatives for learning and assessing learning (see Chapter Five) and that allows for different forms of communication and multisensory understanding, where people can see, hear, and feel what they are actively learning. Bear in mind that the five entry points for multiple intelligences accommodate many cultural styles, as do the collaborative learning procedures discussed in Chapter Two. The Kolb model of learning described below is another procedure for incorporating a variety of ways of learning. Focus groups can also be helpful, yielding ideas about some of the predisposed ways of learning among course members. Creating a community of learners with openness to each other's characteristic ways of thinking, acting, and communicating is a good beginning.

Experiential Learning—The Kolb Model

Often among diverse learners for particular subjects of study there will be a lack of common experience or prekindled interest in the topic at hand. Relevance may have to emerge through immediate experience and teachers need a flexible framework for lesson or course design that provides such experience while accommodating cultural and style differences among learners. Kolb's experiential learning model (Smith and Kolb, 1986) affirms active learning and provides a theoretical configuration for selecting and organizing learning activities that can serve an array of culturally derived differences. It also provides a rich set of possibilities for the experiential as well as some of the other academic entry points advocated by Gardner (1993).

As shown in Figure 3.2, the cycle begins in clockwise cyclical movement with the learner's direct involvement in a concrete experience. The learner then uses the processes of observation and reflection, considering the experience from personal and/or multiple viewpoints to understand its meaning. Out of this reflection the learner forms generalizations or abstract concepts. These may be generated with the aid of the theoretical constructs of others. The resulting constructs are then, through decisions and actions, tested or experimented with, leading to new concrete experiences and thereby starting the learning cycle anew.

Figure 3.2 also portrays two bipolar intersecting dimensions

Figure 3.2. The Experiential Learning Model.

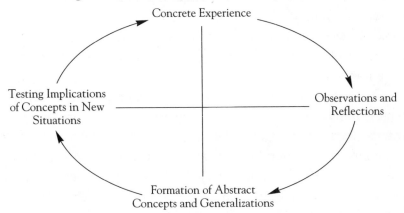

Source: Smith and Kolb, 1986. © Experience-Based Learning, Inc., 1981, revised 1985. Developed by David A. Kolb. Reprinted with permission from McBer and Company, Inc., 116 Huntington Ave., Boston, MA. 02116. 617-437-7080.

representing along the vertical axis, on a continuum from concrete to abstract, how we take in information and, along the horizontal axis, on a continuum from reflective observation to active testing, how we process information. Through learning sequences that allow movement through the full cycle, learners should be able to learn more comprehensively than they would via a single dimension. Yet each of the four aspects of this model can be understood to represent a learning style and a preferred entry point for learning for individual students. Although our suggestion for implementing this model is to begin with concrete experience as a starting point for learning sequences and to move through the entire cycle to ensure students a more balanced exposure to all four dimensions, there are many occasions when other entry points and/or use of less than all of the dimensions would be appropriate. An example is a graduate research seminar where abstract conceptualization (formulating hypotheses) leads to active experimentation (to test these hypotheses) and then to reflective observation (analysis of experiments and discussion) without the need for concrete experience to occur in the cycle. Another example is a history major who prefers to begin by hearing a lecture about a particular topic (abstract conceptualization), then moves on to reading original manuscripts about the topic (concrete experience), followed by writing a reflective paper (reflective observation). In this sequence there is no need for active experimentation.

Figure 3.3 (Svinicki and Dixon, 1987) offers learning activities representative of each of the four dimensions of the learning cycle. Interviews, field work, observations, reading primary sources, and so on give the learner direct, personal experiences with content. Activities such as discussion and journaling help learners to reflect on their experiences and the experiences of others. Creating hypotheses, listening to lectures, and building models can evoke abstract conceptualization. Role playing, developing case studies, and laboratory work can promote active experimentation.

**Figure 3.3. Sample Learning Activities
for Dimensions of the Kolb Model.**

CONCRETE EXPERIENCE
Interviews
Laboratories
Primary text reading
Simulations/games
Field work
Trigger films
Problem sets

ACTIVE EXPERIMENTATION	REFLECTIVE OBSERVATION
Artistic creations	Journals
Simulations	Discussions
Laboratory	Brainstorming
Projects	Thought questions
Field work	Reflective papers

ABSTRACT CONCEPTUALIZATION
Lectures
Papers
Model building
Analogies/metaphors
Creating hypotheses

Source: Adapted from Svinicki and Dixon, 1987, p. 142.

Typically, to create a complete cycle, teachers and learners would generate activities from each dimension and move through them in order (Svinicki and Dixon, 1987). For example, Exhibit 3.4, a unit designed for political science focusing on ethnic variables related to political attitudes, might begin with reading recent studies on this topic and conducting interviews in learner-selected neighborhoods (concrete experience). Individual learners or col-

Figure 3.4. Learning Sequence According to the Kolb Model for a Political Science Course.

CONCRETE EXPERIENCE

Read studies focusing on ethnic variables
related to political attitudes. Conduct related
interviews in ethnic neighborhoods.

ACTIVE EXPERIMENTATION

Test predictions among
identified ethnic groups with a
follow-up questionnaire.

REFLECTIVE OBSERVATION

Categorize observations and
brainstorm about differences in
political attitudes among
ethnic groups.

ABSTRACT CONCEPTUALIZATION

Generate hypotheses to predict how different ethnic
groups respond to various political issues.

---

laborative groups of learners could categorize their observations and make initial speculations on differences among the ethnic groups represented (reflective observation). Then the class as a whole might pool its results and identify patterns among ethnic groups to generate hypotheses (abstract conceptualization) that predict how members of different ethnic groups are likely to respond to various political issues. Finally, the entire class could test its predictions by a follow-up questionnaire with members of the identified ethnic groups (active experimentation).

A specific activity such as a laboratory experiment or conducting an interview may fit into more than one dimension depending on the learning goal. In the political science unit just discussed, interviewing was used twice, first as a concrete experience and then as an active experiment. In the first instance this method was to "see what is" and in the second instance to verify a set of predictions based on various hypotheses. Thus, the functional purpose of the activity governs its selection and placement in the learning sequence. In practical use, reflective observation often becomes a form of examining, abstract conceptualization becomes a form of explaining, and active experimentation becomes a form of applying (Svinicki and Dixon, 1987).

Another way to utilize Kolb's model and to accommodate learner style preferences is to vary the degree to which the learner is active or passive. Figure 3.5 illustrates such an improvisation. The activities at the outer edge of the ellipse most actively engage the learner, while those closer to the center involve the learner far more passively. Others have substituted dimensions such as verbal and visual in a similar manner to extend this model to a greater range of styles (Anderson and Adams, 1992). Almost playfully, the Kolb model not only allows for a more systematic and broader selection of learning activities but centralizes the importance of experience in learning and flexibly accommodates some of the more important culturally derived differences among learners.

A Structure for Developing a Positive Attitude

Culturally responsive teacher-learner conferences are important because a teacher-learner conference is often the first formal means of appeal or dissent for a learner. (We prefer the word *conference* to *meeting* because it is defined as the act of consulting together for the interchange of views [*Webster's Dictionary*, 1993], suggesting a more honored voice for the learner.) It is also frequently the only means for teachers and learners to cooperatively resolve issues and to personalize learning. Consider the following case:

Adrian Chan is a twenty-one-year-old Chinese-American student in a public policy course made up of mostly African-American and European-American learners. The course is conducted as a roundtable discussion with case studies serving as stimuli for eliciting theory and opinion from among the learners. On occasion, the teacher, Joshua Giles, an African American, will use role playing as a method of increasing perspective taking and of personify-

**Figure 3.5. Degree of Direct Student Involvement
in Various Teaching Methods.**

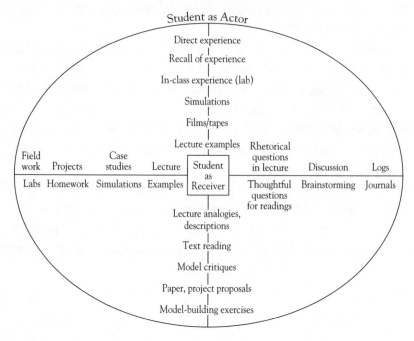

Source: Svinicki and Dixon, 1987, p. 146. Reprinted with permission of the Helen
Dwight Reid Educational Foundation. Published by Heldref Publications, 1319
Eighteenth St., N.W., Washington, D.C. 20036-1802. Copyright 1987.

ing some of the conflicting ideas offered by himself or the other class
members. In this typically lively setting, debate and expressions of
strong feelings are common.

Mr. Giles has noticed that Mr. Chan rarely participates. He has
also observed that the one time Mr. Chan's viewpoint was challenged he became silent, and a tension quickly emerged in the
group when Mr. Giles good-naturedly encouraged him to respond
and he continued to remain quiet. Since that time Mr. Chan has
appeared more withdrawn and sullen in class. His last reaction
paper was superficially done, and Mr. Giles realizes he has begun
to avoid calling upon Mr. Chan for class participation because of

the discomfort that might arise. At the end of a recent class, Mr. Giles drew Mr. Chan aside and asked him if anything was wrong. Mr. Chan politely responded, "No, nothing is the matter," and quickly left.

This case brings up the following questions:
- What cultural influences may be affecting Mr. Chan's behavior and manner of expressing himself?
- Should he and Mr. Giles have a conference?
- If so, how should Mr. Giles conduct the conference and what should he say at the outset?
- Without a conference, should the course be adjusted to be more relevant and inclusive for Mr. Chan? If so, how?

As teachers we are probably more sensitive to attitudinal problems among our learners than we are to academic ones. Learners who are apparently sullen or uncooperative affect the mood of a class as well as get our attention. When these learners are also culturally different from ourselves, we are likely to be more wary and uncertain about what to do. How does one conduct a culturally responsive conference with a learner? We have found most postsecondary teachers have no training in how to conference with learners. We begin our teaching careers knowing we will post office hours for the explicit purpose of having conferences with learners. Yet, rarely do we receive any formal training in this most important process. What follows are eight basic guidelines for culturally responsive conferencing when attitude or other motivation and learning issues prompt us to use this more intimate form of understanding.

1. *The more the conferencing process and goals are seen as appropriate by the learner the more likely the meeting will be an effective and helpful one* (Sue and Sue, 1990). Conferencing parallels counseling in this sense. It means making the language and strategies used in the conference as consistent as possible with the values, life expe-

riences, and culturally conditioned ways of responding of the learner. It also means agreeing upon goals that are preferred by and make sense to the learner. In the case of Mr. Chan, he may not wish to discuss his feelings or how he emotionally reacts when he is challenged but may prefer to focus on academic issues. Forced self-disclosure to strangers may not be comfortable for Mr. Chan if his cultural norm is to reserve expression of personal feelings for the intimacy of family. Creating optional learning activities that more fairly demonstrate his knowledge may be more helpful than finding ways to make Mr. Chan more comfortable in class.

Studies have consistently revealed that self-disclosure may be incompatible with the cultural values of Asian Americans, Latinos, and American Indians in particular. Many ethnic minority learners may prefer an active-directive approach to discussing academic problems to an ambiguous, nondirective approach filled with pauses, paraphrasing, and reflected feelings (Sue and Sue, 1990). However, because groups and individuals differ from one another, the rigid application of these generalizations to all situations is, of course, ludicrous.

In the area of diversity, consistency and flexibility often appear to be in conflict. Conferencing especially brings this to mind because so often the outcome is an adjustment in one's teaching or assessment practices to provide an equitable chance for learning for a particular student. Other students may resent such accommodation, deeming it preferential treatment. Such confusion occurs through misunderstanding the distinction between the objectives of equal access and opportunity and those of equal treatment. For non-majority and underrepresented learners to have equal opportunity to learn, it is often necessary to use a different approach, given the backgrounds and experiences of different learners. Being inflexible and using the mantle of equal treatment to offer the same approach to learning to all students, which in effect favors the dominant groups, is discriminatory.

2. *Taking the role of an empathic and diplomatic teacher who follows*

the learner's lead is often a good beginning for a conference. At the out-set of a conference this usually means listening without interruption to the student's reasons for requesting the conference. When the teacher has requested the conference, this means giving the student ample opportunity to respond to the teacher's stated reasons.

3. *Create a collaborative attitude that avoids blame.* Using descriptive language, avoiding labels, and showing authentic compassion helps to build trust as well as focus on the issue at hand.

If the teacher has requested the conference, she or he will have to state the reason initially. For example: "I've noticed your last two test scores have progressively declined. I'm concerned about this trend and how we might work together to turn it around. What's your opinion about this matter?" (more open ended) or "Let's consider what might be done to improve things" (more directive). In the case of Mr. Chan, Mr. Giles might say, "I'm beginning to wonder if the way we're conducting class is giving you the best chance to learn and demonstrate what you know. What's your opinion about this concern?" (more open ended) or "If you agree, let's explore some ideas about what we could do to make this a better learning situation for you" (more directive).

4. *Although finding and mutually agreeing upon the understanding of the issue or problem is usually helpful, being lucid and in agreement about the goal of the conference is most important.* Many people do not see the world in linear cause and effect terms. Probing for possible explanations may only add to the discomfort of the situation and stimulate further argument. Also, discussing possible reasons for conflict or difficulty may make some learners feel unsafe and/or embarrassed. This is why tone and demeanor are so important. One can convey empathy and care without being unnecessarily analytic. In the case of Mr. Chan and Mr. Giles it may be they arrive at a common understanding that the way class is conducted is argumentative to a degree that diminishes Mr. Chan's wish to participate. Or they may, after a short dialogue that does not focus on specific reasons for Mr. Chan's ostensible distress, mutually agree to

look for other acceptable ways for Mr. Chan to learn and demonstrate his knowledge while in class.

5. *Flexibly consider specific goals or solutions. Mutually agree upon the selected ones.* Such prompts as "Let's take a look at the different approaches we might use" or "Let's think about this and see what comes to mind" may be good starting points. Brainstorming may be used to generate possible strategies. In the beginning all ideas are valid. After the ideas have been exhausted, they are evaluated for effectiveness. In Mr. Chan's and Mr. Giles's situation, three possible alternatives may be: (*a*) Mr. Chan is excused from any role-playing activities until he decides otherwise, (*b*) class is reconfigured to precede the roundtable discussions with small-group discussions after which only volunteer representatives of the small groups debate, or (*c*) Mr. Chan corresponds in a journal with another student or Mr. Giles regarding his reactions to the issues debated in class.

When goals are complicated and involved, the following two strategies may be beneficial:

• *Means-ends analysis:* The goal is divided into a number of subgoals, and then a means of reaching each one is worked out. For example, a learner wants to improve the quality of her or his next case study. The teacher and learner decide to break this task into several shorter objectives, each one allowing for feedback from the teacher, such as selecting a topic, locating sources of information, reading and organizing the information, visiting a field site and conducting observations, making an outline, and documenting and creating the case study. Depending on the situation, the learner and possibly the teacher can then develop a plan to accomplish each of these tasks.

• *Working backward:* Some goals are best considered by looking first at the goal and moving back from it to see the order and timing of what needs to be done to reach it. Let's say a small group of learners wants to meet with the teacher for the purpose of improving their scores on the next exam. At the conference it's decided that they will collaboratively study, organize and share their notes, and receive a list of study questions from the teacher; they will also study individually. They might begin by looking at the date of the next exam, decide how much time they would individually want to prepare the day before the test, figure out how much time they need to prepare and organize their notes, and then decide on a schedule to collaboratively consider the study questions, working backward from the day before the exam.

6. *Make a plan that both the teacher and learner record when desirable.* When the outcome of the conference is taking an action for which someone is responsible or upon which a grade may be based, it is important to have a record to avoid possible confusion or disagreement. Also, when the goals and their procedures are complicated it improves clarity to organize and write them down. This does not have to be a laborious or obsessive task. A simple review at the end of the conference with both the learner and teacher taking the necessary notes may suffice as well as bring a sense of closure to the meeting.

Plans and notes also give the learner and teacher a way of keeping track and revising or refining goals as desired. We suggest teachers keep a conference journal as an aid to memory and as a means to make future and continuing conferences more constructive and focused.

7. *Encourage.* When the conference results in a learner goal and/or some kind of expected action on the part of the learner, this person benefits from knowing the teacher believes he or she can do it. Such encouragement also denotes higher expectations on the part of the teacher. A look or a gesture can sometimes be sufficient, or the teacher can provide a few words of appreciation or expectancy. Being culturally congruent at this time is especially powerful. In the case of Mr. Chan, words as simple as, "I think we have some good ideas for better ways of working together. Thanks for coming," may suffice.

8. *When beneficial, evaluate the results of the conference.* Has the goal been accomplished? Is the learner satisfied with the results?

What has been learned? Should another conference be scheduled to refine or improve matters? In some ways this is not as much evaluation or record keeping as it is caring. Reflective attention of this sort signifies to the learner the conference made a difference to us. We took it seriously and organized ourselves so things would change for the better.

If we reconsider the case that began this chapter, we now see that Ms. Kubiak has at least one option that accommodates both her perspective and Ms. Sanchez's need for relevance and self-determination. She could use a contract procedure that incorporates the necessary standards of performance and allows Ms. Sanchez more choices. Also, if she had an understanding of the influence of culture on interaction styles and profiles of intelligences and an awareness of the importance of relevance to learning, she would be more likely to provide greater flexibility in her assignments. She has the means through such procedures as contracting, using problem-solving goals, increasing entry points for projects, and aligning course requirements with the Kolb experiential learning model.

Intuitively we know it is best for people to like what they must do. We want students to feel positively toward learning. However, exhorting, explaining, or cajoling seldom encourage attitudes that benefit learning. Such "talk," if you will, has little impact compared to an integrated set of educational norms, procedures, and structures. When harmonious, these elements create an ethos among diverse students that they are learning something important and they can learn it well.

Chapter Four

Enhancing Meaning

Come and stand in my heart, whoever you are, and a
whole river would cover your feet and rise higher and
take your knees in whirlpools, and draw you down to
itself, your whole body, your heart too.

—*Eudora Welty*

What is meaning? And who determines it? What stands in our
hearts and tells us it is so? If we do not know the messenger, we
often know the medium: words, the gift of language that all people
possess. We use language to comprehend and shape our worlds, to
imagine and draw our futures. Yet there is realization beyond words,
often for the most important meanings in our lives. As Juana Ines
de la Cruz wrote more than three centuries ago, "Sorting the reasons to leave you or hold you, I find an intangible one to love you,
and many tangible ones to forego you." We often cannot explain
feelings and experiences that may hold our destiny and create the
most compelling moments of our lives. What happens between an
event and a person is frequently more significantly rendered through
artistic and spiritual manifestations. A powerful or worthwhile experience does not need a verbal explanation to validate it. In fact,
such an attempt may only fracture or contaminate it, as this
poignant recollection of the Vietnam Memorial by Michael Ventura (1994) attests:

Only when I step back to photograph the wall do I begin to appreciate the genius of its creator, Maya Ying Lin. For you cannot photograph it, not really. There is no angle through which you can see it whole through a lens unless you're standing so far off that the picture would be meaningless. Even with advanced equipment, if you're close enough to see that the names are inscribed, you're too close to contain the whole; if you contain the whole, you can't tell from the photograph alone what it really is. So the wall defies deconstruction and transmission by any other medium. You can't take it home with you. You have to experience it to know it, and you can keep only as much as you've experienced [pp. 5-6].

The realms of emotion, art, and spirituality are historically essential to human experience. They have incontestable meaning, often beyond words, and certainly outside the scope of modern measurement. We make such a declaration not because we doubt its acceptance by teachers but because we see such an absence of regard for these realms in so many postsecondary courses in spite of this awareness. The logical, the verbal, the explainable—the higher-order thinking, if you wish—reign supreme in higher education. We argue not against these ways of knowing but for the inclusion, acceptance, and respect of these other, less "rational" elements, because their absence during learning and their frequent extraction from the concept of meaning exclude the reality and thus the presence of far too many people. Such disregard perpetuates the boring, fear-driven, sterile, demotivating quality of many college classrooms. Since the conformity to a verbal, abstract, scientifically reasoned world is so all-encompassing in higher education, and especially in graduate school, it is quite possible that a considerable number of people avoid this kind of emotional illiteracy out of a sense of self-preservation, while many of those within feel alienated and resistant. To be under the direction of a teacher whose perception of consciousness does not allow for the intuitive or the unexplainable and whose authority determines one's grade or promotion is for many, at the very least, uncomfortable, and for more than a few, dehumanizing.

Meaning—to What End?

Meaning is a constant in learning and motivation. Meaning is also a concept difficult to define, because any definition can become circular (Csikszentmihalyi, 1990). How do we address the meaning of meaning itself? There are a number of ways to unravel this word in a manner that enlightens how the motivation of diverse learners can be deepened. One way to understand this concept is to see it as the order, connection, or pattern human beings create to link perceptions to some goal or final purpose, or questions, as in What is the meaning of life? or What does this event mean to me? This can be expressed as "felt meaning" because such connections and patterns matter to us (Caine and Caine, 1991). The experience of felt meaning intensifies motivation for all people because there is obvious relevance, a sense of connection, and emotional substance. This kind of meaning can be understood on a more profound level and refers to whatever determines our sense of purpose. This "deep meaning" accesses more passionate feelings and can range from a basic sense of territoriality to an awareness of a strong and unified goal to an intuitive connection to something greater than our personal beings (Bohm, 1987; Csikszentmihalyi, 1990; Caine and Caine, 1991). This realm of meaning is also the domain of that which is extremely vital to us but that we may not be able to articulate, such as creative, artistic, and spiritual connections and expressions. Language is a useful mediator between deep meanings and our awareness, but it is not the only mediator, and there appear to be deeper structures within human beings that process such meanings (Caine and Caine, 1991). Regardless of what we as teachers intend, these deeper meanings will contribute to the learner's interpretation of learning activities. Culturally responsive teaching respects and incorporates the learner's deeper meaning to create joyful, absorbing, and challenging learning experiences.

Another way to understand meaning is to conceive of it as the ordering of information that gives identity and clarity, as when we say the word *castle* means a large fortified residence or recognize our telephone number in a listing. This kind of meaning embraces facts, procedures, and behaviors that contribute to our awareness of how things relate or operate or are defined but in a way that doesn't deeply touch our psyche. In the words of Whitehead (1979) this is "inert knowledge." Caine and Caine (1991) refer to it as "surface knowledge," the type of information or skill that is devoid of social or emotional importance to us. Too much of what passes for post-secondary education is constructed as and remains inert knowledge. Introductory textbooks are notorious for this.

Enhancing meaning refers to those norms, procedures, and structures that expand, refine, or increase the complexity of what is learned in a way that matters to learners, includes their values and purposes, and contributes to a critical consciousness. The phrase "that matters to learners" refers to those processes beyond articulation, such as the creative and the spiritual, as well as those processes involved with emerging relevance—when the act of learning creates its own meaning, as in the case of insight or con-firmed prediction. Often, enhancing meaning will involve learners using information, skills, or inert knowledge so that they acquire deeper meaning. In fact, one of the main goals that we advocate for postsecondary education, and therefore for any course within it, is to exalt the significance in learners' lives, to assist them in the real-ization and enhancement of what is truly important in their world. As the philosopher Susanne Langer (1942) has posited, there is a basic and pervasive human need to invest meaning in one's world, to search for and find significance everywhere. Across many cul-tures, achieving purpose appears fundamental to a satisfying life (Csikszentmihalyi and Csikszentmihalyi, 1988).

When an important goal is pursued with resolution, and all one's varied activities fit together, consciousness becomes harmo-nious (Csikszentmihalyi, 1990). People who know their desires and work to achieve them, whose feelings, thoughts, and actions are congruent with one another, are people in a euphoric state of being. Though the consequences of their lives may not always be kind to them, they are likely not to have felt their efforts wasted on doubt, regret, guilt, or fear. Ultimately, it seems inner strength and serenity come from coming to terms with ourselves.

Yet significance is not a path running only toward us. Our purposes influence what we perceive and how we think. They shape the reality we create. In education, we are obliged by the goals we serve to *construct* the individual and society. To be culturally responsive as a teacher means to hold and to contribute to a critical consciousness in order to promote justice in society. Attention to diversity is born out of the realization that issues of race, gender, class, and ethnicity foster the inequitable treatment of many learners. Teachers with a critical consciousness enhance meaning with an awareness composed of four qualities (Freire, 1970; Shor, 1993, pp. 32–33):

1. *Power awareness:* Knowing that society and history can be made and remade by organized groups; knowing who exercises dominant power in society, what their ends are, and how power is currently organized and used in society

2. *Critical literacy:* Analytic habits of thinking, reading, writing, speaking, or discussing that go beneath surface impressions, traditional myths, mere opinions, and routine clichés; understanding the social contexts and consequences of any subject matter; discovering the deep meaning of any event, text, technique, process, object, statement, image, or situation; applying that meaning to one's own context

3. *Desocialization:* Recognizing and challenging the prejudicial myths, values, behaviors, and language learned in mass culture; critically examining society's regressive values, which are internalized and then manifested as racism, sexism, class bias, heterosexism, excessive consumerism, narcissistic individualism, aggressive militarism, and national chauvinism

4. *Self-education:* Developing a perspective that shows how school and society can be demeaned by undemocratic, unequal distribution of power; initiating and facilitating constructive social change, ideas, and projects

Within the transformative perspective of a critical conscious-ness, learning of any sort gravitates toward deeper meaning. With this frame of reference the motivational goal of enhancing mean-ing discloses a personal and global frontier, a very exciting possibil-ity for learning.

Engagement, Challenge, and Intrinsic Motivation

Even though the cognitive revolution of the last twenty years has held sway in academia, the legacy of behaviorism dominates. Suc-cess, achievement, and performance are primarily measured by tests and coded with grades, vastly overshadowing the quality of experi-ence of the learner. Common factors cited in support of this ap-proach are global competition and the maintenance of quality standards. This perspective frequently forces learners to fit an extrinsic criterion in a prescriptive manner, often sanctioned through the process of instructional design. This is an assimilationist model of learning. For those learners who are less attracted by the "rewards" of success and achievement, there can be a significant motivational problem.

However, the issue is larger than this. By starting with and focusing on how well something is or should be done, attention is drawn away from the subjective appeal of the process itself. Effi-ciency and standards take priority over the needs, values, and per-spectives of the learners, making their concerns seem frivolous.

The teaching of math and psychology are two examples. For decades, students have frequently complained about how poorly their math courses have been taught, employing problems of little or no relevance, using a lecture format, shunning concrete appli-cation and manipulations, and grading on a normal curve, imply-ing that lack of student ability and effort, not poor teaching, are the reasons for failure. Psychology has been dominated by a Eurocentric male perspective for a century. From examples in textbooks to the-ories of personality and pathology developed on the basis of studies of largely male populations (Brown and Ballou, 1992), psychology has offered a skewed perspective. Student judgment of such material as irrelevant or strange has often been disregarded by teachers. The priority goes to passing the test, which seldom includes information drawn from the students' perspectives.

The issue of standards can camouflage how *systematically inaccessible* high grades and test scores are. They apparently have to be limited for reasons of rigor and excellence, with the privileged having the greatest access and chance of achieving them. We have a system of higher education where in 1989 students from the bottom quartile of family income distribution had a 6 percent chance of graduating from college by age twenty-four, while their peers in the next quartile only stood a 12 percent chance (Mortenson and Wu, 1990).

From the perspective of intrinsic motivation, a goal is significant because it allows the learning to occur in a particularly challenging or fascinating way, not because its achievement should dominate or be the ultimate criterion of learning. You need the mountaintop not so much to reach it but because it creates the climb. The goal provides the routes, the journey, the challenge. We need the goal because its accomplishment to a large extent determines the means. That's where the treasure of learning lies. Like the ending to a great novel, it is important because it helps to construct a compelling story, but in and of itself it means less than how we arrived there. This is a critical understanding, because *the more we make the achievement of a specific goal the ultimate reason for learning, the less likely we are to allow learners to enhance meaning as they proceed.*

With this understanding as a context we can address the first criterion for enhancing meaning, *learner engagement.* Engagement is a multifaceted concept and at its most basic level is a meaningful response to something on the part of the learner. There is attention paid by the learner to some entity, with the learner's awareness of the interaction. In this regard, seeing someone on the street, hearing thunder, and touching someone's hand can be very brief but powerfully engaging. For purposes of teaching and learning, engagement is usually of much longer duration and includes involvement, participation, engrossment, and transcendence, as in involvement in an experiment, participation in a project, engrossment in acting out roles, and transcendence of an ideological model. In engagement the learner is active and might be searching, evaluating, constructing, creating, or organizing some kind of learning material into new or better ideas, memories, skills, values, feelings, understandings, solutions, or decisions. Often there is a product created or a goal reached. Frequently, concepts have been transformed, and mental, emotional, and physical energy has been exerted (Corno and Mandinach, 1983).

Critical to engagement are the voices of the learner and the teacher in dialogue with one another. Both are heard, and their meanings are entwined as they define themselves as active authors of their worlds (Giroux and McLaren, 1986). Self-expression and dialogue affirm their identities and perspectives as they negotiate the meaning of their separate and mutual experiences. Such dialogue recognizes rather than negates the realities of both the teacher and the learner.

Since engagement so frequently implies a challenge, let us immediately discuss the second criterion for enhancing meaning. *Challenge* includes any opportunity for action that humans are able to respond to (Csikszentmihalyi, 1988). This broad definition of challenge could encompass talking with a friend, writing a letter, riding a horse, performing a ritual, or completing an experiment. In this manner a challenge may be seen as *the available learning opportunity* and engagement as *the kind of action* the learner takes in the situation. The challenge often has a goal-like quality to it. The form of engagement requires and contains some degree of capacity, skill, or knowledge on the part of the learner. We prefer the word *capacity* to *ability* because the latter concept so often refers to a genetically endowed, test-measured, fixed capability that is used to exclude learners. Also, the concept of capacity embraces the idea of multiple intelligences and culturally influenced ways of knowing, which the teacher has a responsibility to accommodate in the presented learning opportunity (challenge).

For example, an older woman who is an adult education student wants to investigate the influence of gender in the development of her field of study. She agrees with her teacher to conduct an historical research study. The historical research study is the challenge or learning opportunity. Although the student has never conducted a study and has scored below the average of the other graduate students in her program on both the math and verbal components of the Graduate Record Exam, she has the organizational skills to complete such an investigation and the capacity to effectively use primary and secondary resources as well as to learn how to compose a survey with the support of her teacher. She also wants to conduct some oral interviews because of the qualitative information they can bring to this research. Her teacher accommodates this request. Carrying out the study—the reading, writing, organizing, surveying, and interviewing—make up engagement.

A challenging learning experience in a flexible and highly engaging format about a relevant topic is intrinsically motivating, because it increases the complexity of skill and knowledge required for learning and the range of connections to those interests, applications, and purposes that are important to the learner. This enhancement of meaning is at the core of learning and motivation, because human beings by their very nature need to maintain an ordered state of consciousness (Csikszentmihalyi, 1990) and seek integration and cohesion both within themselves and with others (Deci and Ryan, 1991).

Highly engaging and challenging learning activities often lead to the experience of *flow*, one of the most enjoyable forms of involvement possible in learning (Csikszentmihalyi, 1990). We have all had a flow experience outside of an educational context. It is the feeling and concentration that sometimes emerge in a closely contested athletic competition, in a challenging board game such as chess, or, more simply, in reading a book that seems as if it were just written for us or in the spontaneous exhilaration that accompanies a long, deep conversation with an old friend. In such activities we feel totally absorbed, with no time to worry about what might happen next and with a sense that we are fully participating with all the skills that are necessary at the moment. There is often a loss of self-awareness that results in a feeling of transcendence or a merging with the activity and the environment. Writers, dancers, therapists, surgeons, pilots, and teachers frequently report feelings of flow while they are working. Flow has been found to improve the quality of human experience in very different cultures across the world (Massimini, Csikszentmihalyi, and Delle Fave, 1988).

Learners can have flow experiences as well when they are engaged in meaningful learning. Studies, regardless of culture, suggest there are eight elements that create the conditions for this optimal experience. We will present these as a context for the procedures we introduce in this chapter.

Norms for Enhancing Meaning

The essence of enhancing meaning is to create with learners opportunities to accomplish work they can honor. In this manner they will become more effective at what they value, which is the core of personal competence (the motivational goal discussed in the next chapter). Central to this outcome from a culturally responsive perspective are learning processes that encourage people to think holistically and critically about their conditions, to realize the dynamic relationship between critical thought and critical action, and to feel empowered to make the changes needed. This kind of critical consciousness reflects one of the highest developments of thought and action possible among people (Freire, 1970). For postsecondary courses to advance this potential, *learners have to participate in challenging learning experiences involving higher-order thinking and critical inquiry that address relevant, real-world issues in an action-oriented manner.*

Included in this norm are consistent opportunities for learners to manipulate information and ideas in ways that transform their meaning and implications, such as when learners combine data and concepts in order to synthesize, generalize, explain, hypothesize, create, or critique some conclusion or interpretation. If one were to observe learners at work, one would see them clarifying distinctions, developing arguments, constructing explanations, creating hypotheses as well as artistic inventions, and dealing with complex understandings. One would also see learners in dialogue, often with the goal of promoting collective understanding and social equity. It would also be obvious that learners are frequently connecting their understanding to relevant, real-world issues in an effort to influence an audience beyond their immediate environment, for example, by communicating their ideas to others, promoting solutions to social problems, offering assistance to particular people or causes, and generating performances or outcomes with pragmatic political and/or aesthetic value (McLaren and Leonard, 1993; Newmann and Wehlage, 1993). In general, learners are constructing their own evidence that they are moving significantly beyond what they knew and could do before they began the course.

A central question (Sheared, 1994) related to enhancing meaning is, How are we as teachers to deliver course content in such a way that the discourse acknowledges all voices—the multiple ways in which people interpret and reflect their understanding of the world? To enter into dialogue and uncover and acknowledge the voice of each student is necessary for understanding that whatever each of us offers is grounded in a political, social, historical, sexual, and economic context that is unique yet related to the cultures of others. We all—not just a select group or those in academe—hold and build knowledge (Flannery, 1994). Too often, even in engaging and challenging learning experiences, the teacher's voice reflects unilateral authority and universal truth. The learners' role is to answer questions in the teacher's language and usually not to question, especially in their own ways of speaking and seeing. Since speech indicates position in school and society, the domination of the teacher's language, no matter what the learning activity, keeps the class teacher-centered (Shor, 1992). To avoid this undemocratic discourse and to enhance dialogue, mutual inquiry, and the support of learners as knowledge builders we propose the second norm: *learner expression and language are joined with teacher expression and language to form a "third idiom" that enables the perspectives of all learners to be readily shared and included in the process of learning.* Learners' language brings a conversational and concrete quality to the frequently more abstract and conceptual nature of the teacher's language, offering both parties an accessibility to the knowledge and realities of each other (Shor, 1992).

This language fusion is essential to the reinvention of a democratic relationship between teachers and learners. The process is not formal; it occurs in an evolutionary manner as the teacher encourages learner expression and gradually uses and reflects back the learners' language in their dialogue with careful attention to talking and lecturing less, and as the teacher creates with learners more activities and opportunities to use their voices. As Ira Shor (1992) states, an alternative form of communication, a third idiom, is vital to the democratic transformation of education to a construction that is truly equitable and multicultural:

> The knowledge and language that exist in daily life and in the academy cannot by themselves produce social and intellectual empowerment. The culture of schooling and the culture of everyday life in non-elite communities need something from each other to transcend their own limits. The current academic canons of language and subject matter need to be transformed in a multicultural way with and for students, to reflect their language and conditions [p. 255].

The third idiom is, of course, not a static language. With each new learning group it is invented in process anew and reflects the particular learners, subject matter, and political climate of the school or community. Without speech to pose learning within the language and experience of learners, it is impossible for them to speak as members of an authentic learning community.

Procedures for Enhancing Meaning

As we consider the procedures for enhancing meaning we realize content is only as important as the learners' interaction with it. Since we accept multiple realities and differing profiles of intelligences we need ways of creating knowledge that embody these perspectives. Dealing with relevant and larger concepts while learning offers this possibility. Numerous disciplines, from critical literacy and constructivism to multiple intelligences theory and brain-based learning, support this approach and respectively advocate the use of generative themes (Shor, 1992), primary concepts (Brooks and Brooks, 1993), essential questions (Gardner and Boix-Mansilla, 1994), and thematic attractors (Caine and Caine, 1991). All of the latter terms are synonymous with broad conceptual themes that present issues or ideas of such magnitude and meaning that they can provide a relevant focal point as well as elicit intrinsic motivation among diverse students. Broad conceptual themes also evoke deeper meanings within learners, kindling their desire to actively pursue personal learning goals. As an example, each of the following questions could be used to generate a broad conceptual theme among students: How could we find out if competition is necessary for learning to excel? What key concerns do the following words— slum, land, food, work, salary, vote, profession, government, and wealth—urge us to express? Why do the ideas of justice and conflict seem to so frequently be related to one another in personal life as well as in history? Which social systems do you belong to that do not rely on a hierarchy of authority for their operation? Why? What keeps us healthy? In the case of the last question, the themes of health, illness, and prevention easily come to mind. All students could find a relevant and, perhaps, deeply personal perspective to bring to one or more of these themes.

The procedures that follow are excellent ways to extract meaning from major conceptual themes. In most cases we as teachers exercise the role of representing ideas and skills, engaging in *dialogue* with learners, and encouraging their *reflection*. To encourage knowledge building rather than authoritarian truths we must allow different perspectives to exist as a valid part of reality without unnecessarily placing them in competition with each other (Lather, 1991). In addition, as we consider dialogue to be a transformative exchange of voices where teachers and learners are involved in a co-learning process, learner participation informs us about how students think and learn, helping us to successively deepen levels of thematic inquiry. To make authentic dialogue (Shor, 1992) a constant process throughout these procedures we need to

- Analyze with learners' participation
- Avoid jargon or esoteric references that intimidate learners into silence
- Encourage learners to come up with thought-provoking questions for discussion
- Be patient in listening to learners and giving them time to think on their feet
- Invite learners to speak from experience, realizing that knowledge consists of one's everyday lived experiences, and integrating that material into social issues and academic themes
- Include the narrative method, in which people tell their stories in print or by voice, allowing the whole to give meaning to the particular
- Invite learners to suggest themes for study and ask them to specify reading matter
- Draw learners out with questions after they speak and encourage them to respond to each other

With this kind of dialogue as integral to the procedures that follow, learners have a good chance to arrive at personally meaningful and conceptually coherent learning respectful of a multicultural perspective. Indispensable to this entire process for many learners is reflection, a chance to spend time considering their experience in order to more fully grasp the implications and inferences. Reflection allows teachers and learners to be simultaneously open-minded and discerning, with opportunity for spontaneous creativity (Fellows and Zimpher, 1988). Shön (1987) makes a useful distinction between reflection *in* action and reflection *on* action. The former is an on-the-spot analysis and dialogue, excellent for dealing with the variety and unpredictability inherent in such real situations as teaching, medical practice, experimenting, and computer work. The latter is a post hoc examination, often with feedback and dialogue, of what has transpired after the event—what might be learned looking back in fields ranging from politics to music. Both of these forms of reflection imply the need for self-observation and openness to multiple perspectives. In Chapter Five the essential role of reflection for self-assessment is specifically addressed.

Most of the procedures that follow tend to be analytical. However, an excellent way to sometimes deepen meaning is through *contemplation*, placing ideas and experiences in the mind and observing them without any form of analysis or deliberation. Like patiently and calmly watching a child or remembering a dream *without* seeking to understand, patterns, insights, and perspectives can eventually emerge. Allowing learners time to "look" at a problem without trying to solve it or to move away from a project without the demand to map its completion, may be the best way to nurture resolution. There is no formula for the optimal use of dialogue, reflection, and contemplation. Yet their sensitive and continual merging with the procedures that follow is crucial to the enhancement of meaning while learning.

Cultivating Flow

Earlier, we discussed the feeling of flow—the deeply satisfying experience of an intrinsically motivating activity. All of the procedures that follow have the potential to be flow occurrences for teachers and learners alike. Flow is associated with eight major conditions (Csikszentmihalyi, 1990). Not all of these elements have to be present for a person to experience a state of flow, but when all of them are contextual to the learning activity, the moments spent learning are likely to be extremely gratifying. We take a closer look at each condition below. We have specifically adapted these elements to learning situations from broader discussions by Csikszentmihalyi (1990, 1988).

1. *When our knowledge or skill is just right for coping with the demands of a situation, and when compared to the entirety of daily life the demands are above average, the motivational quality of the experience improves noticeably.* This is an excellent way to understand challenges. When they are just balanced with our capacity to act and at least a bit beyond what we consider "the usual" of our customary lives, exhilaration can appear. Thus, a learning activity should have a range of challenges broad enough and flexible enough to engage learners with a variety of backgrounds and profiles of intelligences.

2. *We are able to concentrate on what we are doing.* Our attention can be invested totally in the activity at hand. We are absorbed and unaware of ourselves because the relevant experience so takes up our attention that none is left to think about anything else. The action carries us forward, giving us the feeling of the merging of activity and awareness. We are part of the game, part of the dialogue, or part of the story we are reading, moving with it, fluid and harmonious—in flow. Immersion of this sort occurs more easily in a physical space designed or designated for it. As in many things, aesthetics and mood influence engagement or withdrawal.

3-4. *We can be so involved because what we are doing has relatively clear goals and provides rather quick and unambiguous feedback.* It is difficult to become immersed unless we have some idea of what needs to be done and how well we are doing. This is more obvious in an experiment or case study, but let's take a dialogue where the outcome is unknown. Conversations seek to make sense to all parties. No matter where it ends up, the immediate goal is to create further meaning by talking and listening. Words, facial expressions, and gestures give immediate feedback. And a good dialogue is usually animated. When we experience insight, agreement, or think of deeper questions, we often feel a sense of accomplishment. Our intentions and personal sense of aesthetics serve as guidelines throughout the dialogue, as they would in any creative act.

5. *Involvement removes from awareness the worries and frustrations of everyday life*. This does not mean we should not confront our problems and concerns or deal with matters of social consequence while learning. It does mean there are limitations to what can be considered if flow is to be maintained, and therefore issues that provoke self-consciousness or personal and ethical reflection may, at times, be incompatible with flow. For example, a dialogue about racism or heterosexism may cause us to be uncomfortable as we consider other opinions or personal behavior. Although absorbed, we may have feelings of anxiety, guilt, or sadness. These emotions may not only be unavoidable but necessary in order for us to move into new areas of personal awareness and learning. At such times we may shift in and out of flow, with certain topics or comments commanding our complete attention, skill, and knowledge to the exclusion of self-consciousness, much as surgeons, air traffic controllers, and therapists often do as unpredictable, spontaneous challenges enter their lives. We see flow as a desirable state during learning, frequently more possible than we often realize, but not a matter of primacy to the exclusion of issues of substance.

6. *We are not worried about losing control*. This is not the same as *being in control*. In fact, paradoxically, unless we give up some degree of certainty or see the outcome as having some shading of unpredictability we won't really know we can influence the process

and feel a sense of our own determination. A "sure thing" is too easy to absorb our concentration; it requires robotic, not humanly sensitive, responses. Feeling in control is a relative state in which we can exercise judgment and influence without being overwhelmed by threat or fear. For very challenging situations, we at least have a "lifeline," a "safety net," a back-up plan, a second chance, or a mentor or a community of peers we can join with for added strength or insight. This helps us to feel relaxed and alert—two commonly aligned descriptors of the flow experience (Wlodkowski, 1985). All or nothing situations are the antithesis of flow experiences.

7. *Concern for the self tends to disappear,* yet paradoxically our sense of self emerges more strongly after the flow experience is over. What falls below the threshold of awareness is the *concept* of self, the information we use to represent to ourselves who we are. Being able to forget temporarily who we are seems to be delightful. During such self-transcendence we often further develop personal intricacy. Being egoless frequently leads to greater feelings of harmony and power, as when we are part of a team, moved by the same purpose, as in an activist group or a dance troupe. As Csikszentmihalyi (1990) writes, "When a person invests all her psychic energy into an interaction—whether it is with another person, a boat, a mountain, or a piece of music—she in effect becomes part of a system of action greater than what the individual self had been before. This system takes its form from the rules of the activity; its energy comes from the person's attention. But it is a real system—subjectively as real as being part of a family, a corporation or a team—and the self that is part of it expands its boundaries and becomes more complex than what it had been" (p. 65). When a flow activity is over is often a good time to reflect on the self, to realize how we may have changed or been enriched.

8. *Our sense of the duration of time is altered.* Hours can seem like minutes and minutes can stretch out to seem like hours. Time seems to bear little relation to the passage of time as measured by the absolute convention of the clock. The interaction sets its own pace

and rhythm. When dialogue is in flow it may seem as though there were only a few questions and the class period has completely passed. One sits down to read, and hours fly by. Yet making a difficult turn in ballet or hearing the pained response of a colleague can certainly make seconds move like minutes. Thus, for learning activities in flow, it is sometimes wise to let the sequence of events set transitions and pace rather than set a prior schedule.

Because flow can be found across cultures it may be a sense that humans have developed in order to recognize patterns of action that are worth preserving and transmitting over time (Massimini, Csikszentmihalyi, and Delle Fave, 1988). When it occurs as part of the process of learning it makes learning an end in itself. Those who experience flow have not only a better chance of learning but also a better chance of wanting to learn more. Creating flow with learners regardless of ethnicity, gender, or class is the challenge imbedded in every procedure that follows.

Critical Questioning and Guided Reciprocal Peer Questioning

The first procedure we address is critical questioning practices because if teachers and learners are to realistically engage in the coconstruction of meaning, where everyone, at times, is a teacher and a learner, then they must frequently be co-inquirers mutually capable of thinking about information in ways that transform that material into new knowledge. Thought-provoking questions can prompt everyone to make connections as well as raise contradictions between what they already know and what is the presented "knowledge." Raising critical questions reveals individuals' differing perspectives on ideas and issues.

However, there is research to show that fewer than 5 percent of teacher questions are higher-order questions (requesting complex thinking) and that the frequency of student-generated questions is infinitesimally low, averaging 0.11 per hour per student in classrooms in several countries; of these student questions, most are factual (Dillon, 1988; Kerry, 1987). Questioning is thinking, and critical thinking requires critical questioning. Critical thinking, critical literacy, problem solving, decision making, creative thinking, and research are all aspects of thoughtfulness, sets of related and overlapping skills. Most definitions of critical thinking directly or indirectly address the skills of analyzing, inferring, synthesizing, applying, evaluating, comparing, contrasting, verifying, substantiating, explaining, and hypothesizing (King, 1994). In addition, critical thinking is as much an operative philosophy and disposition as it is an isolated skill. Educators make a distinction between a make-sense epistemology and a critical epistemology (Perkins, Allen, and Hafner, 1983). In a make-sense orientation, the criteria for the validity of a statement are that it seems to hang together and fit with one's prior beliefs. If something appears self-evident and makes sense, there is no need to think any more about it. In a critical epistemology, it is not sufficient for the statement to hang together or match prior beliefs. There is still a need to examine the data and reasoning for inconsistencies, to take alternative perspectives, to construct counterarguments, and to look for bias and overgeneralization. Some of these elements you may recognize from our discussion of constructive knowledge (Belenky, Clinchy, Goldberger, and Tarule, 1986).

Attitudes and beliefs found to support critical thinking and, by implication, its related epistemology are openness to others' ideas and arguments, confidence in one's own ability to solve problems, desire to look for meaning in complex situations, willingness to think adventurously, and acceptance of the ideas that thinking (rather than luck) can lead to the resolution of problems and that there is nothing inherently wrong with changing one's mind on an issue (Baron, 1988; Ennis, 1986).

With the opportunity to use mindful questions, learners can affirm and extend the critical thinking they bring to postsecondary educational settings. Such occasions can also foster the deepening of those attitudes and beliefs that support critical thinking and critical consciousness. Alison King (1994) has developed and extensively tested an instructional procedure for teaching university learners to pose their own thought-provoking questions. She has found that, once learned, this procedure becomes a thinking strategy that learners can use either on their own or in groups.

In using this procedure, the teacher provides the learners with a written set of generic questions or such question starters as, What do we already know about . . . ? and How do you think . . . would see the issue of . . . ? These questions encourage knowledge construction because they serve as prompts to induce more critical thinking on the part of learners and the teacher as well. Learners use these *generic* questions to guide them in formulating their own specific questions pertaining to the material to be discussed. Exhibit 4.1 contains a list of thoughtful question stems that can be adapted for use by "filling in the blanks" with information relevant to the subject being covered. The critical thinking skills these questions elicit are also listed (King, 1994).

When the teacher offers these question stems to students for their conversations and dialogue, students can use their own information and examples to deepen the content of what is to be studied. In this manner a bridge can be formed between the usually more academic language of the teacher and the everyday language of the learners progressing toward a more mutual language (third idiom) and increased dialogue.

Exhibit 4.1. Guiding Thought-Provoking Questioning.

Generic Questions	Specific Thinking Skills Induced
What is a new example of . . . ?	Application
How could . . . be used to . . . ?	Application
What would happen if . . . ?	Prediction/hypothesizing
What are the implications of . . . ?	Analysis/inference

Exhibit 4.1. Guiding Thought-Provoking Questioning, Cont'd.

Generic Questions	Specific Thinking Skills Induced
What are the strengths and weaknesses of . . . ?	Analysis/inference
What is . . . analogous to?	Identification and creation of analogies and metaphors
What do we already know about . . . ?	Activation of prior knowledge
How does . . . affect . . . ?	Analysis of relationship (cause-effect)
How does . . . tie in with what we learned before?	Activation of prior knowledge
Explain why . . .	Analysis
Explain how . . .	Analysis
What is the meaning of . . . ?	Analysis
Why is . . . important?	Analysis of significance
What is the difference between . . . and . . . ?	Comparison-contrast
How are . . . and . . . similar?	Comparison-contrast
How does . . . apply to everyday life?	Application to the real world
What is the counterargument for . . . ?	Rebuttal argument
What is the best . . . , and why?	Evaluation and provision of evidence
What are some possible solutions to the problem of . . . ?	Synthesis of ideas
Compare . . . and . . . with regard to . . .	Comparison-contrast
What do you think causes . . . ? Why?	Analysis of relationship (cause-effect)
Do you agree or disagree with this statement: . . . ? What evidence is there to support your answer?	Evaluation and provision of evidence
How do you think . . . would see the issue of . . . ?	Taking other perspectives

Source: King, 1994, p. 24. Used by permission.

To King's list we add the following examples of the five types of questions Paul (1990) associates with a Socratic dialogue:

1. *Clarification:* "What do you mean by . . . ? Could you give me an example?"
2. *Probing for assumptions:* "What are you assuming when you say . . . ? What is underlying what you say?"
3. *Probing for reasons and evidence:* "How do you know that . . . ? What are your reasons for saying . . . ?"
4. *Other perspectives:* "What might someone say who believed that . . . ? What is an alternative for . . . ?"
5. *Probing for implications as consequences:* "What are you implying by . . . ? Because of . . . , what might happen?"

For guided practice in the use of both of these lists of questions, a teacher could set up a "fishbowl" discussion. One-third of the class sits in a circle and discusses a relevant topic using the questions as prompts. The rest of the class, in a circle around the others, listens and takes notes, then has a dialogue about the discussion.

In the individual or self-questioning version of King's instructional procedure, learners can use the question stems to guide them in generating their own critical questions following a presentation, a class, or a reading. We have found students' use of these question lattices enhances the composition of their journals and self-assessments.

Guided reciprocal peer questioning (King, 1994) is the group version of this procedure, and it can be implemented in any course. After activities such as seeing a project presentation, listening to a short lecture, or reading agreed-upon material, learners use the generic question stems and work independently to generate two or three questions based on the material. Next, in pairs or small groups, they engage in peer questioning, taking turns asking their questions of their partner or group and answering each other's questions in a reciprocal manner. This approach encourages a deeper dialogue and helps learners to check their understanding as well as to gain other learners' perspectives.

Let us say I and my class have read Ralph Ellison's *Invisible Man.* We have agreed to each bring along two questions based on the list in Exhibit 4.1 regarding any aspect of the book that we find applicable to our lives. We break off into dyads, and my partner and I each place our two questions before us. They read:

1. How does the last line of the book, "Who knows but that, on the lower frequencies, I speak for you?" apply to our everyday lives?

2. What is the *brotherhood* analogous to in our own contemporary society?

3. The book has many strengths, as it has been heralded as the greatest American novel of the second half of the twentieth century. From your perspective, what were its weaknesses?

4. What are examples of invisibility at this college?

With these queries, we have an opportunity to relate ideas from this novel to our own knowledge and experience. We can have an extensive discussion that may clarify some inadequacies in our comprehension, and each of us has a chance to guide, to some extent, the thinking that will occur. There is opportunity to infer, compare, evaluate, and explain, all of which can lead to better understanding, fuller awareness of social issues, and the possibility of modifying one's own thinking.

Both teachers and students *learn* to pose critical questions, to clarify, extend, and refine their thinking, and to realize the social implications of any idea from different perspectives. As Perkins and his colleagues point out (Perkins, Faraday, and Bushey, 1991), the meaning that we make in our lives is what constitutes our lives. Critical thinking, and therefore critical questioning, precede and abet critical consciousness. They can broaden the quality of our lives, allow us to include a wider human panorama, and ultimately offer a means to more equitably influence what can be known.

Posing Problems: From Emerging Relevance to Relevance

In a very broad sense, a problem can be characterized as any situation where a person wants to achieve a goal for which an obstacle exists (Voss, 1989). If relevant and within the range of human capacity, problems, by definition, are challenging and engaging. Review of the research in the area of culture and cognitive development indicates that the use of concepts and processes for solving problems is to a significant extent culture bound (Hofstede, 1986; Scribner and Cole, 1981; Schkade, Romani, and Uzawa, 1978). Perceptual differences, information processing, constraints in terms of social and ethical codes, and technical materials and procedures are all culturally determined and do influence how a problem may be conceived and approached. From building a home to settling a divorce, the variance across the world is extraordinary. The interesting and important issue here is that the enormous variety among humans in how problems are perceived, constructed, and resolved is extremely valuable to what can be learned inside and outside of schools.

We distinguish between *problem-posing* and *posing a problem* as procedures because the former term is synonymous with a model of Freirean pedagogy (Freire, 1970) that will be explicitly considered in the structures section of this chapter. However, Shor (1992), an exponent of critical teaching and student-centered learning, offers a very useful taxonomy for the kind of problems that may be presented (posed as a problem) during learning. These are problems identified as generative themes, topical themes, and academic themes. All of them may be offered as questions, as most problems usually are.

Generative themes grow out of the learners' culture. They express problematic conditions of daily life. Learners find them deeply meaningful because they directly relate to their anxieties, fears, and dreams. They are the unsettled intersections of personal life and society based on experiences such as voting, working, housing, and community activity (Shor, 1992). When learners see their own words and experiences in the problems constructed and considered, intellectual work becomes compelling and based in the diversity of the learners' present. Learner subjectivity initiates learning and is often the leading edge but not the end. There is eventually a syn-thesis between the teacher's knowing and the learners' knowing.

The beginning of posing a problem based on a generative theme is to draw attention to a personally relevant and substantial issue or situation. We offer the following scenario as a composite example from the experience of one of the authors.

For a research course for adult learners I begin with the ques-tion, "If you believed research could really help you, and you were able to conduct the study yourself or with your family, friends, or colleagues, what is a personally relevant issue or problem you would like to study?" I then ask the learners to think about the question for a few minutes, usually in silence. Then I ask them to "free write" their response in a narrative form for five to ten minutes (for exam-ple: "A problem that comes to mind . . . ," "I was just thinking the other day that I wish I knew . . ."). After they have completed their free writing, I ask them to break into triads and to read and discuss their compositions, acting as research colleagues to give support and feedback and to deepen their thinking about what has been shared. When these discussions are completed, I ask each learner to review and, if desired, revise their problem or issue into a statement or question and to copy it onto a four-by-six card. All of these cards are then posted on a wall and read by us. After reading the cards we look for three or four themes to emerge that might unite the vari-ous problems that have been posed—for example, children, work issues, or financial concerns. We then reassemble into three groups according to the theme that is of most individual concern, with the purpose of surfacing a problem that all members of that group would find personally worthwhile to research. The three problems that emerge are:

1. How could I find out if my children's diet is really healthy?
2. How would I know if the way I teach immigrant students, whose first language is not English, to use personal computers is as effective as it can be?
3. What are socially responsible ways to invest money?

Using each of these questions as a starting point and asking questions that elicit the learners' language and experience, I begin to teach them how to "operationalize" a question for research: What does healthy mean to you? How do you know when your children are healthy? How would you measure health? and so on. We now have three generative themes to use in considering other elements of research design. If we decide to, we can stay with these problems for as much as a quarter of the entire course. Eventually, we will learn together about action research and carry out projects in our communities based on these or other generative themes. Some of the learners will go on to publish their work in newsletters, magazines, and journals. Others will come back to the next course and share their thinking and support with another community of learners. I doubt if any of these outcomes could have occurred without generative themes.

"The *topical theme* [our emphasis] is a social question of key importance locally, nationally, or globally that is not generated directly from the students' conversation. It is raised in class by the teacher" (Shor, 1992, p. 55). Topical themes are often introduced because learner conversation and thought may not include important issues in society. Frequently, it is a problem the teacher presents based on her or his critical knowledge of the world at large and the learners' experiences in it. A topical theme can be a way to encourage learners to step into an area ignored or covered uncritically by the conventional curriculum and mass media. Commercial text-books frequently diminish consideration of diverse opinions as well as people. Topical themes can offer original and thoughtful conversations and exploration of social issues not yet being discussed by learners in daily life.

However, in a critical-democratic class, the topical theme is open to rejection by learners because a "problem-posing" course is a negotiated experience with a mutual curriculum (Shor, 1992). Therefore, in more conventional courses, teachers ought to choose topical themes with a sensitive awareness of learner needs and perspectives to avoid subjecting them to personal, political, and social harangues. In either case we agree with Shor (1992) that topical themes fit when they are relevant to work in progress, when they are introduced as problems for collaborative study, and when they are in an idiom learners can understand. If these minimal criteria are not met, then topical themes subvert culturally responsive teaching into another teacher-dominated experience for learners.

The following are examples of topical themes we have introduced in courses we have taught:

- Assertive discipline (Canter and Canter, 1976), a behavior control method frequently used in schools that negates cultural differences and punishes critical thinking and self-determination in students.

- Criterion-referenced tests that many people see as preferable to norm-referenced tests but that are frequently normed to the values and orientations of the dominant culture and do not necessarily negotiate cultural or other relevant characteristics of learners.

- School-business partnerships (Molnar, 1989–1990), which often provide a pretext for corporate advertising and in frequent cases reduce learning to a process of supplying simplistic material rewards for behavior—for example, pizzas for reading books, gum for solving math problems, and so on.

- Positive self-esteem as a primary personal and social goal that masks a self-reliant ideology and diverts society's attention from systematic inequality and institutional discrimination based on race, gender, age, class, and sexual preference. (In one course, learners rejected this topical theme and found the perspective offered to be inadequate and biased.)

In general, topical themes should be introduced as participatory problems rather than as a lecture, so that the floor is consistently open for learner voices to reflect, comment, or disagree. If learners are not interested in the problem or do not wish to discuss it, their position is to be respected. Culturally responsive teaching is not about indoctrinating learners. Their right of refusal is equal to the teacher's right of presentation. In the case of the self-esteem theme noted above, learners in one course did not see it as a problem they wished to investigate. They saw it more as a reflection of the male author's bias—white men, especially college faculty, have less of a tendency to regard self-esteem as a problem because of their privileged status in this society.

The third kind of problem is the *academic theme,* which represents a scholastic, professional, or technical body of knowledge that the teacher wants to present or has to put forward as a requirement (Shor, 1992). This material is usually drawn from a specific subject area, such as science, history, or nursing. Often it is a particular knowledge or skill from the teacher's field of study and not part of the learner's culture. Academic themes are generally unfamiliar to learners and are composed of their own jargon and sets of particular skills. Learners bring many of their own ideas about "scholarly topics" like math, science, and statistics, but they seldom call what they know "knowledge." (Although we have both taught research courses, and baseball is a popular topic among many different learners, especially during the spring and summer months, we have yet to hear a single student say, I wonder how much age accounts for the percentage of variance in number of home runs hit? Yet many learners would say a player is getting older and does not have the eye or the power to hit as many home runs as in younger years.) By presenting problems, often posed as questions, we can integrate what learners know with our academic themes to co-create learning.

A heuristic way to consider academic themes as posed problems is to envision the following different ways to frame the problem:

1. The academic theme is a relevant problem.

2. The academic theme solves a relevant problem.

3. The academic theme is made relevant by an intriguing problem.

The first possibility is to present the subject matter itself as the problem. The second is to pose a relevant problem from the experience of the learners that the academic theme may help to solve. The third possibility is to identify a problem with little or no initial relevance that is nonetheless intriguing, where the academic theme is made relevant through teacher mediation. In all cases we use learners' language, perspectives, and suppositions to contextualize and create the problem-solving process.

The Academic Theme Is a Relevant Problem. From the broadest to the most specific academic theme we can incorporate learner perspectives, experiences, needs, and interests by sequential "what" and "how" questions. In an educational psychology course: In the broadest sense, what do we know about psychology? What do we want to know about psychology? How is psychology important in our daily lives? How has psychology helped or hindered people in our families? In a narrower sense, what do we know about learning disabilities? What do we want to know about learning disabilities? What does learning disability mean as we live our daily lives? How has the label *learning disability* helped or hindered people in our families? With writing, reflection, dialogue, critical incidents (Brookfield, 1987), primary materials, and so on, we can take either of these topics and follow them along the path of our learners' perspectives to create challenging problems to pursue for a day, a week, or perhaps the length of the course.

Academic Theme Solves a Relevant Problem. When an academic theme solves a relevant problem we are looking for situations that draw out learner concerns and interests. They need to understand the academic theme to resolve the issue, comprehend what action to take, find relevant insights, and so on. For example, one way to introduce multiple academic themes is to ask learners to take a role or a particular view to solve a relevant problem: the learner who distrusts an historical viewpoint and becomes an historian reading the primary material and writing her or his own historical account; the learner who finds a psychological interpretation too individualized and wants to offer a sociological analysis; or the learner who wants to take a systemic view of what is presented as a criminal problem. Most forms of research, creativity, and invention find their initial impetus in a relevant problem.

Another approach is to place the learner in a relevant problem. For courses in accounting, math, organizational planning, and so on, the problem might be stated: You're the treasurer of a community organization and you are losing this amount of money per month. With these assets, liabilities, dues, and so forth, what would you do? For ethnic studies or courses on social policy or the law, the posed problem might be: You are a twenty-one-year-old African-American male; you have your first automobile accident, for which you are not at fault; you have no driving violations; your insurance is cancelled. You will need to understand actuarial records and predictive statistics to investigate this matter.

Academic Theme Is Made Relevant by an Intriguing Problem. Human beings are oceans of curiosity. Every day we are challenged to bring order out of chaos and meaning from paradox. What is puzzling, bizarre, and surprising attracts our attention not so much because it is relevant but because it is intriguing. The same wonder that makes a beach a miracle of small astonishments for a child elicits amazement from an adult in the presence of a gifted magician. To some extent our capacity for beguilement is beyond relevance, anchored in our need to remain alive. We anticipate to survive, whether to take a step or to enter traffic on a high-speed freeway. Human beings make countless predictions as we live our lives. When the outcome is something unexpected our reactions can range from a reflexive startle to an enduring fascination. Add to this our need for feedback about personal competence (Csikszentmihalyi, 1990), and we have the genesis of engaging and intriguing problems that can create emerging relevance for academic themes.

In culturally responsive teaching, central to the use of provocative problems is reciprocal interaction (Cummins, 1986), where there is a genuine dialogue between learners and teacher and where the teacher evokes meaningful language use by the learners rather than merely employing gimmickry to foster attention and passive learning. Problems of emerging relevance (Brooks and Brooks, 1993) are basic to constructivist pedagogy, in which learning is understood to be a self-regulated process of resolving inner cognitive conflicts that usually become apparent through concrete experience, collaborative discourse, and reflection. Teacher mediation for problems of emerging relevance is used to elicit learner perspectives and hypotheses. Effective problem-solving situations of this sort usually ask learners to make predictions, are complex enough to evoke multiple responses, and can include group efforts to test hypotheses.

As a prototypical example of an academic theme made relevant by an intriguing problem, we offer the following example adopted from the work of Jacqueline Grennon Brooks and Martin Brooks (1993), which invites learners to better understand the concepts of momentum and energy.

The teacher presents a set of five hanging pendula (see Figure 4.1) with metal balls of equal size all touching each other in a

Figure 4.1. A Set of Five Hanging Pendula.

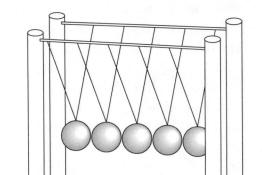

Source: From Brooks, Jacqueline Grennon, and Martin G. Brooks. *The Case for Constructivist Classrooms,* p. 37. Alexandria, VA: Association for Supervision and Curriculum Development. Copyright 1993 by ASCD. Used with permission.

resting position. By raising one ball and releasing it, the teacher allows the learners to note that one ball swings out on the other side. Then raising and releasing two balls the learners observe that two balls swing out on the other side. Then raising three balls the teacher asks the group to predict what will happen when the three balls are let go. Having engaged diverse groups in this activity, Brooks and Brooks have found at least four of the following responses articulated by every group: (1) one ball will go out, but higher; (2) two balls will go out, but higher; (3) three balls will go out; (4) the balls will "go crazy"; (5) the balls will stop; and (6) the balls will swing together. They report they always ask learners to explain their responses, react to others' responses, and indicate whether they have changed their minds upon hearing others' predictions. Because learners are given time to ponder the question, form their own responses, and share their thoughts in a manner that remains open to the opinions and questions of other learners and the teacher, interest develops in a context where immediate feed-back by the apparatus itself can enlighten all possible responses. In fact, Brooks and Brooks write that within about half an hour most groups *demand* the release of the three balls in order to test their theories.

Brooks and Brooks develop labs and experiences that focus explicitly on the students' thinking. For example, those who claim the two balls will swing higher might examine the variables that influence the swing of a pendulum using balls of different weights and strings of different lengths to determine what gets a pendulum to swing higher. Further activities are developed based on the learn-ers' emerging interests and understandings.

Presenting learners with discrepant events and contradictory information is a corollary to this general method. For example, learners may become more interested in the academic theme of heat transference when they have a chance to consider why the bottom of a paper cup does not burn from the flame of a lighter when the cup is filled with water. In fact, making academic themes relevant through learner engagement in intriguing problems is a process that relates to learner background and perspective. It requires the teacher to know her or his learners well enough to understand what to do to encourage them to sincerely wonder about an important academic theme. But there must also be respect for the learners' contributions, the reciprocal interaction that leads to a real dialogue with a view toward the social relevance of what is being learned. Without it, this method remains little more than an expedient trick to enliven conventional learning.

In a broad sense most of the procedures that follow can also be characterized as problem-solving processes. Yet they possess suffi-cient differences to merit their own classifications as, for example, decision making or research. In all instances, although we may offer guidelines and examples, we will not present precise or prescriptive steps for their use. We understand real-life problems as dialectical, where the ability to zig and zag between contradictory lines of reasoning, using each to critically evaluate the other, is necessary. Because culturally responsive pedagogy potentially embodies the social contexts and consequences of all learning, problem-solving processes cannot be limited to a technical or algorithmic set of operations.

Decision Making

Decision making is a process used to arrive at a course of action, a policy, a plan, or a particular choice. It answers such questions as What is the best way ? and Which idea is most suitable? The evidence generally includes estimated or imagined consequences, often arrived at through consideration of several options. Learners usually have to assemble information in the needed topic areas, compare advantages and disadvantages of alternative approaches, determine what additional information is needed, and justify their judgment of the most valued or effective response (Presseisen, 1985). Often the process includes the identification of criteria to determine the selection made.

Decision-making learning activities can be used in a wide variety of content areas. When based on learner interests, concerns, and perspectives, they can be used to address generative, topical, and academic themes. Because this process is well suited to real-life events and direct action, it is an excellent medium for the development of critical consciousness and intrinsic motivation.

The following example could be used in almost any of the social sciences as well as courses in social and health policy, international studies, research, and statistics. The teacher asks the learners to form collaborative groups and to examine the Sunday paper for any article whose topic deeply concerns them and that they see as relevant to the course. One group brings the article found in Exhibit 4.2.

Exhibit 4.2. Newspaper Article.

AIDS Is Likely to Reverse Gains in Life Expectancy

Notwithstanding floods, famine or wars, the overall quality of life in the third world has been improving for two decades. But now, there is evidence that hard-won gains in life expectancy and childhood mortality are being reversed in many places by a new scourge: AIDS.

Last week demographers at the Census Bureau's Center for International Research said that by the year 2010 AIDS will cut overall life expectancy in 13 sub-Saharan nations, Haiti, Brazil and Thailand. Life expectancy had been rising in all of them, but in some, like Uganda, the epidemic will lop off 27 years from the average life span.

The decrease is expected to be particularly sharp because transmission of the H.I.V. virus in places like Africa is almost always through heterosexual sex. This means the disease is passed on to unborn fetuses more often than in the West, and that childhood mortality rates are expected to soar.

In Zambia, for example, demographers predict that by the year 2010 the epidemic will increase the death rate among very young children to 160 out of every 1,000 live births. If the epidemic did not exist, the rate would be 56 out of every 1,000.

Source: Holmes, *New York Times*, May 1, 1994, Section 4, p. 2. Used by permission.

After a dialogue about the meaning and ramifications of the information contained in the article, the learners and teacher agree to a project in which the learners will assume the role of a task force to further examine the materials and data used by the Census Bureau's Center for International Research to make these predictions. Afterward, they will conduct their own study to arrive at a set of realistic and defensible recommendations regarding United States international policy and the AIDS epidemic. The learners also want to collaborate to write an article based on these recommendations for the opinion column of the local paper. They have decided that central to this entire project is their mutual agreement about the criteria that will be used to create and select their recommendations. The report of their study will include explanations of why they chose these criteria and how well the recommendations meet these criteria along with a discussion of salient alternatives that may have failed to meet the criteria but remain worth consideration.

Authentic Research

Creative problem solving, research, and critical consciousness serve a number of similar functions. All three enhance meaning. All three question the status quo. All three use active-participatory methods. All three give evidence that knowledge is not fixed but constantly changing. And all three offer an opportunity to rethink experience and society. Within them, scrutiny is an art form.

In a general sense, research is an in-depth study of something. It involves detailed investigation and extensive explanation in order to understand, predict, apply, create, and/or evaluate some phenomena. Much research also has an action agenda, with the researcher sharing results to have an impact on an audience, as in the case of a medical researcher submitting findings to various health professionals. Although most people do research—for example, studying *Consumer Reports* and reading newspaper articles to purchase a decent car—the term is popularly associated with scholars, scientists, and graduate students. Also, to many learners, research is often interpreted to mean the coerced ritual of writing a *research paper*: using secondary sources to expound on a teacher-determined topic resulting in dull encyclopedic information and a negative attitude.

Culturally responsive teaching advocates authentic research as a learning procedure in which learners actively investigate a problem or question of personal interest where there is no present answer and use primary resources and real-world information and data to share results with people who might benefit from the findings or take action themselves based on these findings. Authentic research can be conducted in any discipline or across disciplines and used for generative, topical, or academic themes. As a procedure, it helps learners to know that their questions and perspectives matter and to acquire the skills and knowledge to pursue any interest in a competent and critical manner.

Authentic research also allows teachers to be co-researchers with their learners, acting as colleagues collaborating in the pursuit of knowledge. Because authentic research requires a researchable question of genuine interest to learners, it emphasizes—as most culturally responsive teaching procedures do—the need for the teacher to know the concerns, cultural conditions, speech, and ways of learning present among the learners in the classroom. Not surprisingly, encouraging learners to do authentic research means teachers must do a kind of research themselves about their learners, using learner-centered discourse and writing to arrive at questions and problems of mutual interest. In addition, brainstorming, concept mapping, and interviewing learners are other possible ways to find authentic research interests with learners.

In the rest of this section we discuss four forms of authentic research. Each is distinct because of the type of investigation that is conducted. We have adapted the categorizations from the work of Robert Marzano (1992). This is not an exhaustive list, but it does afford an exploration and exemplification of the range of possibilities.

Definitional Investigation. Definitional investigation involves clarifying or identifying the defining characteristics or important features of a concept, event, or situation for which such characteristics are unknown, in question, or not readily apparent (Marzano, 1992). In society there are many evolving concepts and events that have an emerging quality or debatable interpretation for which a definitional investigation could make important distinctions and lead to learner enlightenment, emancipation, or action of social consequence. For example, depending on the course, among the many current possible topics are abortion, sexual harassment, and bilingual education. What does each term mean? How do race, class, gender, and ethnicity affect how we understand the contemporary issues related to these terms and their defining characteristics? What personal concerns or experiences make any of these three terms more salient to us? A definitional investigation would research how any of these terms are commonly portrayed in the media or textbooks. Research tools would include primary source materials, direct studies, and interviews to explore less diluted information and data. Careful attention would be given to identifying contradictions, confusions, and misrepresentations. The process of learners offering and justifying solutions or actions based on their definitional investigation becomes a preeminent motivational force for their learning.

As a result of their discourse, learners may offer their own conception of a situation or a generative theme for definitional investigation. This was the case for Daniel Solorzano (1989) at East Los Angeles College, who offered a course jointly listed by the sociology and Chicano studies departments to learners who were mostly Chicanos from the local area.

In the late 1970s, when this class was first offered, gang violence was receiving much attention in the press and in the film industry. Just as the course began, the *Los Angeles Times* ran a three-part series on Chicanos in the mass media. By examining these texts and the theme of youth gangs, the students and their teacher engaged in a dialogue centering on the negative stereotypes of Chicanos and on the Chicano-white culture clash as presented in Hollywood gang movies. After two weeks of discussion, Solorzano and his students arrived at two questions: Why are Chicanos portrayed negatively in the mass media? and Whose interests are served by these negative portrayals of Chicanos?

Based on these queries, extended research began with the class dividing itself into three research groups: (1) a library group to research contemporary and historical images of Chicanos in the media, using among their resources Hollywood trade papers, the *Readers' Guide to Periodical Literature, Sociological Abstracts,* the *Social Sciences Index,* the *Los Angeles Times Index,* and the *New York Times Index;* (2) a group to research public information data on youth gangs in East Los Angeles, using the area census on Chicanos, information from the sheriff's office and from the police department, sociological theories of gang and deviant behavior, and first-hand reports from gang members; and (3) a group to research the film industry, including representatives of Universal Pictures and Warner Brothers studios, Chicano community members and groups working as consultants to moviemakers, and groups who were beginning to challenge the negative images of Chicanos in the media.

Among the findings of the teams was that the gang problem was blown out of proportion, with the percentage of Chicano youths joining gangs not 10 percent as reported in the media, but closer to 3 percent. Another finding was that in films and media, "Chicanos were stereotyped disproportionately in subordinate and demeaning occupational roles such as bandits, thieves, and gangsters" (Solorzano, p. 221). After analyzing and discussing their research, the learners more clearly realized how film companies were exploiting Chicano stereotypes to make a profit. Consequently, they organized a boycott and an informational picket against some of the insulting films. Collaborating with outside organizations for assistance led to the founding of the ad hoc Gang Exploitation Committee. Solorzano reports that no new Chicano youth gang movies appeared in the decade after this class. Public protest and the mixed profitability of these films seem to have stopped their production. It was apparent to him that these learners developed commitment to and confidence in their own ideas and research and succeeded in doing something they considered important and positive.

Historical Investigation. Historical investigation involves determining, understanding, and evaluating past events in order to comprehend them, often with the purpose of clarifying present or future incidents and actions. This procedure is usually concerned with why or how something happened (Marzano, 1992). Every academic discipline has historical relevance, and questions can range from Why did the dinosaurs die? to What was the crucial chain of events leading to the dismantling of apartheid in South Africa? The history inherent in any subject area is often replete with contradictions and confusion. For this as well as other reasons historical research can be an exciting and engrossing context for dialectical thinking. When we begin to ask whose interests are served by certain interpretations of historical events and whether particular actions were justified, we quickly move into the realm of multiple perspectives and critical consciousness.

Learners frequently have questions about the accuracy or authenticity of historical information. Working with them as actual historians and investigating primary sources of data such as original documents, diaries, journals, photo collections, letters, and oral histories can be a fascinating enterprise. The following example, adapted from Giroux (1978), offers a dialectical approach for conducting historical research that can be extended to numerous topical and academic themes.

In this instance the academic theme is immigration law, and the question is, Were the (nineteenth century) restriction laws limiting immigration to the United States justified? A way to initially proceed and develop a relevant context and a variety of perspectives is to ask learners to consider data from their own lives about the impact and fairness of immigration laws. Using this dialogue as a bridge, the teacher could present an overview on the passing of twentieth-century restrictive immigration laws to enhance the learners' awareness of a broader historical context.

At this point, learners could engage the concept of "frame of reference." This could be done by having the learners read two specific historical accounts from the nineteenth century, each covering the same subject and a very similar set of information but arriving at two very different ideas: (1) Immigrants played a positive role in the growth of United States cities and industries by providing valuable skills and labor; (2) Immigrants displaced native workers from jobs by lowering wages and intensifying unemployment.

After the learners conclude their readings, they can discuss the possible frames of reference represented by these two different historians and the meaning of this exercise for themselves. With this background they can form historical research teams to investigate the primary materials (congressional records, newspaper accounts, and so forth) relevant to the restriction laws limiting immigration in the nineteenth century. Through facilitation by the teacher they can agree to pay attention in their research to the same set of possible historical influences, for example, political machines, the growth of the Catholic church, and mass immigration from southeastern Europe. They can also add pieces of their own information about other influences based upon their team's frames of reference and possible findings. When they have concluded their research they can compose a paper answering the question, Were the nineteenth century restriction laws limiting immigration justified? In this paper they can identify the unique pieces of information they selected and identify how their frames of reference emerged, what they were, and how they as historians were influenced by them.

The research teams can read each other's papers and meet with one another or as a whole group to compare and contrast the differences and similarities of ideas that resulted from their investigations. This dialogue can lead to an individual reflection paper and/or some form of artistic expression that indicates the meaning and learning constructed by the learners from this entire experience. The possibility remains that the group can continue with this theme and explore the justification of current restrictive immigration laws—for example, toward the people of Mexico or Latin America—with a consideration of collective action based on what is learned.

Projective Investigation. Projective investigation is concerned with the hypothetical. It involves researching what will happen if certain circumstances continue or change, or if some future event occurs (Marzano, 1992). Current apprehension about the severe global consequences of rain forest and old growth forest depletion is due, in part, to projective investigations. Another form of projective investigation is to predict the consequences if some past event had or had not occurred. For example, students predict the likely political outcomes if Nixon's presidency had continued to term beyond Watergate, or they estimate the potential agricultural production in the United States if the great floods of 1993 had not happened.

Again, as in the previously discussed forms of investigation, learners research what is conventionally accepted about the topic, look at primary source material, collect data, and identify contradictions and confusions and seek to resolve them with justified solutions and actions. The following is an example of a projective investigation that might be conducted in courses ranging from sociology and public policy to economics and education.

For many, the stereotypical image of a homeless person is of a ragged and squalid man drinking wine from a bottle in a paper bag, begging for money, or lying crumpled on a grate. Even with the inaccuracy of this depiction, until the early 1980s almost all homeless people were men; but now, families—typically women with two children under age five—make up about 30 percent of the homeless population (DeAngelis, 1994). Almost half of all homeless women are ethnic minorities. Poverty continues to be the major contributing factor to the increase in homeless families, with the poorest 20 percent of families becoming even poorer during the 1980s. In the latter part of that decade, research swung away from focusing on individual factors to looking at system-level influences that contribute to homelessness. Structural factors, like the amount of affordable housing available for the poor, appear to play a key role. Since homeless rates vary from country to country, cultural and economic influences seem to interact as well. For example, while Italy has a low rate of homelessness, it has a weaker economy, a weaker social service system, and a higher rate of substance abuse than the United States (DeAngelis, 1994).

With this kind of background information and after considering their own experience and awareness of homelessness, the teacher and learners could begin to address the following questions: Can the rate of homelessness or the kinds of people who become homeless be predicted in a city or a local community? What are the relationships among such factors as gender, unemployment, income, affordable housing for the poor, and homelessness? What trend or pattern among such factors can be historically discerned and applied to the future? What can be done politically to prevent or reduce homelessness? In addition to viewing public and real estate records, interviewing "key informants" is essential to research in this area. Informants include the homeless themselves, shelter administrators and volunteers, religious leaders, community mental-health workers, and police officers.

Through dialogue, learners could identify the aspects of homelessness they are most interested in researching for a projective investigation. Research teams might then be divided across a number of variables: those working with public records and those doing the interviews, those assigned to families and those assigned to single women and men, and those contacting religious leaders and those contacting the police. Tasks for the teacher and learners would include structuring the interviews, organizing the data, and analyzing the findings. In addition to learning more about homelessness and what might be predicted in one's own community, there is the emotional and social impact of this entire process on the teacher and learners. Journal writing and self-assessment procedures found in the next chapter may be extensively used. Eventually, the teacher and students ask, "Now that we know what we know what do we want to do about it?" "What actions ought we to take?" The problem is often challenging. No study is definitive. In a real-life situation, R. Pamela Reid and her graduate students at City University of New York, who were studying stress levels in homeless and poor housed children, did take action. Recognizing the need among these youngsters for peer support, they set up an after-school and summer program where older homeless and poor housed children tutored their younger peers and the graduate students tutored the older children (DeAngelis, 1994). Their program lasted for two years before it ended due to budget problems within the local school.

Experimental Inquiry. Experimental inquiry approximates the conditions of a true experiment to explain something, to better understand how or why something occurs, or to explore if certain hypotheses can lead to specific predictions. In its most fundamental form, experimental inquiry involves observing phenomena, analyzing or generating explanations about those phenomena, making predictions based on one's analysis, then testing those predictions and reflecting on the results to arrive at insights and greater understanding (Marzano, 1992). Most people have conducted experiments in science courses, but our purpose here is to bring this kind of inquiry to all content areas and across disciplines as an elegant and intrinsically motivating way of learning for both teachers and learners. In fact, our experience is that experimental inquiry increases the validity of multiple perspectives and allows more challenging discourse regarding the status quo in most fields of study. We especially want to advocate its use on a spontaneous basis: "Given that observation, why don't we try an experiment?" and as a means for the teacher to improve educational practice. With the latter goal in mind, we offer the following example from one of the author's own experiences.

Observation: Having used films and videos for many years to illustrate various ideas and perspectives, I noticed that the learners' pleasure and sense of humor regarding the content seemed to vary according to the guidelines I gave to learners before watching the films. With one film—of a professor teaching physics—I observed that when I gave no prior instructions, learners seemed to laugh more and react more strongly than when I would advise them, before the film began, to analyze scenes within the film. This was a film used to heighten student awareness of the impact of "unpredictability" rather than to teach a particular concept or skill.

Analysis: One thought I had was that different groups have different senses of humor, and fate or randomness favored the groups without guidelines. Another thought, the one I preferred, was that humor is often a narrative and holistic experience, and analysis, as requested by the teacher, fragments humor and distracts the learners' attention from it. Because of my instructions, learners were literally looking for something else.

Prediction: Learning groups *without* prior instructions to analyze will evidence and report greater enjoyment in response to the physics teacher film than learning groups receiving prior instructions to analyze the film.

Test: I showed the film to eight groups of graduate students in teacher education courses. Four groups received no prior instructions and four groups received the same prior instructions to "look for the quality of unpredictability in the professor's examples of various principles of physics." I used the process of *triangulation*, collecting observations or accounts of a situation (or some aspect of it) from a variety of perspectives (Elliott, 1991) in order to gather sufficient evidence. I could then compare the data for possible support or contradiction. The three perspectives represented were those of myself, a colleague, and the learners. After seeing the film, each group of learners was asked to respond to the Likert scale shown in Exhibit 4.3. My colleague and I observed each group and agreed to use the evidence of attention, smiles, and laughter as indication of learners' enjoyment and expressions of distraction, boredom, and discomfort as signs of the learners not enjoying the film as we completed the Likert scale for each group.

Reflection on results: For the learners' self ratings I had decided to use "interest" as the descriptor because a group could appear to enjoy a film less than another group but be equally interested. Also, for purposes of learning I believed interest was a more important distinction. The results of the experiment supported my prediction. Learning groups without prior instructions had higher self ratings of interest and were observed to enjoy the physics teacher film more than learning groups receiving prior instructions to analyze the film.

Exhibit 4.3. Likert Scales and Learners' and Teachers' Ratings.

Learners' self ratings
I found this film to be:

1	2	3	4	5	6	7
very dull						very interesting

Teachers' ratings
The learners appeared to be:

1	2	3	4	5	6	7
not enjoying the film						enjoying the film

Ratings for groups receiving instructions[a]

Learners	Colleague	Myself
5.2	4	4
5.9	6	5
5.6	5	5
5.5	5	5

Ratings for groups not receiving instructions[a]

Learners	Colleague	Myself
6.5	6	6
6.5	6	7
6.6	7	6
6.4	6	6

[a]Ratings are mean scores.

The major lesson from this for me is how subtle but powerful an orientation or "mental set" can be, how looking for one thing or having an analytic perspective may diffuse, diminish, or distract from realizing certain aspects or qualities of a given experience, in this case, humor in a film. Indirectly, this small experiment heightened my respect for the obviously more powerful effects of language, experience, and culture on perception. Specifically, it supported my intuitive notion that with regard to the particular film, learner enjoyment is indicative of learner interest; my directions probably detract from the learners' total interest in the film. In general, it contributed to making me more sensitive to how learners and I create a goal or frame of mind for a learning activity in which we participate. And finally, for this film, the experiment provided me with information to make a decision that on future occasions I would abstain from giving instructions prior to viewing it.

Although the experiment cited above was not technically rigorous, it did give the author more information about a teaching practice that was important to him and his students. It also broadened his understanding of perspective and how it is influenced and affects what is eventually perceived. Experimental inquiry does not prove something or determine knowledge. It allows us better to understand something, improve something, and arrive at information in which we have more confidence and trust. It also helps us to understand the insufficiency of much research and the need for multiple perspectives to validate understanding. Part of the fascination of research is that it is an endeavor that leads us to know more while constantly reminding us how little we do know. With modest instruction and support most learners can carry out intriguing experiments in any academic discipline.

A book of this scope cannot deal adequately with action research (a disciplined inquiry as part of professional improvement or reform), but we highly recommend it as an additional way to enhance meaning and critical inquiry as well as to improve educational practice. The works of John Elliott (1991) and Dixie Goswami and Peter Stillman (1987) are informative. Also, although written for teachers of youth, *Chi Square Pie Charts and Me* (Baum, Gable, and List, 1987) is a clearly written resource for acquainting postsecondary teachers who have modest research experience with a variety of research processes and statistical techniques.

Invention and Artistry

Invention and artistry are creative ways to express oneself, respond to a need or desire, react to an experience, and make connections between the known and the unknown, the concrete and the abstract, the worldly and the spiritual, and among different people, places, and things. With art and invention, people attempt to answer such questions as, What do I want to express? What would I like to create? What is another way? What is a better way? What do I imagine? What do I wish to render? We discuss invention and artistry together because the conceptual and subjective differences between them is difficult to discern and because we believe both ought to be integral to learning and not, as is so often the case with art, a separate entity or curriculum within education. Artistry can be considered embedding art in learning as opposed to a separate and frequently disenfranchised experience. As Jamake Highwater (1994) has said, "Knowledge is barren without the capacity for feeling and imagination." Art is a vivid sensibility within life and learning across all cultures throughout the world. The lack of meaning so frequently discerned in academic learning is due in part to its distillation of artistry from learning.

Although invention is more frequently associated with a specific product and technology, it is very difficult to tell the difference internally between when one is being inventive and one is being artistic. Both processes can be used in every subject area. Both processes are open ended and mean kindling an awareness of creative possibility while considering generative, topical, and academic themes. For example, one of our colleagues, Michele Naylor, teaching a course in foundations of education approached her learners with the question, "As educators in our communities, what are the things we most deeply want to contribute and accomplish?" The learners were then given about an hour to reflect, write, and sketch their reactions to this question. Afterwards they met in small groups to share their responses. This led to the mutual agreement to post their sketches and conduct a large-group dialogue. From this activity it was suggested that the group compose a mural depicting the theme of community and learning. Using poster paints, a large roll of paper, and masking tape they collaborated with their ideas and sketches to create a mural that covered the entire bottom six feet of the circumference of the classroom. This took about six hours and a Saturday of their time. Although the classroom was heavily used by other learners from other disciplines, the mural stood for approximately six months. During the creation of the mural one of the learners took photographs of the process and created a collage. Each learner also wrote a reflective paper discussing the process of creating the mural and the ideas represented. At the next class session, encircled by the mural they created, the learners summarized their reactions and made connections between this process and the work they do or intend to do in the community.

To exemplify invention we recall a small cadre of learners who were struggling to comprehend systems theory and decided to invent a game, played according to systems theory, that could teach the fundamental concepts and principles of this theory to other learners in a pleasurable way. The game board was a narrow roll of cloth with simulated steps that when extended created a serpentine figure across the width of a small room. In order to be eligible to play the game one had to have completed a "systems reader" identified by the learning group. The game could be played by teams or individuals. Along its path were several stations where players would be interviewed or asked to complete activities and draw graphic models of systemic processes. These stations were operated by the game's inventors themselves. When players appeared confused about or unaware of systemic concepts, they could talk with the inventors, explore relevant examples, and find out about other references. The game was not competitive and had three objectives: (1) to comprehend systems theory, (2) to have an enjoyable learning experience, and (3) to improve the game itself. Because systems theory is a foundation for a number of disciplines at this university, the inventors had no difficulty finding players. They put the game through several revisions based on the feedback they received at post-game interviews. In order to maximize its use by other learners, the game was given to the university library with extensive directions and explanations on a computer disk.

Our experience has been that learners across many cultures welcome the invitation to infuse their academic work with such artwork as sketches and poetry. We have also found that projects that include as a core or as an essential component works of fiction, play writing, visual art, musical composition, songwriting, and performance art offer access to and legitimization of some of the most profound knowledge and understandings that learners gain from their educational experiences.

Simulation

Simulation is defined by Meyers and Jones (1993) as an umbrella term for learning procedures that include role playing and simulation exercises and games that allow students to practice and apply their learning in ungenuine yet sufficiently realistic contexts. When learners can sincerely experience perspectives, ideas, skills, and situations approximating authentic instances of life, they have a real opportunity to enhance the meaning of what it is they are learning as well as to become more proficient.

Role playing is acting out a possible situation by personifying another individual and/or by imagining another scene or set of circumstances. *Simulation exercises* refer to situations in which a whole class is involved, with learners assuming different roles as they act out a prescribed scenario. These scenarios allow learners to acquire or put into practice particular concepts or skills. Simulations often immerse learners in another social reality to allow them to feel what might remain only abstract in textual materials—such concepts as power, privilege, stereotyping, and discrimination. Among intercultural simulations, BaFa' BaFa' (Shirts, 1977) is probably the most widely known. In it, learners become members of one of two different fictitious cultures, each with its own set of values, expectations, customs, and communication styles. Through assuming roles and interacting with the other group as well as by formulating hypotheses about how to interact more effectively with them, participants have a chance to gain personal appreciation for the powerful effects of language, stereotyping, and communication style on relationships between different cultural groups. *Simulation games* are very similar to simulation exercises, but they are usually very structured and have a competitive, win-lose quality. Because of this, they often seem contrived. (For further information on simulation development, see Alley, 1979.)

Since role playing has broad, cross-disciplinary applicability and allows for the most flexible and learner-centered perspectives among simulation approaches, we see it as a very useful procedure for culturally responsive teaching. Role playing gives learners a chance to try out ideas, skills, and perspectives that have been introduced formally from textbooks and learning materials as well as more informally from teachers and peers. Depending on the degree of prescriptiveness and formality of the given scenario, role playing can blend into a simulation exercise. The main goal with either procedure is that the learner is genuinely involved with intellect, feeling, and bodily senses so that the learner's experience is a deep and realistic one (Brookfield, 1990).

Role playing gives learners the opportunity to think in the moment, question their own perspectives, respond to novel or expected circumstances, and consider different ways of knowing

(Meyers and Jones, 1993). Role playing can be used to practice a specific skill such as critical questioning, a collaborative skill such as collective bargaining, a problem-solving skill such as a computerized simulation of the procedure for a biochemistry experiment, or a synthesizing skill such as how to organize a learning plan using procedures from throughout this book (Meyers and Jones, 1993). Role playing is also excellent for the development of empathy and validation; it gives learners and teachers a chance to take on the viewpoints and rationales of people from different backgrounds, as in the case of an African American or a European American offering opinions about a local case of school desegregation, or a lesbian couple and a heterosexual couple discussing the merits of a proposed law concerning domestic partnerships. When there is a chance to reverse roles so that learners act out roles from two opposing perspectives (for example, labor and management) or from an unfamiliar or conflicting perspective (as in the case of a police officer taking on the role of a gang member or vice versa), learners have a chance to consider and feel from a position they may never have engaged.

We have had extensive experience with role playing in academic as well as community settings when the perspectives of administrator, teacher, student, parent, and community member were in conflict. Role playing is an excellent procedure for shifting perspectives, adding insights, and starting conversations that may have been unimaginable before the introduction of the simulation process. A unique use of this procedure by Loretta T. Johnson in history courses (Meyers and Jones, 1993) is to have learners create their own character at a particular time in history, giving that person a series of characteristics related to, say, gender, religion, class, occupation, and ethnicity. Learners write out the character's personality and role in society. As history continues and historical events occur, whether they are the Hiroshima bombing in 1945 or the French Revolution, the learners describe their character's actions and reactions to circumstances of the times as they continue their reading and research. By consciously chronicling and imagining the effect of historical events on a realistic person in a context the learner has actively constructed, and by also understanding that person's impact on those events, the learner gathers meaning from history and employs a level of analysis beyond textbook superficiality.

Using a scenario of a teacher and parent in conflict about a student's performance, we offer the following series of guidelines, adapted from the work of Meyers and Jones (1993), for creating effective simulations.

If you have not done simulations before, observe a teacher you trust who uses them routinely so you can see the process first-hand with your own teaching situation in mind and are able to ask relevant questions before you begin.

Know where and how the simulation conforms to your teaching situation. Is it a good "fit" given who your learners are, where the learning is heading, and what they expect to do? Nothing is worse than a simulation that feels contrived or trivializes an important issue or concept.

Plan well ahead. Have some degree of confidence that your learners are familiar and proficient enough to use the concepts or skills to be practiced. Have they seen models or read cases that acquaint them with what they are expected to do? Do they have fairly solid knowledge or background about the cultural roles they may assume? If they are uncomfortable, can learners excuse themselves or observe until they are more at ease to play a role? For example, before role playing a conferencing method we teach, all teachers (whose students' parents vary in background, social economic class, and ethnicity) have read this approach and seen it on video as applied by three different teachers. Also, each simulation scenario uses an observer (a role learners may choose if they prefer) to facilitate the role playing process and to give feedback and guide the discussion that follows.

Make sure everyone clearly understands the roles before you begin the role play. Allow for questions and clarification. Often it is helpful to write out a script with learners that contains the role's attitudes, experiences, and beliefs. This is studied and used by learners to deepen their familiarity with the role. For example, an excerpt from our script for the parent includes such statements as, I am a single parent. I work nights in a service job. I often feel exhausted.

Make sure enough time has been set aside for the simulation and the discussion that follows. The discussion and analysis are as important as the simulation itself. What are the different perspectives, reactions, and insights? What are the learners' concerns and what has not been dealt with that still needs attention? Has the desired learning been accomplished? How? What about the process itself? How can it be improved? This is the time to raise issues of critical consciousness, when impressions are fresh and resonant.

When role playing seems potentially embarrassing or threatening, it is often helpful for the teacher to model the first role play and discuss it. This may alleviate some initial hesitation and allow learners to see our own comfort (we hope) with our imperfections and mistakes. In some cases, starting out slowly, with only those learners who are interested in role playing serving as initial models, can lead to working up to exercises involving all learners (Shannon, 1986).

Freezing the action during a role play can serve many purposes, such as critiquing a given perspective, exploring learner reactions to a poignant comment, allowing learners to make beneficial suggestions and comments to the actors, and relieving tension that may be becoming overwhelming.

Some people suggest ending a simulation at a high point so that discussion will be more enthusiastic and compelling. This depends on the purpose and narrative of the role play because some issues may need to be further encountered to explore their depth and ramifications.

The follow-up activities to simulations are extremely important in connecting what is learned to learner concerns and greater academic and social consequences. For example, creating action plans to use what has been practiced and discussed is often a beneficial next step.

For many learners and teachers, simulations may be the only way to enter worlds that seem too distant or to try out actions initially too uncomfortable. In some instances this procedure not only enhances meaning but also nurtures courage, the willingness to step beyond the self-consciousness of our own misgivings to encompass other realities and to act with new understanding.

Case-Study Method

A case study is a narrative of real events that presents provocative questions and undercurrents in a way that compels learners and teachers to analyze, deliberate, and advance informed judgments that integrate an array of perspectives and concepts (Christensen and Hansen, 1987; Shulman and others, 1990). The hallmark of cases is their authenticity. With lifelike, concrete details and characters expressing a personal voice, they put flesh and blood on otherwise abstract and ambiguous concepts. Because cases present dilemmas and are open ended, they tend to stimulate extremely different reactions and propositions across a group.

The case-study method enhances meaning and is ideal for culturally responsive teaching for the reason that it fosters "an ethos of critical inquiry that encourages multiple interpretations, conflicting opinions, and equal participation" (Mesa-Bains and Shulman, 1994, p. 7). Yet, it does so in a manner that permits learners and teachers to be more open and less defensive, because the situation is someone else's (Hutchings, 1993). In addition, we can share our uncertainty as well as our knowledge and experience, because this is a knotty problem, not one given to glib resolution. When we face a relevant predicament with an opportunity to learn something important for our own lives, solidarity is more likely to emerge among us. The ethos of inquiry—a group spirit that is not limited to merely exchanging opinions but rather is imaginative and visionary enough to consider the universe of ideas—mediates and results from this process (Mesa-Bains and Shulman, 1994).

As in our discussion of the previous procedures in this chapter, our goal is to be specific enough about the way to use case studies so that you can make use of this method in your own setting, and to offer guidelines general enough to allow for your own creativity, situational conditions, and self-determination.

Most practitioners are dogmatic about only one thing: having a thorough understanding of the case and its nuances before teaching it (Meyers and Jones, 1993; Mesa-Bains and Shulman, 1994). By reading the case a few times over one can begin to see if it meets such criteria as relevance, authenticity, narrative strength, complexity, and so on to merit selection for use. If it does, then rereading the case will provide the opportunity to construct discussion notes and a possible outline for dialogue. Some useful questions to reflect on as one is reading a case are suggested by Amalia Mesa-Bains and Judith Shulman (1994):

What is your first impression?

What excites you?

What bothers you?

What is this a case of?

What are the different ways to interpret this case?

What are the teaching and learning issues?

How will events in the case bear a cultural impact?

What are the pressures or stress points (for example, high emotion, confusion over a dilemma, doubt, or crisis) of the narrative?

What needs to be asked or said to take the discussion beyond acknowledgment ("This is racism") to analysis ("What seem to be the root causes of this problem?")?

How can people deduce principles and applications from this case?

Please keep these questions in mind as you read the case in Exhibit 4.4, which was composed for use by faculty for collaborative discussion about improving college teaching. It describes the first day of a course in which students will be working to improve their writing skills.

Exhibit 4.4. Case Study.

"See You on Wednesday!"
by
Deanna Yameen
Instructor and Critical-Thinking Specialist
Massachusetts Bay Community College
and
Elizabeth Fideler
Recruiting New Teachers, Inc.

The first class meeting seemed to go smoothly enough. I went in, introduced myself, and ran through the course syllabus and calendar. The students seemed pretty much like the students I taught at State U.—maybe a little older. They asked the same questions about how long the paper should be and which books to buy. They made no comments about the journal assignment for the next class. They filled out my survey readily enough. In fact, class ended twenty minutes early.

In my eight years of teaching at State U., I never saw anything like the survey responses received from this class. Can community college students be that different? I just don't know how I'm going to cope.

I used the same survey I used at State U., with exactly the same directions: "I'm just looking for some information to get a feel for the class. Tell me (1) why you are taking the class, and (2) what you want me to know about you. Please be honest. You don't have to sign your name if you'd rather not."

Then I read their responses. What have I gotten myself into? What am I going to do on Wednesday?

Take a look at the responses for yourself:

I want to write very, very well.

I want you to know is that the main reason for me to learn, is because I wanna go to computer afterwards.

This is my first class in college. Since I graduated I wanted to try writing to see if I didn't have the ability.

Exhibit 4.4. Case Study, Cont'd.

I am a international student. Sometimes I don't speak or tell what I want to say well.

I want to how to use research information then write paper.

To enter nursing program, and have a good abilities.

You should know that I have a learning disable.

I have a Learning Disability in Reading and I think my writing is Poor.

I would like to prove to myself that I am am now ready to be a serious student and that I can get an A in this class.

I failed out of school and it has taken me a long time to get the guts to try again. I really want to do well.

I have taken this course last semester and wrote three essay.

A lot of things come very easily to me but what does not I become easily frustrated which makes it that much harder. I have to read lips. I am slightly tone deaf.

I would like to learn how to get my thought down in an organized fashion. I would like my writing to be impressive and express how I feel.

I would like to write a paper on my own that really makes sense.

I want to be able to write a good essay, or other papers I might have to write in my college days.

I want to be prepared for the other courses for my college education. I want to improve my writing skills.

I'd like to read different kinds of books and I want to try to like writing.

I want to learn to read and think about a situation or article and know what to write about.

Source: Hutchings, 1993, pp. 35–36. Used by permission.

It is often a very good first step to be sure that learners comprehend the goals of the particular case study (Mesa-Bains and Shulman, 1994). In this instance, possible goals could include the following:

1. Increase understanding of how to improve teaching and learning among diverse learners.

2. Improve understanding of multicultural issues, such as bias, class, privilege, and disability that often powerfully influence teaching and learning.

3. Analyze and explore multiple perspectives of the issues found in the case.

4. Learn how to find out more about learners at the beginning of a course so that teaching can be more effective and culturally responsive.

Discussion notes can be helpful in designing a plan for moving the learning group through the case—how to introduce the case, questions and probes for analysis, cues for taking the case to another stage, and what to ask if discussion stalls. However, none of these options should be rigidly used, because learners may create perspectives and insights beyond the teacher's imagination. For "See You on Wednesday!" an initial and partial discussion outline is found below.

Suggested Discussion Outline

1. Which items in this case stand out as significant teaching and learning issues?
   Probes: Which of these issues are you familiar with from your own teaching? Which of these issues have you had some success in resolving?

2. What kind of diversity is represented in this case?
   Probes: How might this kind of diversity be constructed as a greater opportunity for learning for everyone? Which issues of diversity in this case arouse apprehension? Why?

3. How effective is the assessment strategy used to find out about the learners?
   Probes: How could this assessment strategy be improved? What alternative assessment strategies would you suggest?

4. What does one do on Wednesday?

Depending on such factors as the kind of material covered in the case and the experience, trust, and sense of community among the learners, cases can be processed in small groups or with a single larger group. Opening the discussion of the case in a manner that invites wide participation and relevant and interested commentary is very important. Some ways to start (Hutchings, 1993; Mesa-Bains and Shulman, 1994) include the following:

- Ask learners to "free write" for a couple of minutes after reading the case so they have something to offer based on reflection.

- Ask each learner to talk with a partner for a few minutes about key issues in the case before requesting individual responses.

- Ask a couple of learners to summarize the case before asking others to join in.

- Ask each learner to remark about one element she or he felt was important in the case and record these comments publicly. This lets everyone know there are a range of interpretations before discussion begins.

During the discussion the kinds of questions asked by the teacher can serve different purposes, such as to further analysis, challenge an idea, mediate between conflicting views, and draw learners to generate principles and concepts. For the teacher the role is one of a facilitator who provides opportunities for everyone to contribute but also has the responsibility to provoke and inform, but never to indoctrinate or impose preconceived conclusions (Mesa-Bains and Shulman, 1994). At times, role-playing aspects of the case may be very effective ("What would be your first remarks to the learners on Wednesday? Let's hear them and we can react as they might"). Other times it may be beneficial to record key information on the board or a chart. Direct quotes from the case can serve to focus the group, and, at times, playing the devil's advocate may be a way to surface missing issues or counterpoints. In general, after reading the case, the pattern of learning moves incrementally from reflection and analysis to problem-solving hypotheses to application to one's own practices or social action. You may recognize this sequence as the Kolb experiential learning model discussed in Chapter Three.

How to close the case discussion is critical. As Hutchings (1993) points out, there is disagreement among practitioners about the degree of closure appropriate to the case-study method. This approach, more than some other procedures presented in the chapter, has a structure and style for which looking for "the answer" is not the appropriate kind of thinking. Yet *ending* the case-study process in a suitable manner is desired by most teachers and learners. There should be some opportunity to reflect on what has been learned, to synthesize and identify new understandings, to air unresolved conflicts or questions, and to make plans for making changes or taking action. Some approaches (Mesa-Bains and Shulman, 1994; Hutchings, 1993) include the following:

- Spending some time writing answers to such questions as, What new insights did you gain from this case study and its discussion? What are your lingering questions? What new ideas do you want to try out? What resources would be useful to you?

- Brainstorm (in small groups or as a large group) insights, personal changes in thinking or action, or new areas to explore as a result of the case study.

- Go around the group and allow each learner to provide one insight, question, lesson, change, or good that has emerged as a result of this process.

Using case studies in technical fields such as chemistry may require a more structured approach, but the challenge remains to

The following guidelines can be kept in mind when creating and carrying out projects:

- Whether the project is individual or collaborative, learners should be involved in its conception and planning.
- The creation of the project can involve the questions and procedural identifications found in the next list.
- Consider goal setting or some of its elements as a means to explore and plan the project.
- Request an outline of the project with some schedule of agreed-upon documentation and a completion date.
- Arrange for the presentation of the project to a relevant audience who can offer authentic acknowledgment and feedback.
- Assess the project—including a thorough self-assessment (see Chapter Five)—from numerous perspectives (Gardner, 1991), which may include project planning, execution, and presentation; the challenge level; creativity and originality; employment of resources; and what was learned. Include the evaluation of other learners and knowledgeable people outside of the course.

One way to begin creating actual projects is to reflect on the questions found in the list below and to identify relevant issues and their related procedures. For each selection sketch and outline the actions and resources that would appear necessary to carry out the identified procedure. Further reflection on what emerges from this process can lead to choosing a compelling issue with an appealing and reasonably challenging procedure.

Decision making: Is there an unresolved issue that learners find relevant that calls for a course of action, a policy, a plan, or a choice?

Definitional investigation: Is there an unresolved issue that learners find relevant that calls for clarifying or identifying the defining characteristics or important features of a con-cept, event, or situation for which such characteristics are unknown, in question, or not readily apparent?

Historical investigation: Is there an unresolved issue that learners find relevant that calls for determining, understanding, and evaluating past events?

Projective investigation: Is there an unresolved issue that learners find relevant that involves researching what will happen if certain circumstances continue or change, or if some future event occurs?

Experimental inquiry: Is there an issue that learners find relevant for which conducting an experiment will provide greater understanding?

Invention and artistry: Is there something learners find relevant—a problem, an issue, a state of being—about which they want to deeply and artistically express them-selves or create a conceptual or material invention?

Simulation and/or case study: Is there something relevant to be learned for which the creation of a simulation or case study affords learners the kind of authentic understanding or skill acquisition currently unavailable through other academic procedures or direct experience?

The Problem-Posing Model

In theory and espoused practice, we view the problem-posing model of teaching (Freire, 1970; Shor, 1992) as one of the most consis-tently authentic forms of culturally responsive pedagogy. It has crucially informed our teaching and our writing. By situating all classroom discourse in the learners' language, experience, per-spective, and community life, the foundation of its curriculum is the learners' cultural diversity. In the problem-posing classroom, the learning process is negotiated with learners rather than unilaterally imposed, the discourse is co-developed rather than teacher dominated, and knowledge is examined rather than prescribed. Such significant differences as these make problem posing a genuinely alternative structure for learning and authority in postsecondary education.

With such strong culture-centeredness and a methodology that immerses the learner in challenging questions and research, this approach to teaching, if done well, elicits intrinsic motivation. Problem-posing presents all subject matter as an historical product to be questioned rather than as a universal wisdom to be received. The current canons of knowledge and usage are not considered a common culture, because they have largely ignored the diverse themes, idioms, and achievements of such nonelite groups as women, minorities, lesbians, and poor people (Shor, 1992). However, this orientation does not mean that any subject, whether it be chemistry, mathematics, sociology, or education, has nothing to offer as it now exists, or that the expertise of the teacher counts for very little. As Shor (1992) states: "Formal bodies of knowledge, standard usage, and teacher's academic background all belong in the critical classroom. As long as existing knowledge is not presented as facts and doctrines to be absorbed without question, as long as existing bodies of knowledge are critiqued and balanced from a multicultural perspective, and as long as the students' own themes and idioms are valued along with standard usage, existing canons are part of critical education" (p. 35).

A problem-posing computer science teacher might integrate the following questions into the framework of the course: Who controls the design and marketing of computers? Which groups in society use them and for what purposes? Which groups don't have access to them? In which schools are they more accessible to learners? How could groups deprived of computers be enabled to use them? How do computers promote or diminish democracy in school, at work, and in society?

228 Diversity and Motivation

Problem-posing teachers use lesson plans and predeveloped questions and materials, but they also abide with change, being open to exploring outside their plans based on what emerges from learner articulation and dialogue. Learners have considerable flexibility but do not have license to do whatever they want.

Based on his extensive college teaching experience with this approach and the philosophy of a critical-democratic pedagogy, Ira Shor (1992) outlines the possible phases of a problem-posing model for a term-long course as

1. Posing a generative, topical, or academic problem to students and conducting a dialogue about it
2. Asking students to write on the posed problem
3. Inviting peer-group, collaborative editing and discussion of the rough drafts
4. Conducting a whole-class dialogue based on the essays
5. Questioning student responses and encouraging them to question each other
6. Posing a second-level problem based on the class dialogue
7. Following this posed problem with a second cycle of student writing, peer editing and discussion, and whole-class dialogue
8. Continuing these cycles as appropriate and integrating reading materials and other media along the way
9. Conducting an interim class evaluation and adjustment of the process.
10. Offering a lecture (dialogic) based on the teacher's view and expertise concerning the currently identified problem
11. Hearing student feedback and challenges to the lecture
12. Discussing solutions and actions regarding the problem
13. Taking action if possible and reflecting on it
14. Posing a new problem based on action and reflection
15. Conducting the end-term evaluation

Problem posing is a creative approach with the above frame-work flexibly adapted to the learning process under way in a particular course. As a way of teaching, problem posing is very difficult to convey in outline form or with short declarative statements. It needs a lengthy narrative voice to flesh out its qualities of dialogue and reflection-in-action. For comprehensive examples of problem posing, read *Empowering Education* (Shor, 1992).

As the problem-posing model and the other elements of this chapter have indicated, personal meaning is essential to learning and motivation. However, culturally responsive teaching does not impose meaning. The norms, procedures, and structures offered in this chapter present a holistic means to bring to existing knowledge a multicultural perspective. Again, in this process the balanced interaction between teacher expertise and student experience integrates the authority of an academic discipline with the validity of a student's perspective. How to create this symmetry in the area of assessment of learning is in our opinion one of the critical challenges to genuinely implementing a culturally responsive pedagogy. We encounter this often contentious educational responsibility in the next chapter.

Chapter Five

Engendering Competence

How did it come to be that our main goal as academics
turned out to be performance? I think the answer to
the question is fairly complicated . . . but the main
component is fear. Fear is the driving force behind the
performance model . . . I became aware recently that
my own fear of being shown up for what I really am
must transmit itself to my students, and insofar as I
was afraid to be exposed, they too would be afraid.

—*Jane Tompkins*

Assessment is a procedure for gathering information about learning
and the learning process that utilizes multiple indicators and sources
of evidence. We propose that the essential purpose of assessment
is to engender competence. This function of assessment should
not and need not be secondary to such other purposes of assessment
as providing evidence of learning and determining levels of proficiency. With this perspective in mind, in this chapter we present interactive processes of assessment that honor the origin of
this word, that is, *assidere*, or "to sit beside" (*Webster's Dictionary*,
1986). We believe that we as teachers must, figuratively and sometimes literally, sit beside our students to collaboratively understand
what has been learned, how that has come to be, and how to create the conditions that will further inspire intellectual growth.

Assessment exerts powerful motivational influence on students because it provides socially sanctioned meaning about their academic competence. Competence is the human innate need to realize desired internal and external outcomes and to be efficacious in performing the requisite actions (Deci, Vallerand, Pelletier, and Ryan, 1991). To put it succinctly, all people want to be effective at what they value. The circumstances most prevalent in college for understanding how competent one is being and can be are generally feedback and assessment procedures.

The desire to be competent is an extraordinary force in our lives. Activities involving manipulation, exploration, and making meaning often provide satisfaction because they are instinctual ways to become effective in our environment. Researchers have demonstrated that infants as young as eight weeks old can learn particular responses to connect with their environment. In one such study, infants were placed in cribs with a mobile above each of their heads (Watson and Ramey, 1972). By turning their head to the right, they activated an electrical apparatus in their pillow causing the mobile to move. Not only did these children learn to move the mobile, but they displayed more positive emotions (smiling, cooing) than infants for whom the mobile movement was controlled by a researcher. Similarly, when learners can actually sense their insights and progress or accomplishment, their motivation is enhanced. Although culture largely determines what is worth accomplishing, across cultures motivation is evoked by the desire to be effective at what one values.

For the record, teacher assessment, more than any other action, validates student competence. Teacher judgment is also vulnerable to subtle forms of bias. From personal experience, most of us are aware that teachers make subjective judgments about such affective qualities of learners as effort, initiative, and commitment. We also know that these judgments can influence expectations of learners and consequent grades. Research at Northwest Regional Laboratory suggests, for example, that there may be a tendency for teachers to unduly reward white male students who appear atten-tive and aggressive during class. The implication is that students who are most prepared culturally to fit the stereotype of "learning" may be disproportionally rewarded through higher grades (Stiggins, 1988).

In this chapter we introduce criteria, norms, procedures, and structures that are less likely to disguise bias and are consistent with the best we know about intrinsic motivation. Our emphasis is on procedures that engender competence through clearly negotiated processes that support and illuminate the learner's authority, strength, and sense of cultural and academic identity. These processes simultaneously reveal authentic information about what has been learned and how that has occurred.

Authenticity, Effectiveness, and Intrinsic Motivation

Assessment that engenders competence meets two primary criteria: authenticity and effectiveness. Let us first examine the meaning and relevance of authenticity.

As students, most of us spent a good deal of time feeling right or wrong, smart or dumb, expecting that the teacher held the truth about where we fit among our peers and why this was so. The mea-sures of our learning were recitations, worksheets, weekly quizzes, tests, and examinations, most of which were structured around spe-cific bits of information.

When we think back on our formal learning many of us remem-ber a sadness that recalls the invisibility of our experiences, the silencing of our feelings and beliefs, and the artificiality of an iden-tity as a learner that is dependent on extrinsically imposed goals, tasks, and judgments. To persevere, we usually did not allow our-selves to dwell on how learning might be both viable and non-competitive, on ways in which self-reflection and self-expression could deepen and sustain our education, and on how real-life appli-cations or at least plausible challenges could reveal not only what we learned (even beyond the expected outcomes) but what we could understand about our strengths and identities as lifelong learners.

Authenticity within assessment engenders competence among culturally diverse learners by valuing and appraising learning as an interaction of the milieu in which education takes place, the nature of the curriculum, the teachers and their approaches to teaching, and the infinitely varied student population. It includes multidimensional and multiple "measures" for a range of skills or intelligences. For example, authenticity within assessment as well as in learning requires students to solve problems that have an equivalent in their real world or in their future work lives, involving use of resources, consultation with other people, integration of skills, and so forth. This kind of assessment avoids "blaming the victim" by exploring factors that have contributed to or impaired learning and emphasizing relationships that have developed within a learning context in a manner akin to apprenticeship (Gardner, 1993).

The apprentice learner and the guiding teacher are able to co-create processes for improved learning because success and the reasons for success, and limited success and the reasons for limited success, are more contextualized and more apparent to all concerned in situations approximating real life. Further, when there is a trust relationship, the apprentice is able to more openly listen to sensitive information concerning necessary adjustments. This is particularly important to students of color who may have been typically misunderstood by teachers' assumptions of deficit (Villegas, 1991), who may distrust the perceptions of instructors who are inaccessible and perpetuate asymmetrical power relations, and for whom sensitive personal information may be carefully reserved for family or extended-family members (Vasquez, 1990). When such authentic approaches to assessment are contrasted with the decontextualized and impersonal formal testing model exemplified by a multiple-choice exam followed by posted grades and class standing, it is easy to see how, to many students, learning seems one-dimensional, tedious, and irrelevant beyond the certificate.

For these reasons, as well as those of the added burdens of cultural marginality, displacement from personal experiences and values, and—at times—significant financial debt, a one-dimensional means-ends orientation to assessment can seriously impair the motivation of many diverse students. The overarching value of authentic assessment is to support intrinsic motivation. Intrinsic motivation is supported when learners see the locus of causality for learning within themselves, when the act of learning and application of knowledge is considered primary, and when the learning context is examined for ways in which the capacities and talents of all learners can be strengthened.

While authentic assessment seeks a broader, more realistic picture of student learning, it requires a genuinely supportive environment. We have previously examined this issue in Chapter Two. Nonetheless, it is important to emphasize once again that activity and colorful innovation can produce the same kind of isolation, fear, and boredom as homogenized routines, memorization, and competitive grading. It is essential to demonstrate a sincere spirit of support and responsiveness to the needs, interests, and orientations of learners. At times, this requires a critical shift in authority where distinctions between "teacher" and "learner" converge for mutual reward. The instructor does not abdicate responsibility for establishing and maintaining the highest and most reasonable expectations. Rather, there is heightened sensitivity to learners as individuals so that we not only value autonomous thinking and initiative but also respect the reasons some learners may prefer caution, deference, and/or the appearance of conformity; so that we are willing to engage in personal and professional dialogue but respect the reasons for silence and privacy; so that as we affirm and encourage, we are also willing to live with contradictions—our own as well as others'.

From a practical as well as culturally responsive perspective, *effectiveness* is the learners' awareness of their command or accomplishment of something they find to be important in the *process* of learning or as an *outcome* of their learning. Therefore, both the

process as well as the result of learning are important forms of information for learners. The questions How well are we doing? and
How well did this turn out? are a critical duet during any learning
activity. Intrinsic motivation is elicited when people know they are
competently performing an activity that leads to a valued goal. This
affirms their innate need to relate adequately to their environment.
The process and the goal are reciprocal and, to our way of thinking, indivisible—one gives meaning to the other. If someone wants
to learn how to use a computer because it is a valued skill and
increases one's range of occupational opportunities, that awareness
will evoke motivation as one learns. The progress and competence
one gains while learning will influence the motivational value of
the original goal. In other words, becoming more effective often
increases the value of the goal. With increased competence, computer skills and related occupational opportunities acquire even
greater value for the learner.

However, the transaction that informs learners of their effectiveness may crucially affect their motivation. These events can be
seen as either informational or controlling (Deci and Ryan, 1985).
Informational transactions tell learners something about their effectiveness and support their sense of self-determination for learning.
Controlling transactions tend to undermine self-determination by
making learner behavior appear to be dependent on forces that
demand, coerce, or seduce the learner's compliance. They encourage the learner to believe the reason for learning is some external
condition outside of the learner such as a reward or teacher pressure. When verbally communicated, they often contain imperative
locutions such as "should" and "must." For example, a teacher might
say to a learner, "Your performance was clearly presented and relevant to your audience" (informational). Or the same teacher might
say, "Your performance was excellent. You did exactly as you should
do" (controlling). The difference between these two statements
may seem subtle but is, nonetheless, very important. The former
encourages self-determination, while the latter places much more

of the emphasis for learning in the direction of the teacher's control. The following norms and procedures for engendering competence will emphasize the informational approach, which encourages empowerment and is more likely to be culturally responsive.

Norms for Engendering Competence

The norms that foster authenticity and effectiveness rely on the necessity for each instructor to become more conscious of his or her "assessment philosophy." An understanding of how new approaches to assessment fit with our overarching beliefs about learning helps us achieve greater consistency in our actions and to manifest our true intentions. Our recommendations for developing an assessment philosophy are straightforward: (1) decide what sorts of information and skills are really needed; How often are they needed; To what end?; (2) examine assessment procedures for bias and for their consistency with how you teach; (3) consider the relevance of high standards for kindness and cooperation as well as academic work (Perrone, 1991).

We advocate the following assessment norms:

1. *The assessment process is connected to the learner's world, frames of reference, and values.* As discussed in Chapters Two and Three, people only feel a part of something that is relevant to them. As with all aspects of the learning process, this applies to assessment. Pragmatically, this has two primary implications: assessment ought to be contextualized in ways that hold meaning for students given their experiences, frames of reference, and values, and assessment ought to allow for personal interpretations of "truth"—that is, linkages between traditional academic perspectives and personal experiences and the generation of valid alternative perspectives to conventionally held beliefs.

Real and significant contexts for demonstrating understanding enhance the relevance of learning, the responsibility for learning, and the coherence of learning. These are motivationally powerful

conditions. Undergirding these conditions, and a key to motivation, is affirmation of one's own experiences (Knowles, 1980;
McLaren and Leonard, 1993). When we standardize approaches to
and judgments about assessment, we often constrict connections to
students' experiences, thereby constricting the relevance of the
assessment process and requiring conformity and subordination.

Beyond contextualized assessment are opportunities for personal
interpretations of truth. Assessment that allows for individual interpretations of truth, rather than a litany of fixed realities, validates
the unique cultural lenses through which individuals view the
world—in addition to expanding understanding beyond dualistic
"right" and "wrong" (Butler, 1993; McIntosh, 1989). Once again,
this is especially important for learners whose opinions and ways of
understanding have been subjugated to or patronized by dominant
norms. Many learners from underrepresented groups are well aware
that their instructors' opinions and ways of understanding generally conform to dominant norms. The experience of assessment
processes, then, that reward students who best conform to the
instructor's norms and values present overt evidence of cultural bias.
For example, are the conventions of a discipline immutable or are
they representative of a partiality? There can be a huge difference
between the necessity to solve a problem with a predetermined
algorithm and the necessity to comply with a teacher's conceptual
model of a mental disorder or a "discipline problem."

The limitation of the culturally mediated knowledge of external authorities can be used to encourage passivity and depen-
dence—or it can provide a rationale for developing assessment
procedures that, to the degree possible, create opportunities for
well-substantiated alternative points of view. That is, as teachers
we can choose to ignore or to acknowledge the inherent biases
within our systems of belief. The latter choice provides a window
for promoting the emergence of multiple perspectives within a community of learners. This is not to suggest that "anything goes" or
that there are not valuable lessons from the past. It is a reminder

that the personal construction of knowledge is a salient feature in motivation to learn (Belenky, Clinchy, Goldberger, and Tarule, 1986) in addition to being essential to the overarching goal of creating a just, pluralistic society (Gilligan, 1982; Lather, 1991; Oldfather, 1992).

2. *Demonstration of learning includes multiple ways to represent knowledge and skills and allows for attainment of outcomes at different points in time.* This is a value that has been consistently advocated in research on assessment and evaluation (Gardner, 1982; Perrone, 1991; Shepard, 1989; Alverno College Faculty, 1979; Ewell, 1991). Nonetheless we appreciate that it is a value that makes many educators run for cover. The vast amount of professional time devoted to the task of assessment and information processing is already consuming the profession of education, and considering more new ways to conceptualize and implement assessment tasks can appear overwhelming.

Upon further consideration, what could be more defeating to a learner than to realize that critical judgments about students are based on vague or superficial criteria, inadequate communication about what students really should know, insufficient opportunities for students to learn from mistakes, and dismissal of alternative approaches to encouraging success given the motivational limits of grades, especially for lower-achieving students (Stiggins, 1988)? As we move from the once popular view that intelligence or ability is a single, fixed capacity to current intelligence theories that stress the existence of a variety of human talents and capabilities (Sternberg, 1993; Gardner, 1982; Herman, Aschbacher, and Winters, 1992), we are further compelled to find ways in which learners can engage their unique talents.

3. *Self-assessment is essential to the overall assessment process.* All learning is about change. This can create confusion as well as opportunity. In this light, posing our own learning as a problem to be solved has the potential to be a compelling enterprise (Freire, 1970). Self-assessment allows us to gain perspective on how

we understand ourselves as learners, knowers, apprentices in a discipline, and citizens in a complex and paradoxical world (MacGregor, 1994). With adequate guidance, we can identify our growth in ways that nurture respect for ourselves and the learning process. We can better understand those *metacognitive* processes (those that make us aware of our own thinking) such as internal questions and self-monitoring strategies that increase our motivation and learning.

Interestingly, several recent studies in higher education provide evidence that undergraduate women consistently underestimate their abilities, and that men overestimate theirs (Astin, Green, and Korn, 1987; Light, 1990). Self-assessment offers all students a way to transcend stereotypes and to make well-reasoned connections between their actions and present learning opportunities. Self-reflection about their learning also allows students to validate their authenticity as learners and as human beings. This is especially important for underrepresented students who may feel, at times, like impostors in the culturally isolated, often competitive, lonely, and disconnected universe of academia. Thus, self-assessment, in a larger sense, provides an opportunity for students to develop new ways of understanding "community" or lack thereof and to gain insight into the various contexts and conditions—outside of themselves—that inhibit or promote learning and beliefs about their identity.

Based on his studies, Vincent Tinto (1987) addresses the learner's need for validation and connectedness. His research indicates that unless a student finds a place in a new cultural setting and feels connected to it, he or she will often "give up" and leave that culture. When we are able to tell our own story and be given credit for it in a new cultural setting, the validation assists us with finding a sense of place (Waluconis, 1994). The positive motivational implications of realizing this new cultural connection are profound.

Our discussion of self-assessment would be incomplete without consideration of possible sources of cultural discomfort, given expectations of self-disclosure and candor about academic accomplishment. Requests for self-disclosure, to some learners, may feel intrusive. Many students of color, as well as members of other underrepresented communities, prefer to confine their confidences to family and intimate relationships. It is important for instructors to be respectful of this and to collaborate with students to negotiate the content of the self-assessment. In addition to recognizing the primacy of family as confidants and counselors, it is important to remember that many underrepresented students bring to the classroom longstanding memories of personal humiliation and rage at myriad forms of institutionalized racism, classism, sexism, heterosexism, ablism, and so forth. Choice and confidentiality are essential. With the best of intentions, instructors can create an irreparable gulf between unilateral expectations of openness and a student's right to privacy.

A second consideration is the impact of personal recognition on the individual. Some learners may view personalized claims of academic accomplishment as self-aggrandizing, whether they emanate privately from themselves or emerge from dialogue with an instructor. For some students, if a person stands out, it is because the *community* recognizes the individual, not the individual himself or herself (Reyhner, 1986). Although self-assessment can provide a unique platform for self-definition (MacGregor, 1994), we encourage instructors to respect the value of community over individual accomplishment and to consider making ways available for all learners to circumvent the need for psychologically intimate narratives about self. We offer suggestions for this purpose in the next section.

Procedures for Engendering Competence

The procedures for engendering competence are categorized as follows: feedback, alternatives to paper-and-pencil tests, well-constructed paper-and-pencil tests, and student self-assessment. Each of these categories and their related approaches embrace the criteria and norms discussed earlier in this chapter. Although they sometimes appear prescriptive, we invite adaptations of these procedures that better fit your professional responsibilities. We encourage using multiple measures or instruments as well as longitudinal approaches to develop a range of perspectives on academic accomplishment. In other words, learners need multiple opportunities and multiple approaches to demonstrating what they know. The most "authentic" forms of assessment involve long-term programs of study, activity, and practice while simultaneously enhancing the learners' understanding of themselves in relation to others. The shorter-term generation of products, activities, and services that are also associated with authentic and/or performance assessment are often, however, more practical to implement. The most important point is to avoid limiting judgments to one or two high-stakes testing occasions or one particular kind of assessment task. This can seriously skew generalizations about student accomplishment, especially with learners whose experiences, orientations, behaviors, beliefs, and values challenge our own understandings.

Feedback

Feedback is information that learners receive about the quality of their work. Knowledge about the learning process and results, comments about emerging skills, notes on a written assignment, and graphic records are forms of feedback that teachers and learners use. Feedback appears to enhance learners' motivation because they are able to evaluate their progress, locate their performance within a framework of understanding, maintain their efforts toward realistic goals, correct their errors efficiently, and receive encouragement from their teachers and other learners.

In general, feedback is probably the most powerful process that teachers and other learners can regularly use to affect a learner's competence. It can also be far more complex than a few words about a learner's progress during a learning activity. The following types and characteristics of feedback are most likely to engender competence.

Feedback That Is Informational Rather Than Controlling.
Feedback that relates to the learner's increasing effectiveness or creativity and self-determination is to be emphasized. For example: "You've identified three critical areas of concern. Your writing is well organized and concise. I appreciate the clarity of your work," rather than, "You're making progress and meeting the standards I've set for writing in this course."

Feedback That Is Based on Agreed-Upon Standards. Learners appreciate feedback based on how well they have met an agreed-upon performance standard. This clarifies for them the criteria against which their work is being evaluated and may explicitly indicate what needs to be done for further effective learning. They can use this information to more accurately guide their effort, practice, and performance. This is especially important for learners for whom ambiguous learning criteria are yet one more unknown barrier to success. For example: "We agreed that any project containing more than six errors would be returned for revision. I've indicated where those errors are located as well as some explanatory references you might want to consider if you need them."

Feedback That Is Specific and Constructive. It is difficult to improve performance when one is told only in general terms how well one has done. Most people prefer specific information and realistic suggestions for how to improve. For example: "I found your insights on government spending compelling. To emphasize your conclusion, you might consider restating your initial premise in your last paragraph."

Feedback That Is Quantitative. Sometimes quantitative feedback has definite advantages. It is precise and can provide evidence of small improvements. Small improvements can have long-range effects. One way to understand learning is by *rate*, which is to indicate how often something occurs over a fixed time. For example, learners are told they completed thirty laps during a one-hour swimming practice. Another way is to decide what percent of learning performance is correct or appropriate. Percentages are calculated by dividing the number of times the learning performance occurs correctly by the total number of times the performance opportunity occurs, as in batting averages and field-goal percentages.

Another common form of quantitative feedback relates to *duration*, which is how long it takes a learning performance to be completed. For example, a lab technician might receive feedback on how long it takes that person to complete a particular chemical analysis. These are not all of the forms of quantitative feedback that are possible, but they are a representative sample. Whenever progress on learning a skill appears to be slow or difficult to ascertain, quantitative feedback may be a realistic and relevant means to enhance learner motivation.

Feedback That Is Prompt. Promptness refers to feedback that is ready and quickly given as the situation demands rather than immediately. Sometimes a moderate delay in feedback enhances learning, because such a delay is culturally sensitive or polite. For example, some learners may experience discomfort with direct mention of specific performance judgments shortly after the occasion. Also, a short wait may allow learners to more easily forget incorrect responses and reduce their anxiety, as in the case of a public performance. In general, it is best to be quick with feedback but to carefully pay attention to whether any delay might be beneficial.

Feedback That Is Frequent. Frequent feedback is probably most helpful when new learning is first being acquired. In general, feedback should be given when improvement is most possible. Once errors have accumulated, learners may see improvements as more difficult to accomplish. Also, once multiple errors become established, the new learning encouraged through feedback may seem overwhelming and confusing to learners, making further progress seem even more remote.

Feedback That Is Positive. Positive feedback places emphasis on improvements and progress rather than on deficiencies and mistakes. It is an excellent form of feedback because it increases the learner's intrinsic motivation, feeling of well-being, sense of competence, and positive attitude toward those who have given the information. People prefer positive feedback because when they are trying to improve, emphasis on errors and deficiencies (negative feedback) can be discouraging. Even when learners are prone toward mistakes, the pointing out of a *decrease in errors* may be considered positive feedback. Also, positive feedback can be given with constructive feedback. For example, a teacher might say to a learner, "You've been able to solve most of this problem. Let's take a look at what's left and see if we can understand why you are getting stuck."

Feedback That Is Personal and Differential. Differential feedback is self-comparison and focuses on the increment of personal improvement that has occurred since the last time the learning activity was performed. In skill or procedural learning, such as writing, operating a machine, or learning a particular sport, emphasizing small steps of progress can be very encouraging. The time allowed before such differential feedback is provided can be quite important. For example, learners are able to see larger gains and feel a greater sense of accomplishment when improvement is noted according to a daily or weekly schedule rather than after each performance.

In addition to the specific characteristics of feedback just listed, some refinements in the composition and delivery of feedback may be helpful, depending on the circumstances. Sometimes *graphing* or *charting* feedback can be encouraging to learner motivation because it makes progress more concrete and shows a record of increasing improvement. *Asking learners what they would like feedback on* should be considered. Their needs and concerns may be different than ours, as teachers, and the knowledge gained from such discussion can make the feedback more relevant and motivating. Learner *readiness to receive feedback* is also important. If people are not ready to hear, they are not likely to learn. For example, this may mean holding off on feedback until a personal conference can be arranged or until learners are more comfortable with the learning situation. There are times when *checking to make sure our feedback was understood* can be important. This is certainly true for complex feedback or situations in which English is not the learner's first language.

Everything that has been said about feedback thus far could also apply to *group feedback*. Whether it is a team, a collaborative group, or an entire class, feedback on their total performance can affect each individual and help to enhance group cohesiveness and morale. This is because group feedback consolidates their mutual identification.

Sometimes the best form of feedback is simply to encourage learners to move forward to the next learning challenge. Too much comment by teachers tends to emphasize the teacher's power and can contradict the norm that we are co-learners with our students.

Alternatives to Pencil-and-Paper Tests: Contextualized Assessment

In recent years, several terms have been used to describe innovative assessment procedures. Among the most common are authentic assessment, alternative assessment, performance assessment, and portfolio assessment. Although there is significant variation in purpose and application, all four procedures can be considered *contextualized assessment*. This means that the assessment is intended to show growth in multiple, integrated, and concrete ways; is meant to inform instruction; and is not a standardized or conventional test. Further, contextualized assessment is authentic to the extent that it reflects (1) the breadth, depth, and development of learning; (2) goals and learning experiences connected to real-life needs and applications; and (3) student reflection and self-monitoring. For further distinctions and elaborations of alternative assessment, performance assessment, and portfolio assessment, see *Performance and Portfolio Assessment for Language Minority Students* (Pierce and O'Malley, 1992).

Contextualized assessment encourages students to make what they learn their own and to fit emerging meanings to personal cultural milieu. Contextualized assessment avoids asking, Do you know this material? and instead asks, What do you know? Because students are invited to exhibit what they have internalized and learned through application (Brooks and Brooks, 1993), this process extends—rather than merely tests—learning. For example, *focused dialectical notes* (a collection of student written agreements, disagreements, questions, and so forth) provide an opportunity for learners to create a critical dialogue around statements encountered in assigned reading in order to practice critical thinking skills. *One-sentence summaries* ask students to reorganize a particular concept in a single grammatical sentence (Cross and Angelo, 1988). These techniques encourage learners to apply their understanding and analysis of information rather than regurgitate narrowly defined "correct answers." Such techniques have been extensively field-tested, particularly in community college settings, and have proven powerful tools for focusing faculty attention on what constitutes good learning (Ewell, 1991).

Comparing Personal Assessment Values with Actual Assessment Practice. Exhibit 5.1 lists key qualities and characteristics of effective contextualized assessment. It provides an opportunity to compare your assessment-related values to your actual practices. With the insights provided by this exercise you can consider possible changes and suggestions as they are discussed in the rest of this chapter. We cannot overstate the importance of two of the items in the exercise: using simulations or real-life challenges where new

Exhibit 5.1. Considerations for Contextualized Assessment.

Circle your own assessment (on a scale of 1 to 5, from weak to strong) of your current personal *values* and *practices* for engendering competence. Compare your values with your practices to determine areas in which to focus your attention for improvement.

Your value Weak Strong	"Test" components	Your *actual practice* Weak Strong
1 2 3 4 5	Convincing evidence that students can *use* their new knowledge and skills effectively and creatively.	1 2 3 4 5
1 2 3 4 5	Simulations or real-life challenges where new academic knowledge or skill is required.	1 2 3 4 5
1 2 3 4 5	Tasks where a multifaceted *repertoire* of knowledge and skill must be applied with good judgment. Simple recall is insufficient for performing well.	1 2 3 4 5
1 2 3 4 5	A chance to produce a *quality* product and/or performance.	1 2 3 4 5
1 2 3 4 5	Demystified criteria and standards that allow students to thoroughly prepare, self-assess, and self-adjust with apt resources available.	1 2 3 4 5
1 2 3 4 5	Opportunities for students to learn from the experience itself and to improve before the course or class has ended.	1 2 3 4 5
1 2 3 4 5	Reasonable chances to learn from mistakes without any penalty.	1 2 3 4 5
1 2 3 4 5	Opportunities for students to justify their answers, choices, or plans.	1 2 3 4 5
1 2 3 4 5	Evidence of the *pattern* and *consistency* of student work.	1 2 3 4 5
1 2 3 4 5	Opportunities for teachers to learn new things with their students.	1 2 3 4 5

Source: Adapted from materials provided by the Center on Learning, Assessment, and School Structure, 1991.

academic knowledge or skill is required, and producing a quality product or performance. An implicit goal of each item is, whenever possible, to use assessment as yet another opportunity to bridge the learner's community of origin and the institutional context. Consider, for example, the enhanced meanings and intellectual value of a student-generated questionnaire on unemployment, immigration, or bilingualism for a research, sociology, or statistics class. Imagine the motivational worth of a student-designed workshop on cultural sensitivity and communication patterns for a speech class. Relevant topics with deep meaning for students evoke intrinsic motivation within complex intellectual functions. Simulations, real-life challenges, products, and performances can be interpreted as superficial and irrelevant when they preclude opportunities for affirming cultural identity, building bridges between community and school, and underscoring the practical value of formal education. In addition, they offer classmates and teachers invaluable opportunities to deepen their understanding of critical multicultural issues.

Generating Creative Alternatives to Tests. A number of ideas for creative contextualized assessment can be developed and can, as previously mentioned, be deepened through applications to cultural issues, topics, and themes. For example, a teacher of cultural anthropology might want learners to examine the implicit and explicit rules of a given culture and apply their knowledge by creating "rules of etiquette" to guide unfamiliar visitors. The teacher might deepen this exercise by requiring learners to log the contradictions that emerge as they attempt to explain and prescribe limited rules and procedures for a given group of people. The following list, developed in part by Heidi Jacobs of Teachers College, Columbia University, for the Center on Learning, Assessment, and School Structure (1991), can be used to generate creative alternatives to testing:

Add chapter to a book

Construct an auto-
biography of a
protagonist's or
antagonist's life

Design a brochure

Create a museum
display

Rewrite a constitution

Design a proposal for
funds

Write an editorial

Design a flow chart

Construct a map

Write a movie script

Design a music video

Document an oral
history

Create a photo display

Design a poster

Construct a relief map

Create a resume/cover
letter for a mythical
character or real
person

Design a scale model

Develop a scrapbook

Author a short story

Design and implement
a survey

Design an advertisement

Create original awards

Develop a chart

Create a collage

Design a contract with
relevant data

Write an essay

Research a family tree

Design games/puzzles

Keep a journal

Write a memoir

Paint a mural

Use a musical instru-
ment to express . . .

Use painting/drawing
to express . . .

Write a play script

Use puppets to explore
the relationship
between . . .

Report current events
as a news show

Design and collate a
review of books

Design scenery for a play

Design a sculpture that
expresses . . .

Coordinate a slide show

Create a time capsule

Adapt a biography
to fit a particular
perspective

Build a terrarium

Develop an audiotape

Design a children's
book

Develop a computer
program

Initiate correspondence

Design and construct a
diorama

Write a eulogy

Analyze a flag and
create a design that
expresses contempo-
rary issues

Graph data

Write a last will and
testament for a pic-
torial or historical
person

Author a petition/bill
of rights

Write a poem

Modify a recipe

Outline a research
paper

Create rules of etiquette

Design scientific
equipment

Invent song lyrics

Create a time line

Direct a videotape

The following list (adapted from materials provided by the Center on Learning, Assessment, and School Structure, 1991) offers a
range of higher-order performance verbs for use in designing contextual assessment tasks. These verbs enable teachers to focus analytical attention on the process of learning rather than on merely
documenting outcomes (Light, 1990).

Discern a pattern

Adapt to and reach an audience

Empathize with the odd

Pursue alternative answers

Achieve an intended aesthetic
effect

Exhibit findings effectively

Polish a performance

Lead a group to closure

Develop and effectively implement
a plan

Design, execute, and de-bug an
experiment

Make a novice understand what you
deeply know

Induce a theorem or
principle

Explore and report fairly on a
controversy

Lay out cost-benefit options

Assess the quality of a product

Graphically display and effectively
illuminate complex ideas

Rate proposals or candidates

Establish principles

Make the familiar strange

Infer a relationship

Facilitate a process and result

Create an insightful model

Disprove a common notion

Reveal the limits of an important
theory

Successfully mediate a dispute

Thoroughly rethink an issue

Shift perspective

Imaginatively and persuasively
stimulate a condition or event

Thoughtfully evaluate and accurately analyze a performance

Judge the adequacy of a
superficially appealing idea

Accurately self-assess and self-
correct

Communicate in an appropriate
variety of media or languages

Complete a cost-benefit analysis

Question the obvious or familiar

Analyze common elements of
diverse products

Test for accuracy

Negotiate a dilemma

Make the strange familiar

For example, a group of science class students might design an experiment to analyze the lead content in the college's water supply and teach the results to another science class. Or perhaps a history class would analyze the effects of wars on technological development. They might then use computer graphics to infer the relationship of the country's economic growth to periods of peace and war. The use of higher-order performance verbs can catalyze assessment processes that are common and motivating to all groups of students. They provide opportunities for imaginative problem-solving experiences that allow learners to utilize their own unique culturally mediated learning preferences and strengths. Further, the personal application of concepts and ideas allows learners to develop relationships between new intellectual material and their backgrounds, memories, and values.

In recent years, exhibitions of learning have received favorable attention as a means of revealing competence and performance across curricular areas. Science and technology students, for example, have demonstrated the use of scientific methodology (for example, conducting and documenting an experiment) as well as demonstrating awareness of how science is used in contemporary society (for example, staging a debate or conducting research on a scientific development by analyzing social costs and benefits). Mathematics students, for example, have developed and displayed projects that utilize various numerical calculations for political, civic, or consumer purposes (for example, collating and analyzing social science statistics, generating and analyzing polling statistics, evaluating architectural blueprints, and so forth) (Secretary's Commission on Achieving Necessary Skills, 1992).

One efficient and interactive method for reviewing exhibitions is the poster conference. Poster conferences allow an entire class to simultaneously display and discuss information. A typical format allows 50 percent of the class to display and discuss its visual and written material as the rest of the class interacts with the presenters at their poster sites. This process can be informal, with students spontaneously selecting displays to visit and independently determining topics of discussion. The alternative is a formalized review process in which peers are assigned to review specific displays and are expected to submit as supporting evidence of their peer review such documents as resource lists, questionnaires, and standardized interviews that are consistent with preestablished criteria for excellence.

Exhibitions can also be presented formally to a committee of peers, instructors, and community members (or any combination thereof) serving as "critical friends" who record their perspectives and offer responses in round-robin fashion at the conclusion of the presentation (McDonald and others, 1993). Critical friends can be assisted with their documentation by the creation of a matrix that identifies assessment criteria and space in which to organize both warm and cool responses. *Warm* responses are taken from a believing, supportive, and appreciative perspective, and *cool* responses are taken from a constructively critical, doubting, and discerning perspective (McDonald and others, 1993). These two perspectives combine to support the socio-emotional and academic-professional aspects of informative feedback.

Documenting Learning in Ways That Support Variety in Preferred Approaches, Developmental Orientations, Interests, and Intelligences. With the topic of exhibitions we touched upon the issues of "warm" and "cool" in assessment documentation. We would now like to open the discussion of documentation to other ways in which instructors can support the multidimensional nature of all learning and all learners. This topic is especially compelling because it deflects the efficiency and comfort of quick, finite tests and judgments in favor of multiple indicators of integrated and emerging knowledge, personal meanings, and talents. Further, it encourages multiple opportunities for learners to use and refine their ideas and products. This is congruent with the awareness that learning does not best proceed in discrete hierarchies. However, as with all change, teachers may anticipate with this new assessment a loss of efficacy and confidence. We encourage you to collaborate with others and to create a process of change that allows you to manage your learning with a good chance for success. As many of us tell our students, think big and start small.

1. *Process folios:* The process folio (Gardner, 1993) goes beyond the traditional portfolio, which typically contains select samples of highly polished work. The process folio layers elements of the entire learning experience so that learners are able to document

and reflect upon challenges and emerging understandings over time. It facilitates a continual, ongoing monitoring for new insights, possibilities, and directions. Most important, the process folio allows for the identification of small successes over time rather than binge-and-purge assessment practices where accomplishment is superficially manifested in unsustainable major breakthroughs.

With the process folio, the emphasis is on nurturing habits of the mind and broadening skills and meanings over time rather than restricting learning to discrete units, simple recall, and other narrow outcomes that create the illusion of finality at designated intervals. Recommendations for working with process folios include the following:

- Encourage students to produce several works, exploring many compelling aspects of a given discipline. Match the range of works to important instructional targets and authentic tasks. For example, if the instructional targets of a course on teacher research include the ability for learners to critique different kinds of research articles and construct a research project, the learners might be asked to select two articles—one ethnographic and one experimental design—for critique. Learners would include their critiques in their process folios as an exemplification of the degree to which they have learned to critically assess research design. With respect to constructing a research project, learners might be asked to document for their portfolio (1) a one-page case study about a problematic educational situation, (2) a one-page delineation of the issues contained within, (3) a single issue that can be rephrased as a researchable question, (4) a hypothesis, and so forth.

- Provide fertile (personally and, when possible, culturally relevant) choices that allow learners to use multiple intelligences. Cumulative choices ought to represent what students can really do. This includes taking risks and stretching beyond comfort zones. For example, for a course on educational research, some learners might begin an inquiry process by artistically illustrating a problematic situation, utilizing visual clues for identifying and writing about educational issues that might be embedded within. Other students might prefer to author a short play from which to extract researchable questions. Case studies—like many other instructional tools—need not be limited to conventional modes of conceptualization.

• Create opportunities for learners to share, critique, and extend each other's ideas. Ask learners, however, to identify coached work, independent work, and group work and the amount of support they received for each. For example, students might be asked to work together to refine their personal case studies with portfolio submissions containing comments from peers on personal drafts. Learners might also be asked to work together to critique research articles. Process-folio submissions ought to reflect the original, improved, and final drafts of the critique.

• Determine with your learners a process and time frame for assessing their work, including clear delineation of valuable qualities to consider at different intervals. For example, a teacher might expect learners to review individual process folios four times a term—either with a peer, a review team, or the teacher. Learners should have clear understanding of the specific contents that will be reviewed as well as any indicators of quality that are expected.

• Generate—perhaps with input from a focus group of learners—a document for charting the broadening of skills, meanings, and talents and for linking them with personalized and appropriately high expectations and goals. For example, for a public speaking course learners might create a matrix that charts growth over time with respect to personalized goals. The matrix would include such items as "speaks with feeling" or "gestures to help express meaning," allowing learners the opportunity to set personal goals that respect differences in communication values and style.

• Ask students to judge their own work while it is in process, finally completed, and in relation to earlier or later work. (The definition of "later work" can be extended to include long-range goals for personal, academic, or professional development.)

Essentially, the process folio creates documentation for three primary considerations: the content of learning (what is being learned), the context of learning (how what is being learned fits into a larger framework, one's life and experiences, or other areas), and perceptions of the process of learning (personal reflections on the content and the process of learning, including perceptions about the various influences on learning and ways in which learning can be enhanced) (Moore and Hunter, 1994). For the instructor, process folios can serve as a guide to informed and reflective practice. They are a powerful tool for identifying and responding to the needs of diverse learners and the motivational effectiveness of instructional practice. As Arthur Costa and Bena Kallick (1992, p. 278) forewarn, we do not want to reflect on this era and think, "What was educationally significant but difficult to measure was replaced by what was insignificant but easy to measure." When educators primarily function as a "cult of efficiency," we often fail to uncover the multidimensional meanings embedded in the learning process and to use those meanings to shape the teaching and learning process.

2. *Checklists, logs, graphs, and charts:* Checklists and logs are respectful of time constraints and provide a systematic means of identifying and recording valuable information. Although many of us already use these tools, our focus is frequently limited to such basic issues of accountability as whether or not students are completing independent assignments. Checklists and logs can also be used to encourage students to document such aspects of the learning process as mutual support, modes of inquiry, and study habits. For learners who have not experienced prior opportunities to consistently reflect upon their personal learning processes, these brief experiences encourage metacognition and self-direction within a fairly conventional framework.

The use of different modes of inquiry might be addressed by asking students to identify, from a checklist, approaches to learning they find most effective. Students might then be asked to use a similar checklist to identify other approaches they might utilize for enhanced learning and to outline a process for doing so. (Review Table 3.2 and refer to the lists of assessment product and task ideas earlier in this chapter for creating your own checklist of multiple intelligences and identifying corresponding processes that have relevance for your area of study.)

A note of caution. Just because an assessment is authentic does not mean it is a valid and reliable measure of what a learner knows and can do. One of the reasons we believe that authentic and effective assessment requires multiple approaches to demonstrating learning is that one-event testing of any kind makes it difficult for teachers to judge with any assurance whether the work is truly representative of what a student has learned. Technically, this is a "validity" issue. What happens, for example, when we vary the prompt or the context? What prompt and what context are most respectful of the students' preferred ways of learning and demonstrating learning given the diversity among students? Further, with most teachers testing and grading in isolation, how are we to trust our judgments about quality? This issue has to do with reliability—having enough evidence to infer that a score or grade is appropriate and representative (Wiggins, 1992). And last, will the ways in which the assessment tool is used produce positive consequences for the learning and teaching process for all students? This emerging standard is referred to as *consequential validity* and presses for assessment developers and users to demonstrate that what they are doing works to the benefit of those who are assessed (Shepard, 1993; Darling-Hammond, 1994).

Well-Constructed Paper-and-Pencil Tests

As Grant Wiggins (1992) asserts, tests can be enticing, feasible, and defensible. The critical issue is how to construct tests so that they are worth taking. In this section, we will discuss some of the limitations of tests as well as useful ideas on how to create substantively better assessments. This discussion should make it possible to critique and revise testing decisions within a culturally responsive and comprehensive framework of understanding.

Avoiding Cultural Bias. With respect to cultural diversity, discussion of the limitations of tests must include cultural bias. As Ovando and Collier (1985) contend, it is virtually inevitable that any test that uses language as a means of assessment will have accompanying cultural content. The most common type of bias identified is item content that represents one cultural frame of reference when a broader point of view would call for a different answer (Ovando and Collier, 1985). This type of bias has also been referred to as *culture-loaded* (Jensen, 1974). These issues relate not only to ethnicity but to gender as well. For example, items about baseball averages tend to give males an edge, whereas an item of similar difficulty but focusing on child care may favor females (Pearlman, 1987; Wendler and Carlton, 1987). An item such as "Bananas are (a) black, (b) yellow, (c) red, or (d) green" is clearly invalid to anyone who has traveled south of the United States and knows that all of the above answers are correct depending on what kind of banana one is talking about (Ovando, and Collier, 1985). Although these examples may oversimplify the issue, they are a reminder to examine the assumptions embedded in the items we create or select for use in our classrooms. When tests are biased toward European-American, middle-class, English-language-dominant students they not only are unfair but can exacerbate feelings of resentment and alienation among students who intuit or overtly recognize that they are being penalized for not having been fully socialized in the dominant culture. As with all curricular materials, it is important to consider the following when you select or construct test items:

- *Invisibility:* Is there a significant omission of women and minority groups in testing materials? (This implies that certain groups are of less value, importance, and significance in our society.)

- *Stereotyping:* When groups or members of groups are mentioned in tests, are they assigned traditional or rigid roles that deny diversity and complexity within different groups? (When stereotypes occur repeatedly in print and other media, learners' perceptions are gradually distorted until stereotypes and myths about women and minorities are accepted.)
- *Selectivity:* Is bias perpetuated by offering only one interpretation—or allowing for only one interpretation—of an issue, situation, or group of people? (This fails to tap the knowledge of learners regarding varied perspectives.)
- *Unreality:* Do your test items lack an historical context that acknowledges—when relevant—prejudice and discrimination? (Glossing over painful or controversial issues obstructs authenticity and creates a sense of unreality.)
- *Fragmentation:* Are issues about women or minorities separate from the main body of the test material? (This implies that these issues are less important than issues of the dominant culture.)
- *Linguistic bias:* Do materials reflect bias in language through the dominance of masculine terms and pronouns? (The implication of invisibility devalues the importance and significance of women and minorities.)

Even directions for tests can constitute a form of bias. This is especially true for language-minority students. Second language learners of all ages can benefit from test instructions that are direct and simplified. Whenever possible, instructors ought to avoid the passive voice and ambiguous comments. In addition, test instructions should be in short sentences.

Ovando and Collier (1985) also remind us that the testing situation itself can manifest cultural bias. The discomfort that is familiar to many students can be especially devastating for students who have less experience in such situations or for whom such situations serve as reminders of feelings of alienation or inadequacy. Norms and ground rules for testing should be clear and explicit. There also ought to be adequate processing time for questions and directions to be understood. (For an extensive review on the topic of cultural fairness in testing members of ethnic minority groups in the United States, see Kumar and Treadwell, 1982.)

Avoiding the Imposition of Limitations on Knowledge. Paper-and-pencil tests can take the form of product assessments such as essays, stories, poems, and critiques. They can also be constructed-response or selected-response items. When many of us think of paper-and-pencil tests, we think of *constructed-response* items—that is, filling a blank, solving a mathematics problem, labeling a diagram or map, responding to short-answer questions, and so forth. Although constructed-response tests generally allow for application of a broader and deeper range of knowledge than *selected-response* tests (multiple choice, true/false, and matching), constructed-response items can still have the following limitations:

- The content may be limited in its breadth and depth. The consequence is that imaginative and challenging problem solving is negotiated out of the test content domain (Shepard, 1989).

- The content may not cover the full range of important instructional objectives. The consequence is that instructors may end up teaching two curricula. One involves promoting mastery of the content to be tested. The other involves creative classroom pursuits that are often seen, then, as tangential to measurable success and therefore less important (Popham, 1987).

- Tests may be limited in terms of format. For example, a short-answer question restricts the amount of knowledge students can convey. Therefore, learners may not have an opportunity to demonstrate knowledge, simply because of the way the question is presented (Gardner, 1992).

Bear in mind the previously mentioned limitations as you consider ways to create tests that are fair and equitable and that provide real opportunities for the application of knowledge. Constructed-item responses are only one of many ways in which learning can be measured. *Multiple forms of assessment*—including constructed-response tests, product assessments (essays, stories, research reports, writing portfolios, projects, and so forth), performance assessments (music, dance, dramatic performance, exhibitions, science lab demonstrations, debate, experiments, action research, and so forth), and process-focused assessments (oral questioning, interviews, learning logs, process folios, journals, observation, and so on)—yield more authentic and reliable information about learning experiences and ways of making meaning from those experiences. In addition, we know that learners are most likely to gain understanding when they construct their own cognitive maps of interconnections among concepts and facts. Relying only on decontextualized paper and pencil testing practices can cheapen teaching and undermine the authenticity of scores as measures of what learners really know.

Recommendations for Effective Paper-and-Pencil Tests. To the extent possible, *design tests to resemble real learning tasks that have instructional value.* This is one of the reasons that we prefer open-ended paper-and-pencil tests over multiple-choice tests. An example of a real learning situation that can be represented on paper is an item on an introductory bilingual education midterm that asks learners to outline a letter to the school board explaining the short-term and long-range benefits of bilingual education programs for learners.

Tests should require complex and challenging mental processes. For example, in an introductory course on organizational culture, a test item might require learners to create and present their reasoning for five interview questions that would help to determine which individuals are best suited for working effectively within a culturally diverse workplace. (See the list, earlier in this chapter, of higher-order performance verbs that can be used to stimulate complex and challenging mental processes.)

Tests should acknowledge more than one approach or right answer. For example, in a course on culture and psychology, learners may be asked to select and respond to one of the following two items: (1) Construct a map or schematic chart that illustrates seven to ten key social-political-cultural influences on the psychological well-being of members of culturally diverse groups; or (2) Which of the ten social-political-cultural influences that Don Locke (1992) uses to describe culturally diverse groups are most important in your work or everyday life? Why? Which seem least important to you? Why? Please select at least two influences for most important and at least two influences of least importance.

And perhaps most important, *tests should be meaningful to learners.* This is likely to occur when students see tests as an opportunity for self-enhancement and meaning. Designing tests to fit a range of student interests and "felt needs" supports their own awareness that they have to understand and act in this world. Further, whenever learners are able to make deliberate connections between what is new and what is known, the more likely they are to see learning as a fascinating elaboration on their lives.

As discussed in Chapter Four, tests that are meaningful usually foster a sense of high challenge with low threat. Sometimes called *relaxed alertness*, this is the optimal state of mind for expanding knowledge. We know from language acquisition studies, for example, that people only learn language well when they are relaxed and the emphasis is on communication, not on error. Ongoing relaxed alertness is the key to people's ability to access what they know, think creatively, tolerate ambiguity, and delay gratification (Caine and Caine, 1991). When tests are meaningful, when the topics we choose really matter to learners, and when we are even a bit playful, we help learners lose fear and engage their multiple talents in even the most challenging processes.

As teachers and college graduates, most of us have been educated and socialized to believe that "ability" or "intelligence" is the major determinant of learner success and failure. The best of what we know about assessment reminds us that the systems in which we work and the practices we perpetuate are frequently not matched to the needs, interests, or experiences of the learners with whom we work. Without these considerations, the human capacity to feel, to know, and to make necessary changes for enhanced learning (Freire, 1970) degenerates into feelings of anger and resentment, trivia that means little more than a paper certificate, and diminished motivation for academic success. The limitations of popular testing practices and related recommendations are relevant not only to students of color and other underrepresented learners. Emerging testing and assessment theory and practice applies to everyone.

There are no easy answers to questions of efficiency, accountability, or how to expand testing boundaries in ways that promote consistently accurate judgment (reliability) and conclusions about whether or not our tests reasonably measure valuable outcomes (validity). (See Herman, Aschbacher, and Winters, 1992, and Wiggins, 1989, for a more thorough review of reliability and validity.) Yet circling correct answers to problems only test makers care about is not "knowing," nor is it the aim of teaching (Wiggins, 1989). The language that we use, the values we reflect, the environments we create, and the quality of the tests we select or design demonstrate our fidelity to both equity and excellence.

Self-Assessment

As stated in this chapter's discussion of norms, self-assessment is a reflective process of gaining perspective on how we understand ourselves as learners, knowers, apprentices in a discipline, and citizens in a complex and paradoxical world (MacGregor, 1994). Self-assessment also allows people to validate their *authenticity* as learners and human beings. It is fascinating that so many of us— earners and teachers alike—who have experienced cultural incongruity in educational institutions have learned to mistrust our own cultural forms and behaviors that include history, language, dialect, traditional values, cultural norms, rituals, and symbolism. Self-assessment can help us weave relationships and meanings within even those environments that emphasize the amassing of academic information in ways that seem disconnected from our experiences. In addition to weaving meaning into academic work, self-assessment can provide an opportunity for all learners, regardless of personal and cultural orientation, to reflect upon and negotiate personal orientations in relation to dominant norms that need to be understood if one is to successfully live in the United States. For example, learners in a computer science course might be asked to visit two different corporate settings to observe the ways in which technological skills are utilized as well as to gain insight into corporate norms and expectations. Prior to the field experience, learners are asked to construct a brief set of interview questions in order to respectfully identify salient assumptions about the meaning and nature of work in each corporate setting. Subsequent to visiting two workplaces, learners share interview findings and personal observations and create a short essay on potential value conflicts that they, as individuals, might experience in each setting. They select one particular concern for further exploration and problem solving.

The exploration of values is a complex process and sometimes a lonely one, as social identity theory elucidates (Jackson and Hardiman, 1988; Tatum, 1992).There can be colliding, entrenched world views within the same social groups (for example, male and female students; heterosexual and gay, lesbian, and bisexual students) as well as across social groups (Adams and Marchesani, 1992). Creating opportunities for points of views to be made explicit and examined is, nonetheless, basic to intrinsic motivation. By exposing surprises, puzzlements, and hunches, structured experience with self-reflection enhances the motivation to search for ways to understand the tension we feel when we experience something that does not fit with what we already know (Sigel, Brodzinsky, and Golinkoff, 1981).

For each of the approaches that follow, we recommend that instructors carefully structure opportunities for learners to engage in personal reflection as a process of self-discovery and self-determination, even when self-assessment is primarily intended as a simple record of learning or a moment of accountability. In order to make this feasible we encourage, when needed, developing explicit norms and ground rules for mutual respect, focusing on confidentiality, honesty, nonconfrontation, speaking for oneself, and maximum opportunity to process and reflect. This invites the expansion and deepening of knowledge and helps to avoid cliché or culturally biased "truths."

A word of caution: too much ambiguity may overwhelm beginning students. We encourage you to identify clearly what you would like students to focus on and learn in the process and what you would like to learn with them. It is also a good idea to explain how you will evaluate or respond to self-assessments (MacGregor, 1994). Learners generally appreciate and are encouraged by an instructor's personal interest and timely feedback to their self-assessments. Not everything needs to be read and/or commented upon. But learners are more likely to strengthen their reflective skills if they receive expected, sincere, specific, supportive, and timely feedback.

Self-assessment can be superficial when it is appended to a class as a single episode at the end of the term. To develop a habit or point of view about learning, MacGregor (1994) advises instructors to build self-assessment into the course as an ongoing process through such activities as learning journals, portfolio development, or classroom assessment strategies. Familiarity with shorter processes helps learners develop ease and confidence with long-term forms of self-assessment.

There are several approaches that can be utilized throughout a course for "micro" purposes or aggregated together and summarized for a long-term perspective. In our opinion, some of the most effective are student-invented dialogues, focused reflection, post-writes, journals, closure techniques, and summarizing questions.

Student-Invented Dialogues. At the end of class or as an assignment, ask students to create two different but related roles for themselves in order to apply today's work to their emerging awareness of
how well they are learning (Angelo and Cross, 1993). Ask students
to script a dialogue—not to exceed two pages—based on these
roles. A short two- or three-sentence summary of "insights gleaned"
should be included. For example, a student might choose the roles
of student and instructor:

> *Student:* Sometimes I feel so overwhelmed, I can't believe that
>   I'm actually learning anything.
> *Teacher:* I know how this feels. How can we work together to
>   more clearly focus on what you might be learning?
> *Student:* I suppose frequent ungraded tests—even tests that we
>   could do with partners—might help me become more aware
>   of what and how well I am learning.
> *Teacher:* Do you think you could create a study group to create
>   your own tests?
> *Student:* I wish I had more time, but I work outside of the home
>   and I have a family in addition to going to school.
> *Summary:* I'd like to use class time to understand whether or
>   not I am making reasonable progress toward the completion
>   of course goals. I'd like this to feel relaxed but to also be
>   informative.

Roles can also place the student in conversation with major intel-
lectuals or leaders to derive new meanings from course content.
Consider, for example, a learner in dialogue with the secretary of
defense about military spending (for a United States political science course), or perhaps in dialogue with a theoretical biologist on
confusion about what the structure of DNA means for scientific
research (for a biology course). The possibilities are endless.

Focused Reflection. In focused reflection teachers ask students to
write a brief five-minute reflection prior to the end of class. Topics

can range from issues related to group participation to personalizing the meaning of academic coursework. For example, teachers might ask learners to identify whether, how much, and what kinds of prejudices operated in how learners listened to each other. With respect to content, learners might be asked to identify something new and significant that was learned and why it is of particular interest or value. This technique has also been termed *five-minute writes* (Waluconis, 1994) or *quick writes* (Wilson, 1986). Students write answers to such questions as, What is the most significant thing that you learned today? What question is uppermost on your mind at the conclusion of this course session? These questions have obvious value for an instructor who wishes to build on the interests and needs of learners. However, they also help learners clarify the personal significance of their experiences and more fully understand their responsibility for conceptualizing what may need to be done for enhanced meaning.

Although five-minute writes and quick writes have value, it is important to remember that they may be difficult for students who are in the process of becoming proficient in English as a second language or who are unaccustomed to shifts of authority in which learners evaluate their own experiences. In addition, these brief exercises may trivialize opportunities for self-assessment and self-expression by reduction to "sound bites" of information. They may constrict awareness rather than expand it. With this in mind, you may want to consider extending the time allotted for reflection or allowing time outside of class for students who would like more time or who would like to create partnerships for responding to questions. Self-reflection becomes a natural condition for learning when there is diminished self-consciousness.

Post-writes. Michael Allen and Barbara Roswell (1989) have coined the term *post-writes* as reflection that encourages learners to analyze a particular piece of work. For example, Now that you have finished your essay, please answer the following questions. There are no right or wrong answers. We are interested in your analysis of your experience writing this essay. Questions might include the following:

1. What problems did you face in the writing of this essay?
2. What solutions did you find for these problems?
3. Imagine you had more time to write this essay. What would you do if you were to continue working on it?

According to Allen and Roswell (1989), asking learners to pay attention to their writing problems and strategies for solving them changes the essential meaning of writing assessment from the assessment of writing to the assessment of writers. It is easy to imagine ways in which this technique could be applied across disciplines. Consider, for example, slightly redesigning the previous questions to allow math or engineering students to identify and reflect on a math problem that posed a particular challenge.

Journals. Journals can take a number of forms. Consider, for example, a journal that is used in a science course to synthesize lab notes, address the quality of the work, examine the process(es) upon which work is based, and address emerging interests and concerns. Journals preserve risks, experimentation with ideas, and self-expression. They are, in many ways, excellent complements to more standardized and high stakes forms of assessment.

With respect to multiculturalism and encouraging critical awareness of the origins and meanings of subject-specific knowledge, journals can be used in every course to address the following questions: (1) From whose viewpoint are we seeing or reading or hearing? From what angle or perspective? (2) How do we know what we know? What is the evidence and how reliable is it? (3) How are things, events, or people connected to each other? Is there a cause and effect? (4) So what? Why does it matter? What does it mean? Who cares? (Meier, 1991).

Journals can address interests, ideas, and issues related to course material and processes, recurring problems, responses to instructor-generated questions, responses to learner-generated questions, and important connections that are being made. Important connections can refer to learner observations within the classroom. But, optimally, connections are meanings that emerge as learners apply coursework to past, present, and future life experiences. If we wish to promote this level of reflection, then we must make the classroom a place where this can happen. Providing time in class for learners to respond in their journals to readings, discussions, and significant questions builds community around the journal process and sends yet another message that the classroom is a place in which the skills of insight and personal meaning are valued.

It is important to note that sometimes the act of trying to understand actually prevents understanding (Caine and Caine, 1991). A new idea must have time to "incubate." This involves learning to let go of some of our current beliefs. As most of us know, this is a process that requires reorganizing experience, re-perceiving information, and finding analogies and metaphors to better fit what is learned into our personal world (Caine and Caine, 1991). Powerful journals require time and effort. We recommend that learners pay less attention initially to the mechanics, organization, and whether or not it makes sense and simply try to get their thoughts and feelings down on paper where they can learn from them. They can be reorganized and summarized later, having sufficiently incubated.

Closure Techniques. Closure is a term that implies an ending. For those of us who believe that arbitrary ending points are insufficient markers for learning, the concept of closure can be problematic. Our preference is to define closure activities as opportunities for formative synthesis—to broadly or selectively examine some of what we have learned, identify emerging thoughts or feelings, discern themes, construct meaning, and so forth. Essentially, learners are encouraged to articulate their subjective relationship with course material as an active, ongoing process. For example, we might ask learners to formulate a question that they can take away with them for further consideration. Closure, then, becomes a way of building coherence between the classroom and personal experience beyond. At other times, we might use closure as an opportunity for learners to pose their own learning as a problem to be solved. For example, students identify one particular obstacle they must still overcome to feel effective at a particular learning goal. Additional suggestions for positive and constructive closure follow.

1. *Thematic problematizing:* On a three-by-five card, each learner is asked to identify one issue, challenge, or concern that has emerged as a consequence of the previously completed learning experience. Anonymity is protected by asking learners not to put their names on their cards. With masking tape or pushpins we post all of the cards and work together as a group to organize the cards into thematic categories for collective exploration. For example, in a graduate-level course on designing curricula for cultural diversity, we asked learners at the end of a lesson on alternative approaches to assessment to write down—on a three-by-five card—one fear they have that relates to making changes in their usual approach. We then posted their fears and, as we reviewed them, organized them according to themes that seemed to be emerging. Subsequently, we broke into groups to explore and problem-solve the various issues contained within each theme or category. An example of a category that emerged was "fear of making a mistake in evaluating someone." This category contained all of the cards that identified a particular way in which a mistake might be made or the various perceived consequences of making such mistakes (for example, unfair grade, lowered motivation, personal conflict, and so on).

2. *Head, heart, hand:* Another closure activity that learners often enjoy as a focus for reflection is "head, heart, hand." For "head," learners are asked to identify something they are thinking about as a consequence of the learning experience. For "heart," they are asked to identify a consequent feeling. And for "hand,"

learners are asked to identify an action as a logical next step in the learning process.

3. *Note-taking pairs:* Closure note-taking pairs (Johnson, Johnson, and Smith, 1991) can be used intermittently during a lecture or as a culminating activity. Either way, two students work together to review, add to, or modify their notes. This is an opportunity to cooperatively reflect on a lesson, review major concepts and pertinent information, and illuminate unresolved issues or concerns. Note-taking pairs are especially beneficial when there has been a lecture. Many learners, including but certainly not limited to students who speak English as a second language, benefit by summarizing their lecture notes to another person or vice versa. Students may ask each other such questions as, What have you got in your notes about this particular item? What are three key points made by the instructor? What is the most surprising thing the instructor said today? What is something that you are feeling uncertain about?

Summarizing Questions. There are any number of informative questions for reflecting upon an entire course, semester, or year. Several of the following questions are a part of the Evergreen State College Student Self-Evaluation (Elbow, 1986), a formal document that is suggested but not required in Evergreen students' transcripts. You may find some of these questions useful at the end of a course for your own approach to assessment.

- How do you feel now at the end? Why?

- What are you proud of?

- Compare your accomplishments with what you had hoped for and expected at the start.

- Which kinds of things were difficult or frustrating? Which were easy?

- What is the most important thing you did this period?

- Think of some important moments from this learning period: your best moments, typical moments, crises or turning points. Tell five or six of these in a sentence or two for each.

- What can you learn or did you learn from each of these moments?

- Who is the person you studied that you cared the most about? Be that person and write that person's letter to you, telling you whatever it is they have to tell you.

- What did you learn throughout? What were the skills and ideas? What was the most important thing? What idea or skill was hardest to really "get"? What crucial idea or skill came naturally?

- Describe this period of time as a journey. Where did the journey take you? What was the terrain like? Was it a complete trip or part of a longer one?

- You learned something crucial that you won't discover for a while. Guess it now.

- Tell a few ways you could have done a better job.

- What advice would some friends in the class give you if they spoke with 100 percent honesty and caring?

- What advice do you have for yourself?

Many learners at first omit the "self" in self-assessment, writing instead about the teacher or the course or using vague and abstract language. For many learners, it takes time, practice, and feedback to build the confidence and skill to narrate one's experiences with learning. It is a process that can carry personal risk. Yet the mastery of content is but a single challenge of academe. Experiencing and consciously deliberating one's own authority and knowledge contributes to a personal identity that will affect students for the rest of their lives.

The self-assessment process creates opportunity for dialogue between learners and teachers. In doing so, it provides an opportunity for us as faculty to reflect on our own work. We can gain critical insight into the selection of topics, materials, and approaches to teaching. We can also gain insight into some of our own assumptions about who we are culturally as well as the assumptions we hold about others. As difficult as this unpredictable and unexpected learning can be, when we are willing to use authentic ways to learn from and with our students, they—indeed—are co-learners, as opposed to audiences and critics. In this manner, self-assessment also contributes to building community in the classroom.

We are prone to search for comfort amid the confusion and excitement of diversity—trying hard to identify fixed rules, precise definitions, and logical strategies for successful assessment. The idea that we can currently exercise efficient, effective, and equitable technical control over the processes and outcomes of learning is a fantasy. Like all of curriculum, the perfect assessment process is yet to be found. Our path, as professional learners committed to enhancing motivation among diverse learners, is to set reasonable and fair assessment goals, use multiple approaches, and learn from them as we go along.

Structures for Engendering Competence

In this section we provide an overview of perspectives and approaches to assessment, and alternatives to conventional grading systems. Because one of the consequences of assessment is a historical record of performance that creates a legacy throughout students' academic and professional lives, we take a critical look at the motivational and societal ramifications of grading systems. We recognize that the perspectives offered in this section are inconsistent with most existing institutional policies and public expectations. Nonetheless, we present an alternative point of view based on a careful analysis of the motivational and social consequences of grading.

Overview of Perspectives and Approaches

We suggest that along with your course syllabus you also distribute a general overview of perspectives and approaches to assessment that defines and generally explains your assessment philosophy. It is important to clarify the difference between "giving a test" and the complex processes of assessment. This is new to many learners, and a description of the conditions and practices that create an assessment culture in your classroom can alleviate anxiety and awaken possibility. Specifically, you might want to communicate the following:

• *The reasons* you are using a different, fuller and more contextual form of assessment—for example, to nurture complex learning in which learners can amplify their understandings and apply them in meaningful ways; to develop reflective habits and increased confidence in who we are as learners and world citizens; to document learning that evolves over time; and to make use of assessment as a moment of learning.

• *The conditions* you will try to create for authenticity and effectiveness at what is valued to emerge. Some possible conditions are: clear criteria and standards for each assessment process and for the course as a whole; high and reasonable expectations for all learners; respect for learners as individuals with unique backgrounds, needs, interests, and values; opportunities for learner involvement in such aspects of assessment as determining guidelines and a time line for the development of process folios; safety and confidentiality; and accessibility.

• *The practices* you will utilize. These might include a process folio that allows learners to document and reflect upon their work throughout the semester, or dialogue journals through which learners voice emerging understandings and challenges as they connect coursework to their backgrounds and experiences, regularly exchanging narratives with a peer that they trust. Another possibility might be a mid-semester written test that allows learners to apply knowledge effectively and creatively by simulating real-life challenges facing workers in this particular area of study. There will be advance notice of test criteria and standards, allowing for thorough preparation. An idea for concluding the course could be a final poster conference at which learners display, demonstrate, and/or articulate the application of a term-long research project.

Alternatives to Conventional Grading Systems

Of all the structures in postsecondary education, the one that most systemically holds students of diverse backgrounds and perspectives in hierarchical patterns and hinders equitable opportunity for relevant educational success is the grading system. It is noted for its letter grades, A, B, C, D, and F and its numerical legacy, the grade-point average (GPA). Although this system's claim to objectivity is specious and GPAs serve no legitimate teaching purpose nor accurately predict educational or occupational achievement, grades receive very high status in society and explicitly determine how and what students learn (Milton, Pollio, and Eison, 1986). Grading systems maintain and enforce a dominant perspective and agenda in higher education and legitimize teacher power and control over learners. Further, grades diminish the accessibility of higher education for poor and working-class people (American Association of University Women, 1992). We realize these assertions challenge the basic structure of higher education and will discuss support for them below. Let's begin by examining why a grading system ought to exist.

When people give reasons why grades should be used and recorded, they frequently cite the explanation that grades are an objective measure or indicator of learning. Examining this claim reveals it to be substantially exaggerated and misleading. A grade is a context-dependent judgment, which is assigned and registered as a unidimensional symbol for a multidimensional conglomerate of teacher information, attitude, bias, and error. In most cases, one doesn't know what the symbol reveals or hides; one is *not* aware of the quality of the test, those with whom the learner was or was not compared, the evaluation plan, the content of assignments, the values of the teacher, whether effort was considered, the opportunities for revision of assignments and exams, and the mood of the teacher at the time of grading. So many factors and forces enter into the giving of grades that the realization that we actually rank students based on grades from different subject areas, different teachers, and often different institutions is neither rational nor ethical.

Quantification does not necessarily indicate accuracy or objectivity. And when it is speciously accounted for, or based on invalid comparisons, or calculated from various or unrelated measures, then quantification is a misrepresentation falsely portraying a value whose worth is, at best, unknown. That is a major reason why there is evidence that the GPA is a poor predictor of occupational accomplishment (Nelson, 1975) and graduate and professional school achievement (Warren, 1971). Consider, for example, that in a representative survey study (Warren, 1971), *prediction* means knowing that one-third of the students in the top 20 percent of undergraduate GPAs will remain in the top 20 percent of first-year graduate school grades. However, 10 percent of those in the bottom fifth will rise to the top fifth. Yet at the time of this research, the question of which students shift in which direction was unanswered. With this uncertainty, one can see how GPA offers a form of prediction far short of genuine foresight. In business and the professions, the GPA as an oracle of accomplishment fares no better. A comprehensive literature survey by the U.S. Civil Service Commission (Nelson, 1975) concluded that GPA is a poor calculator of professional achievement.

The questionable forecasting role of the GPA should not preclude a further and more important question: Ought the main role of higher education and its evaluation system be to rank students for a national personnel selection enterprise? We believe not and contend that the GPA serves little viable educational purpose other than to act as a mechanism to sort learners, implying that those with higher GPAs are smarter and better than those with lower GPAs. This continues the myth that progress through higher education is a merit-based system while it camouflages the fact that it is as much a compliance-based system that frequently and unwittingly enforces obedience to unquestioned dominant norms. Low grades serve the gatekeeping function of removing learners from the educational system who do not conform. Low grades may also disqualify students from the graduate schools and vocations to which they aspire. Our consistent observation is that many more students would object to and confront poor teaching, irrelevant content, sexual harassment, unfair evaluation, and prejudiced comments and practices if it were not for the intimidation of teachers lowering their grades.

Often missing from this critique is the understanding of the pedagogical harm that results from teachers attempting to objectively ascertain grades. The main function of grades should be to communicate with learners about the quality and amount of learning that has occurred. Grades seldom do this. Grades do influence the construction of tests, and tests influence what students will study and learn. Since tests have to be quantified to arrive at scores that can be added up and averaged in order to arrive at an "objective" grade, tests are frequently organized in overly simplified formats (for example, multiple choice, true/false, short answer) and evaluate trivial or factual information. This is why some students can cram and do well on tests: because superficial information can be rapidly covered and retained for a short time. In a few days, the information is gone, but the grade has been captured. In short, the grading system encourages teachers to create simple tests that do not teach but can be easily quantified and logically defended as leading to a number indicating a grade. "Look, there were twenty multiple-choice questions. You got five wrong. That means your score is 75. You get a C. How can you say that's not a fair grade?"

The demotivating effects of grading are severe. The responsibility to grade frequently places teachers and learners in adversarial positions. As agents of the grade, teachers often keep a distance, making their position easier to defend and emotionally less vulnerable. As clients receiving the grade, students often resent the power and arbitrary nature of the process, viewing teachers as unfair and authoritarian. When learners experience their language and/or perspective as different from the teacher's, they are likely to feel even more vulnerable. Because grading is so relative, and traditionally a competitive process, learners are wary of one another and uneasy about sharing knowledge or notes, in order to safeguard their chances for a better grade.

Grades are openly employed as rewards and punishments—the prototypical example of the "carrot and stick" mentality. Grading systems obscure the perception that learners are intrinsically motivated in situations they find relevant, challenging, and valued. As we have argued throughout this entire book, learners will seldom be seen as self-motivated as long as reward and punishment structures are used. As an efficient system that rewards compliance and has few checks and balances (appealing a grade is a legalistic, time-consuming, and emotionally draining experience for most students), it is unlikely to significantly change or self-correct.

Our critique reflects our concern as well as that of others (Milton, Pollio, and Eison, 1986) who have carefully studied grading practices in colleges and concluded that reifying grades distorts learning, abuses learners, and is a disservice to society. From a systemic perspective, the conventional grading system is not a problem to be fixed but a flawed universe requiring "radical reconceptualization" (p. 224) of its role and function in contemporary society.

To replace the conventional grading system, we have two suggestions. Either one could help to recompose postsecondary education, more justly serve a diverse population, and improve the information given to learners about their competence.

The first suggestion is to reform college assessment with the use of narrative evaluations. While the number of postsecondary institutions using narratives is relatively small, these schools have for many years sent thousands of learners into vocations and graduate schools. Their impact is more widespread than might appear (Quann, 1993). These include public universities as large as the University of California, Santa Cruz (over 10,000 students), and private colleges throughout the United States and Canada, including Sarah Lawrence College (over 1,100 students) and Nova Scotia College of Art and Design (over 1,500 students).

Narrative evaluations are not a new idea and have existed as far back as 1917. Although they vary significantly from institution to institution, their proponents frequently cite the following advantages:

- When thoughtfully written, they give learners much information about themselves, their work, and their learning.
- They accommodate differences among learners.
- They afford the consideration of varied perspectives and multiple factors.
- They encourage faculty to be attentive to each learner.

C. James Quann (1993) summarizes the disadvantages of narrative evaluations as the added cost and effort to produce, collect, file, and reproduce them; the difficulty of writing them, especially for classes with large numbers of students; and, in some instances, narratives may delay the learner's chances for admission to transfer institutions and graduate and professional schools.

We have had extensive experience with traditional grading and narrative evaluations. We concur with Quann's assessment. We would add that narratives gave us a chance to "talk" with our learners, to have a dialogue about the whole process of learning, to genuinely treat each person as an individual, to focus on important moments of learning and group interaction, to appreciate what we learned, and, with relief and sometimes joy, to be unconcerned about the inadequacy and the unfairness of having to give a grade.

Narratives do not remove the difficulty of sensitively explaining how a learner's work has fallen short of a requirement or agreed-upon goal. But in terms of teacher and learner understanding of the problem and ways to improve, this approach is far superior to the mystery and frustration of receiving a single letter on computerized paper. We have also found narratives to be an excellent assessment process to use in conjunction with learning contracts, projects, and self-assessment formats. In Resource C we have placed, for purposes of illustration, an adaptation of the narrative evaluation form we used for a research course of about twenty-five learners and a copy of the evaluative descriptors (Resource D) that were given to learners for their understanding and, when desired, negotiation.

Our second suggestion is to change the entire grading system to two major units: credit and no-credit. Credit indicates the learner has learned the relevant components and skills of a course or program (Milton, Pollio, and Eison, 1986). This would eradicate the ranking of learners and the GPA. It would allow teachers and learners to decide and candidly state what are the essentials of any given academic field. Teachers could reorganize their efforts to enhancing meaning, giving feedback, stressing critical thinking, and including and respecting differences instead of struggling to convince themselves and others that there really is a meaningful difference between a C- and a D+. Norm-referenced testing would be more irrelevant and more likely to lose its intuitive luster of pragmatism. Far fewer learners would have reason to avoid and drop courses for fear of risking their GPAs.

This shift to credit/no-credit must be complete across the entire institution, because when it exists in the larger context of a letter grading system, this system undermines the credibility and social value of the credit/no-credit system (Quann, 1984). The conditioned reflex response of society that grades are objective indicators is so deep and so strong that a college that retains a grading system continues to be connected to a colossal social norm that eventually overwhelms and depletes a partial credit/no-credit approach.

Under a credit/no-credit system, transcripts would have to change to be more descriptive of course content, process, and outcomes. Employers would have to examine samples such as portfolios, projects, and essays as well as in-house performance exams. This would also apply to graduate and professional schools. We realize all of these suggested practices are subject to classist and racist manipulation. The intent of these changes does not inevitably grace them with a conception and implementation that will be just and forthright. Yet the magnitude of the efficiency and the complicity with which higher education exercises a classist bias to sort people, to prescribe roles, occupations, and opportunities under the false pretense of valid objective quantification, would be seriously interrupted by either a narrative or credit/no-credit system.

For those of us who must continue to give or to use grades, we do not, given the complexity of different postsecondary environments and the variation among learners, presume to have a formula for ascribing a single letter grade for a person's commitment of study and learning over the course of a semester. Because it has a structure that allows for mutual understanding and agreement, as well as a dialogue about the content, process, criteria, and outcomes, generally we favor the use of contracts (see Chapter Three) to arrive at grades for culturally responsive teaching. Contracts can be created and distributed at the beginning of the course to be discussed and negotiated. We believe each teacher should know where and why they will stand firm on certain contractual items. Negotiating ought to be a democratic process, but not a permissive one, or the integrity of the learning experience is in question.

It is advisable to give learners sufficient time to think about the contract, especially if resources or the work commitment are uncertain. For learners who have difficulty deciding, an individual conference may be arranged. Also, there is the possibility of learners proposing their own contracts. Two questions we have found beneficial for designing and negotiating contracts are: Do the learners retain their self-determination? Does the course remain challenging from the learners' as well as the teacher's perspective?

When learners' work has to be evaluated by themselves, others, or teachers, arriving at some common language for such descriptive labels as "excellent" or "unsatisfactory" can be extremely informative for everyone. For an example, please see the matrix (Resource D) we used at Antioch University, Seattle. Learners who are not demonstrating the quality specified in the contract should be informed as early as possible so they may have ample opportunity to rectify the matter.

This chapter has presented norms, procedures, and structures for engendering competence. Assessment that is culturally responsive illuminates the nature of human learning—the connection between knowledge as others have defined it and meaning that is relevant to individual experiences and belief systems.

Change and adaptation to new ways of working with assessment is a multidimensional, interpersonal, and intrapersonal negotiation. Our decisions are mediated by standards of quality and excellence that are defined by individuals, institutions, communities, and cultural agreements. It is our belief that the unique spirit and meanings that motivate us as learners and teachers can be affirmed even amid the confusion of competing expectations and policies. When assessment is conveyed and sanctioned as a trusted medium for understanding learning, it is not something one simply practices or performs. It is an ethical process and one of our most profound responsibilities as teachers.

Chapter Six

Implementing a Culturally Responsive Pedagogy

From the standpoint of democratic pluralism
wherein diversity is a resource, the explosion [of
diversity] is challenging and unsettling but highly
welcome. I thus prefer the metaphor of inchoateness
to the backward-looking metaphor of fragmentation.
We are not staring wistfully at the fragmented ruins
of a temple once whole, but poring over the recently
discovered jottings for a novel whose form or plot
has yet to emerge.
                                        —*Patrick J. Hill*

As the arc of multiculturalism radiates through higher education,
it creates an exciting, unsettled, and kaleidoscopic landscape. It
awakens discourse, confronting the inertia of conventional college
teaching. Rather than a radical notion, however, culturally responsive teaching is an evolution of sound educational practices that
respects the principle that all cultures are significant to the construction of knowledge. Culturally responsive pedagogy is consistent with the historical and central purposes of a liberal education—
that is, to promote intellectual development and the ideal of responsible and active political participation. We have organized this
approach to teaching to offer college teachers more effective ways

to align their professional practice with their commitment to democracy and its basic values of justice and equality.

If there is a tone to the process of culturally responsive teaching as we have rendered this approach, we believe it is embodied in Patrick J. Hill's ideal of "conversations of respect" (1991):

> Conversations of respect between diverse communities are characterized by intellectual reciprocity. They are ones in which the participants expect to learn from each other, expect to learn non-incidental things, expect to change at least intellectually as a result of the encounter. In such conversations, one participant does not treat the other as an illustration of, or variation of, or a dollop upon a truth or insight already fully possessed. There is no will to incorporate the other in any sense into one's belief system. In such conversations, one participant does not presume that the relationship is one of teacher to student (in any traditional sense of that relationship), of parent to child, of developed to underdeveloped. The participants are co-learners [p. 47].

With a framework largely anchored in intrinsic motivation we have created a synthesis of norms, procedures, and structures to untangle the vast array of culturally related philosophies and teaching practices that have emerged in the last ten to fifteen years. Our approach is comprehensive but not exhaustive. As we have integrated many different perspectives from a number of disciplines, we have leaned toward finding mutually resonant theoretical concepts and aligning pedagogical methods as diverse as giving quantitative feedback and multidimensional sharing. This reflects our wariness of doctrinaire as well as political aggressiveness.

We agree with Lil Brannon (1993) that central to the transformation of education is building alliances with teachers and the enterprises of scholarly insight and research. As we discuss how to apply the material found in this book, we want to focus again on what we believe is the major challenge facing postsecondary education in general and culturally responsive teaching in particular: to create learning experiences that allow the integrity of every learner to be sustained while each person attains relevant educational success and mobility. In this way all learners are intellectually and ethically empowered to contribute to the achievement of equity and social justice in a democratic pluralistic society. Awareness of this preeminent goal as a personal and collective responsibility may nurture further insight during consideration of the roles and practices suggested in this final chapter.

Authentic Roles and Practices for Culturally Responsive Teaching

As a democratic community is always a community in the making, teaching also remains dynamic, with attention to its present flaws and a vision of its future possibility. Leading an ethical professional life often means trespassing—not in the sense of a moral transgression, but to infringe upon the status quo, to question unexamined assumptions or media that demean or exclude the experience of women, people of color, lesbians and gay men, and others who are culturally different (Bensimon, 1994). This means starting with ourselves and our own course content, syllabi, and materials, being willing to cross the border from what we know to what we need to know. In our opinion, this is the first requisite for culturally responsive teaching: *a humble sense of self-scrutiny*, not to induce guilt or liberal, knee-jerk responses but to deepen our sensitivity to the vast array of ways we may be complicitous with the inequitable treatment of others and to open ourselves to knowing the limitations of our own perspective and our need for the other.

We must also consider our students. Their history and experience are critical to how we create with them the kind of learning where trust, equal participation, and inquiry are normal ways of proceeding. Our experience and that of other practitioners (Tatum, 1992; Schmitz, 1992) in the field of multiculturalism is that many learners are uncomfortable with the topics, methods, and changing roles of its pedagogy. Learners may resist learning procedures that require active engagement with other learners, faculty, or course materials. Constructing and critiquing their own and other's knowledge may contradict their experience and the paradigm that knowledge is something the teacher possesses at the beginning, transmits to students during the course, and that they demonstrate as their own private possession on a test. Dialogue may make them feel provoked, exposed, or even used as well as sometimes frustrated when other learners seem to talk too much or too little. As we indicated in Chapter One, culturally responsive teaching may violate the unspoken norms of many conventional college classrooms. Since college teaching has not dramatically changed in the last thirty years, the resistance of learners may very well mirror our own.

We have addressed student and teacher resistance at the beginning and end of this book because we respect the enormity of the challenge not only to assist learners to construct and acquire knowledge but to raise their critical consciousness about social justice as well. Culturally responsive teaching often places marginalized views and issues of social inequity in the foreground. This means teachers and learners will, at times, grapple with altering long-held viewpoints as they begin to understand and accommodate other perspectives. Therefore, teaching in a culturally responsive way may require considerable transformation. Being skilled, prepared, and willing to deal with some of the tensions and difficulties that accompany this pedagogy is a continuing responsibility. In this regard, emerging literature related to cultural and intercultural competence is informative (Kim, 1991; Kim and Ruben, 1988; Taylor, 1994). Many people who take up residence in a culture different from their own are able to eventually develop an understanding of and respect for the perceptions, experiences, and values of the other culture. Initially, however, there is a period where sojourners feel dissonance and emotions ranging from fear to overexcitement as they experience the incongruities between their host culture and their primary culture. Through processes involving actively observing, socializing, and developing friendships within the host culture, they eventually arrive at a more inclusive and integrated world view. Very few people are able to do this without some period of uneasiness. As practitioners evolving toward a more culturally responsive pedagogy we offer the following guidelines:

- Proceed carefully and gradually.
- Create a safe climate in which to learn.
- Learn with others.
- Identify new roles.
- Create action plans.
- Acknowledge doubt and anxiety as signs of change and potential professional and personal development.
- Recognize the power of self-generated knowledge.
- Share your work with others.

For our discussion of the above suggestions refer to Exhibit 6.1, which outlines the summary of criteria, norms, procedures, and structures of a motivational framework for culturally responsive teaching.

The recommendations that follow the exhibit are created for consideration by faculty who want to become more competent as culturally responsive teachers. The ideas we offer are meant more as heuristics, rather than prescriptions, to stimulate further ideas about how to move one's professional practice in a culturally relevant direction. As we know from multiple intelligences theory and literature on cultural differences, there are many places to begin, with an array of possible directions and dimensions.

Exhibit 6.1. Norms, Procedures, and Structures of a Motivational Framework for Culturally Responsive Teaching.

NORMS

Establishing Inclusion (Criteria: Respect and connectedness)

1. *Human purpose:* Coursework emphasizes the human purpose of what is being learned and its relationship to the learners' personal experiences and contemporary situations.

2. *Ownership:* Teachers share the ownership of knowing with all learners.

3. *Collaboration:* Collaboration and cooperation are the expected ways of proceeding and learning.

4. *Hopeful view:* Course perspectives assume a non-blameful and realistically hopeful view of people and their capacity to change.

5. *Equitable treatment:* There is equitable treatment of all learners with an invitation to point out behaviors, practices, and policies that discriminate.

Developing Attitude (Criteria: Relevance and self-determination)

6. *Learners' experience:* Teaching and learning activities are contextualized in the learners' experience or previous knowledge and are accessible through their current thinking and ways of knowing.

7. *Choices:* The entire academic process of learning, from content selection to accomplishment and assessment of competencies, encourages learners to make real choices based on their experiences, values, needs, and strengths.

Enhancing Meaning (Criteria: Engagement and challenge)

8. *Challenge:* Learners participate in challenging learning experiences involving higher-order thinking and critical inquiry that address relevant, real-world issues in an action-oriented manner.

9. *"Third Idiom":* Learner expression and language are joined with teacher expression and language to form a "third idiom" that enables the perspectives of all learners to be readily shared and included in the process of learning.

Engendering Competence (Criteria: Authenticity and effectiveness)

10. *Relevant assessment:* The assessment process is connected to the learner's world, fames of reference, and values.

11. *Multiple ways:* Demonstration of learning includes multiple ways to represent knowledge and skills and allows for attainment of outcomes at different points in time.

12. *Self-assessment:* Self-assessment is essential to the overall assessment process.

Exhibit 6.1. Norms, Procedures, and Structures of a Motivational Framework for Culturally Responsive Teaching, Cont'd.

PROCEDURES

Establishing Inclusion

1. Collaborative learning
2. Cooperative learning
3. Writing groups
4. Peer teaching
5. Opportunities for multidimensional sharing
6. Focus groups
7. Reframing

Developing Attitude

8. Learning-goal procedures
   a. Clearly defined goals
   b. Problem-solving goals
   c. Expressive outcomes
9. Fair and clear criteria of evaluation
10. Relevant learning models
11. Goal setting
12. Learning contracts
13. Approaches based on multiple intelligences theory
14. Sensitivity and pedagogical flexibility based on the concept of style
15. Experiential learning—the Kolb Model

Enhancing Meaning

16. Critical questioning and guided reciprocal peer questioning
17. Posing problems
18. Decision making
19. Authentic research
    a. Definitional investigation
    b. Historical investigation
    c. Projective investigation
    d. Experimental inquiry

Exhibit 6.1. Norms, Procedures, and Structures of a Motivational Framework for Culturally Responsive Teaching, Cont'd.

20. Invention and artistry
21. Simulations
22. Case-study method

Engendering Competence

23. Feedback
24. Alternatives to pencil-and-paper tests: contextualized assessment
    a. Comparing personal assessment values with actual assessment practice
    b. Generating creative alternatives to tests
    c. Documenting learning in ways that support variety in preferred approaches, developmental orientations, interests, and intelligences
25. Well-constructed paper-and-pencil tests
26. Self-assessment

STRUCTURES

Establishing Inclusion

1. Ground rules
2. Learning communities
3. Cooperative base groups

Developing Attitude

4. Culturally responsive teacher-learner conferences

Enhancing Meaning

5. Projects
6. The problem-posing model

Engendering Competence

7. Overview of perspectives and approaches
8. Alternatives to conventional grading systems
    a. Narrative evaluations
    b. Credit and no credit
    c. Contracts for grades

Proceed Carefully and Gradually

As we suggested earlier in this chapter, most of us and our learners are products of a conventional college experience. Developing new roles such as co-learners in the classroom and using unique ways of learning and assessing will often initially feel awkward. Stepping into a class on the first day is akin to walking into a theater of strangers—we have a vague mutual goal, but there is no sense of personal attachment and little expectancy of developing a rela-tionship. Rarely are most learners seeking social change or coming with a transformative agenda. As Goodlad (1990) has observed, most students are largely passive, because it best fits the nature of school. There is also the reality that when we change the way we teach we are not just going to learn from this experience, we are going to learn in it, acting in the situation and being acted upon by it (Wilson, 1993). A negative and difficult initial teaching experi-ence, even with an open attitude and new methods, can malform the entire process. Therefore, to proceed gradually and carefully offers a better chance that we and our learners can negotiate the new changes we intend for our courses (Shor, 1992). Rather than choosing rigidly and exclusively between conventional and cultur-ally responsive forms of pedagogy, it may be more reasonable to focus on how to move the course gradually toward more culturally responsive norms, procedures, and structures. In addition, our expe-rience is that unless significant alterations in course structures and procedures are explicitly named and discussed with learners, learn-ers are likely to be confused and resistant.

As you proceed through the many suggestions that follow it may be beneficial to review our idea of culturally responsive pedagogy. It (1) respects diversity; (2) engages the motivation of all learners; (3) creates a safe, inclusive, and respectful environment; (4) derives teaching practices from principles that cross disciplines and cul-tures; and (5) promotes justice and equity in society.

One way to begin to access the materials and information in this book is to review Exhibit 6.1, this time checking off all the norms, procedures, and structures that you currently use when composing your courses. This will affirm what you do and may give you some ideas about what you would like to do next. Another immediate possibility is to check your syllabus and materials for bias. Making changes here can profoundly affect the learning process and clarify how the knowledge of the course is constructed.

Probing a bit deeper, you might take each course syllabus you have and scan the entire composition for the norms it reflects, the integration of various procedures, and the structures that are explicitly noted. After this careful consideration you might reflect on how you would like to revise or remodel the course to be more culturally responsive, using Exhibit 6.1 as a suggestion map. To exemplify this process and as a point of departure and critique, we have provided in Exhibit 6.2 the syllabus for a course, *Introduction to Research*, which one of the authors has recently taught. The four representative questions that follow might be used to examine where a syllabus is consistent with norms, procedures, and structures of culturally responsive teaching and to find areas for possible improvement from a culturally responsive perspective.

Composing a course syllabus is similar to making a map for a particular terrain. It creates definite directions, expectations, and boundaries. Along with the people in class, the course syllabus probably creates the strongest impression at a course's initial meeting. Writing a course syllabus that can reassure students about the value of a course as well as evoke their motivation to learn is a considerable challenge.

1. *Which culturally responsive teaching norms are clearly imbedded in the context of this syllabus?* Norm one (human purpose) is reflected in the *introduction* (discusses the influence of research on society and its connection to learners' experience) and in *potential learning experiences* numbers four (Designing Research to Understand Current Issues), five (Free Wheeling), nine (Conducting Action Research), and eleven (Development of a Research Project).

Exhibit 6.2. Introduction to Research.

Introduction

Welcome to an *Introduction to Research*. The type of thinking and requirements for a course of this nature may appear formidable. Research has a jargon and set of symbols that can seem strange, difficult, and rigid. Yet it is a way of knowing that can be helpful and very creative.

As a graduate student I came to research with a sense of inadequacy and genuine trepidation, and after having worked twenty years as a psychologist and educator, and using and conducting research on a regular basis, I still feel those two emotions about research. They are less intense now and tempered by skepticism. But I am also more respectful of the field of research.

Research as a means of knowing dominates our society. It influences every aspect of our life, from the purity of water we drink to the size of the federal budget. It is the voice of authority for educational and social policy. To understand research and to know how to critique it is a valuable asset in the pursuit of our personal and social goals. Thus, our course aims to increase our conversational and critical skills in the use of research. As the syllabus indicates, our activities are extremely utilitarian. We are going to use research for purposes we value.

Please get the texts as soon as possible and do your required reading. Most of our course activities are guided practice in the application of knowledge about research. No one has to be expert, but if one has not done the necessary reading, the experience will be, at best, confusing. The first few classes will be much like a clinic. We will find out what we know and what we need and want to know about research.

Course Intention

The purpose of this course is to develop an understanding of the primary assumptions, perspectives, and methods that guide research as it can be conducted in the social sciences. This course also provides a framework and a literacy for comprehending, analyzing, and evaluating research studies as they are found in professional journals and reports. Because of the nature of education, action research is offered as a research method to be learned at a level of useful proficiency.

Learning Goals

1. To conduct a dialogue concerning the usefulness, limitations, advantages, and assumptions of research approaches and practices represented by the following topics:

    a. The nature of human inquiry and the scientific method

    b. Inductive and deductive theory

Exhibit 6.2. Introduction to Research, Cont'd.

  c. Correlation and causality

  d. Research designs for exploration, description, and explanation

  e. Reliability and validity

  f. Questionnaire formats

  g. Sampling design

  h. Experimental designs

  i. Survey research

  j. Field research

  k. Unobtrusive research

  l. Evaluative research

  m. Action research

  n. The ethics of research

2. To effectively interpret and critique research articles published in such education and social science periodicals as the *Journal of Teacher Education*, *American Psychologist*, and the *Anthropology and Education Quarterly*

3. To effectively construct and apply an action research method to know what happens as a result of specific educational practices and interventions

Potential Learning Experiences and Class Outline

1. General introduction

2. Overview of current issues in educational research

3. Reaction panels to controversial articles in education and social science. A number of small cooperative groups will be formed. Each will find a different research article that deals with a topic of a controversial nature (for example, consequences of ability grouping, relationship of cognitive ability to social class, failures of direct instruction). Each group will have a chance to publicly critique the article based on its knowledge of research methods.

4. Designing research to better understand current issues in education. Using a small-group format, participants will create or choose a specific description of an important issue in education (for example, parent involvement, drug use in schools, magnet schools). Each group will be requested to design a study to increase a better understanding of the issue. These designs will be presented to the rest of the class and open to further refinement.

Exhibit 6.2. Introduction to Research, Cont'd.

5. Freewheeling. Each participant suggests one social or educational problem about which he or she feels genuine concern. The participant describes it in approximately 100 words on newsprint. These descriptions will be posted, and the class will select one or more for a research study to be designed (in class) to provide information to better understand and respond to the problem. Carrying out this study is optional.

6. Formative test. Each participant will receive a formative test to evaluate his or her knowledge of general research methods. Each participant will receive immediate feedback regarding the accuracy of his or her responses. This feedback will be private. After the evaluation, there will be time for discussion, clarification, and refinement of understanding.

7. Overview of action research.

8. Discussion of models of action research.

9. Conducting action research among ourselves. Using ourselves as a data base, we will conduct a number of studies using survey and interview methods. Participants will be divided into research teams and will have the opportunity to generate their own research questions and methods of investigation. Results of the studies will be reported back to the class.

10. Discussion and exercises for analysis of data.

11. Guidance in the development of an action research project. Guidelines for problem definition, literature review, and action research designs will be offered. Participants will bring their ideas for potential research projects to class. The class and instructor will act as a sounding and advisory board in response to participant research ideas. This will give all participants a good chance for a solid beginning in their research work as well as another chance to apply their knowledge in the area of action research.

Demonstration and Assessment of Learning

1. Unless otherwise negotiated, full attendance and active participation

2. Completion of critiques of two personally chosen research articles; competent analysis and discussion (two to four pages in length) of the research indicated in the article

3. Competent completion of one action research proposal

Criteria for the evaluation of items two and three are an adequate demonstration of knowledge of research methods as exemplified in the body of work required for each project. More specific criteria will be offered in class.

Norm three (collaboration) is reflected in *potential learning experiences* numbers three (Reaction Panels), four (Designing Research to Understand Current Issues), nine (Conducting Action Research), and eleven (Development of a Research Project).

Norm seven (choices) is reflected in *potential learning experiences* numbers three (Reaction Panels), four (Designing Research to Understand Current Issues), five (Free Wheeling), nine (Conducting Action Research), and eleven (Development of a Research Project); *assessment of learning* number two (Critique of Research Articles).

Norm eight (challenge) is reflected in *potential learning experiences* numbers three (Reaction Panels), four (Designing Research to Understand Current Issues), five (Free Wheeling), and primarily eleven (Development of a Research Project).

Norm ten (relevant assessment) is reflected in *assessment of learning* numbers two (Critiques of Research Articles) and three (Action Research Proposal).

2. *Which culturally responsive teaching norms are obviously absent from the context of this syllabus?* I found norms numbers four (hopeful view) and nine ("third idiom") difficult to specifically state in my syllabus, although I would likely behave in a way that would reflect them. These are norms I continue to consciously work on for improvement. Norm eleven (multiple ways) has a chance to come about in those activities where learners generate their own methods of investigation, such as qualitative or quantitative research approaches. Clearly, norms five (equitable treatment) and twelve (self-assessment) are missing. For norm five I am likely to experiment, and instead of writing some form of it into my syllabus, I will state it publicly at the outset of class and assess its effects as we proceed. For norm twelve, I will make a definite change using the summarizing questions of self-assessment (see Chapter Five), including them with the required action research proposal and using instruction such as, "Compare your accomplishment with what you had hoped for and expected at the start of this course."

3. *Which culturally responsive teaching procedures are clearly found in this syllabus?* Procedure two (cooperative learning) is reflected in *potential learning experiences* numbers three (Reaction Panels), four (Designing Research to Understand Current Issues), and nine (Conducting Action Research).

Procedure eight(a) (clearly defined goals) is reflected in *assessment of learning* number two (Critiques of Research Articles).

Procedure eight(b) (problem-solving goals) is reflected in *assessment of learning* number three (Action Research Project).

Procedure fourteen (pedagogical flexibility) is reflected in *potential learning experiences* number nine (Conducting Action Research).

Procedure fifteen (the Kolb model) is reflected in *potential learning experiences* number five (Free Wheeling); for example, concrete experience (the 100-word problem); reflective observation (class selection and discussion of problem); abstract conceptualization (creating a research design); active experimentation (carrying out research).

Procedure sixteen (critical questioning) is reflected in *potential learning experiences* numbers three (Reaction Panels), four (Designing Research to Understand Current Issues), five (Free Wheeling), and nine (Conducting Action Research).

Procedure nineteen(c) (projective investigation) and (d) (experimental inquiry) are both possible with *potential learning experiences* numbers nine (Conducting Action Research) and eleven (Development of a Research Project).

Procedure twenty-three (feedback) is reflected in *potential learning experiences* numbers six (Formative Test) and eleven (Development of a Research Project).

Procedure twenty-four (alternative to test) is reflected in *assessment of learning* number three (Action Research Project).

Procedure twenty-five (paper-and-pencil test) is reflected in *potential learning experiences* number six (Formative Test).

From exploring my syllabus I realized I would like to develop more pedagogical flexibility and use multiple intelligences theory to design an activity in which different research designs emanate from learners who explore a concern or question from such different entry points as foundational, aesthetic, and narrational. An example would be if learners were to write a short story (narrational) about how a particular problem is resolved and then design a study that would be likely to inform that specific process of resolution. I further noted that it might not be clear in the syllabus, but generative and topical themes are likely to be imbedded in the problems posed by learners during potential learning experiences numbers four and five.

4. *What culturally responsive teaching structures do I need or value that are not clear on this syllabus?* The university for which I taught this course used narrative evaluations. My approach to assessment was to provide models to the class of a well-done critique of a research article and an exemplary research proposal. The class then divided into small groups to discuss why these two examples might be considered commendable. They also reflected on other approaches and ways to compose these outcomes that might vary from the examples offered and still be laudable. During a whole-group discussion we listed both sets of these qualities on the chalkboard. Although the assessment was not bound by these criteria, this information was recorded by me and certainly informed my evaluations of my learners. If I had to give grades I would still use a similar process, compose a contracting system based on it, and bring it to the next class session for mutual agreement.

Transforming our courses into the kind of educational settings where learners share responsibility and authority for their learning is an evolving process for them as well as for ourselves. It means coming to class with a well-considered plan but being willing to reinvent some of that structure according to the learners and situation that you find there. Creating a safe climate is essential to easing the doubts and cushioning the risks inherent in any group that may undergo significant change.

Create a Safe Climate in Which to Learn

Creating a safe climate begins with respect—for ourselves and for our students. Such respect means that before we attempt any new approaches or changes we have carefully reflected on them and specifically planned for them to ensure their success and to minimize any possible negative consequences. We can also use focus groups from among our students to test our ideas before we put them into action.

With a non-blameful attitude we can value the risk we are taking to develop our craft and realize that the outcome is not a final judgment of our own or our students' abilities and character but information to reflect on for further improvement. With the use of quick writes, postwrites, and surveys we can learn from our students how our new methods are affecting them and glean suggestions for further refinement before any negative consequences become entrenched. In addition, and where appropriate, we can share ownership of knowing with our students and directly inform them about the rationale, purpose, and process of the change we have selected and request their perspective as we proceed. Finally, there is the counsel of our professional colleagues. Learning new teaching approaches with our peers also contributes to our sense of safety and can be quite enjoyable as well.

Learn with Others

There's an old saying that no one can avoid pain but that most people can escape suffering. One of the key aspects of this adage is "not going it alone," sharing the burden or the challenge, whichever it may be. Taking on something a bit daring alone is often considered risky. Add a few people to the same venture and it could easily be called a sport. The literature on professional development is unanimous in declaring that when one changes teaching practices it is most fluidly and effectively accomplished with support and feedback from other faculty (Joyce and Showers, 1988). As Michael Collins piquantly states, "It is altogether reasonable to learn emancipation, and how to dance, *before* [his italics] the revolution" (1991, p. 115). As Barbara Leigh Smith and Jean MacGregor (1992) have found, faculty collaboration in the development of learning community programs is a powerful means for enabling teachers to build their repertoires and confidence.

A simple and direct way to enlist such collaboration is to form a collegial cooperative group modeled after the work of Johnson, Johnson, and Smith (1991). The principles of positive interdependence, individual accountability, promotive interaction, social skills, and group processing discussed in Chapter Two under cooperative learning groups would apply in this situation as well. The purposes of this small group would be to

1. Provide the help, assistance, support, and encouragement each member needs to improve in the use of culturally responsive teaching practices.

2. Serve as an informal support group for sharing, letting off steam, and discussing problems connected with implementing culturally responsive teaching practices.

3. Serve as a base for faculty experienced in the use of culturally responsive teaching practices to teach others how to use these approaches.

4. Create a setting where friendship and shared success occur and are celebrated.

Collegial cooperative groups should be organized to ensure active participation by faculty, developing such concrete outcomes as syllabi, lesson plans, and learning activities and sharing articles, books, media, and other resources. Once members have established rapport with each other and are ready to deepen their work together, they can consider beginning a modified coaching process. This involves reciprocal observations of each other's teaching using the following guidelines:

1. The members confer with each other to decide whether to focus on student responses, use of critical questions, how problems are posed, or some other aspect of the learning procedure.
2. The feedback is on what occurs and the procedures used, not on teacher competence.
3. The observer provides information the teacher requests and does not impose advice, opinions, or suggestions that are not solicited by the teacher.
4. The observer is confidential about what is seen in the classroom.
5. The observer provides support and participates in the collaborative solving of problems posed by the teacher.
6. The observer is also a learner watching for practices and materials to discuss and consider for her or his professional use.
7. The tone of the entire process is one of respect and trust.

Because of the reciprocity and shared experience, coaching often deepens relationships and generates new teaching practices in collegial cooperative groups. A survey conducted at the British Columbia Institute of Technology (Wlodkowski, 1992) found that better than two-thirds of the instructors who had training in peer coaching reported an improved attitude toward their role as a teacher as well as toward their students and colleagues. In further support of this approach is the understanding that the situation in which we learn to actually practice evolving methods has an enormous impact on our ability to effectively transfer and maintain new ways of teaching (Bredo, 1994). In general, the more authentic the setting, the more likely we will retain and use what we have competently applied.

Identify New Roles

Identity is a powerful influence on our motivation. We do things we would otherwise not do because we adhere to certain roles—teacher, parent, friend. Identities confine as well as expand our lives and the lives of those around us. We reward, we encourage, we prevent, and sometimes we punish because of who we think we are. To change one's identity is to change one's entire motivational system. Those who claim to be reborn or to have reinvented themselves have also reidentified themselves. "Coming out" is a public embracing of one's identity.

Often identity resists change. One of the largest impediments to transforming teaching in colleges and universities is faculty identity. We are professors. We are scholars and researchers. The amount of time we will devote to teaching and the position we believe we should maintain relative to students is in many ways controlled by those identities. Most faculty teach the way they do not because of the way they were taught but because of whom they identified with when they were taught. With respect to teaching, the brilliant theoretician, the renowned researcher, and the mesmerizing lecturer are academic clichés that may have imprisoned more faculty than liberated them. Repeat the roles, repeat the system.

Thus, an important question is: How do you see yourself professionally? What do the words *professor, faculty, instructor, teacher,* and *teacher assistant* mean to you? Jim Cummins (1986) states, "In the absence of individual and collective educator role redefinitions, schools will continue to reproduce, in these interactions, the power relations that characterize the wider society and make minority students' academic failure inevitable" (p. 33).

Culturally responsive teaching recedes from identities that are authoritarian, elitist, or directive and gravitates toward roles that

are collaborative, egalitarian, and consultive. Primary to this pedagogy is the identification of oneself as a co-learner. How could a co-
learner lecture for an entire period? How could a co-learner ignore
another learner's perspective? How could a co-learner completely
avoid collaboration? The identity of being a co-learner makes many
forms of conventional teaching so incongruous as to be humorous
or, at the very least, uncomfortable. With the active, cooperative,
and critical nature of culturally responsive teaching there are more
than a few nontraditional educational roles that may surface from
this approach, such as mediator, advocate, orchestrator, arbiter, and
archivist (Bensimon, 1994). In addition, some of the quite conventional provinces of teaching still hold and are very necessary. There
must continue to be someone to guide, to consult, and to facilitate.
To begin to reference oneself with these roles while thinking or talking about teaching encourages our consciousness to evolve and creates the will to enlist a culturally responsive framework for our work.

Create Action Plans

Earlier in this section we discussed and exemplified a number of
ways one might revise a syllabus to reflect a more culturally responsive pedagogy. We began in this manner because it afforded a holistic and systemic orientation toward an entire course. Often a
teacher may want to try changes on a smaller scale or experiment
with a particular norm, procedure, or structure before formally revising her or his course. In any case an action plan can help to organize and facilitate the use of new teaching approaches. Action plans
work a lot like goal-setting strategies, because they clarify what we
want to do and give us a way to organize and emotionally prepare
for the changes we wish to make. They increase our chances for
optimal implementation. In Exhibit 6.3 is an action plan for applying the use of the case-study method to a research course. A short
discussion follows to model our thinking and to discuss how the
plan was conceptualized.

Exhibit 6.3. Action Plan.

Goals(s): To have learners develop a critical understanding of ethical issues in research—specifically informed consent, right to privacy, and protection from harm—through the analysis of a case study in which homosexuals were uninformed subjects.

Actions to be taken: (1) Write a realistic and complex narrative based on research in the manner of the study of Laud Humphreys (1970) that resulted in the publication of the book, *Tearoom Trade.* (2) Create a discussion outline. (3) Decide how to begin the case study (free writing and discussion with a partner) and how to end the case study (go around the group, with each learner providing an insight, goal, and so forth).

Potential obstacles: None.

Needed support: Have a couple of my colleagues (gay and straight) critique the case before I use it.

Criteria for success: High learner involvement; discussion that references the ethical issues, analyzes the historical and systemic variables, and allows for multiple interpretations.

Post-implementation assessment: Discussion initially very tentative and somewhat self-righteous and accusatory. Dialogue became more integrated and inclusive when we dealt with how research ethics reflect historically what the broader society will condone. For example, use and treatment of animals in experiments has been changing due to activism of animal rights organizations and greater public awareness. After this point in the discussion there was high involvement. Ending activity revealed a variety of critical insights. I need to revise the discussion outline. I learned some of the ways research often engenders its own mistrust.

Source: Action plan format, adapted from Cheek and Campbell, 1994, p. 27.

Some recommendations for proceeding with each stage of the action plan are as follows:

Goal: Although there are exceptions to this (see the discussion of problem-solving goals and expressive outcomes in Chapter Three), most often it is beneficial to start with what you want to do and what you imagine your learners will learn. Sensitivity to the teaching practice and its connection to what is learned is critical to assessing its value.

Actions to be taken: Writing a narrative of the steps that will make the teaching practice a reality ensures a better chance it will be effective.

Potential obstacles: If there are any obstacles, it is best to know them and plan for them.

Needed support: This can be crucial to uncovering or resolving problems with the plan. What if the written case was inadvertantly sexist, homophobic, or otherwise offensive?

Criteria for success: Sometimes there are surprises, but if we know what we are looking for we are more likely to understand when it occurs. Knowing the criteria should support and add consistency to our goal.

Post-implementation assessment: This stage is critical to refining the teaching practice, or, in some cases, to rejecting it. Most first experiences with a new teaching approach are somewhat awkward, and reflection at this time can be immensely helpful for finding ways to improve. The given discussion outline needed a more sensitive and less inflammatory beginning. Acknowledging and including what the teacher learned is important validation of a pedagogy based on the premise that the teacher is a co-learner.

Action plans can be immensely useful to collegial cooperative groups. They create anticipation, focus the group on concrete teaching, assist reciprocal coaching, and can be enjoyable to collaboratively create and assess.

Acknowledge Doubt and Anxiety as Signs of Change and Potential Professional and Personal Development

As we have said a number of times, co-learning—using critical analysis, adapting to local conditions, reshaping course content, sharing authority, and trying new teaching practices—complicates and enriches a teacher's life. All of this takes time to learn and practice. Feelings of confusion and disorientation are not uncomon. Doubt and anxiety are often invitations to flex, to look a bit further, and to realize that we may need to change or are changing and it will not feel comfortable for a while. Collegial support, a sense of purpose, and being aware of the results of one's work help, but they don't completely free us of these emotions.

Recognize the Power of Self-Generated Knowledge

Who speaks in class and how often? How much of the time is the teacher speaking? Do learners talk to one another during class discussions? How multicultural are the examples or perspectives given throughout the course? Who gets the highest test scores and best-graded papers? Are lessons connected to the learners' real worlds? Do learners explain themselves in a number of sentences and with reference to concepts or principles? These are just some of the questions that we can use to concretely understand how culturally responsive our teaching really is. We can answer a number of these questions ourselves, and for the others we can enlist the assistance of a colleague or learner to observe and record. If you have doubts or question the validity of a particular norm, procedure, or structure, you might create an observational process, a survey, or a classroom study (preferably with a colleague) to find out for yourself. We encourage you to test assumptions related to your own practice.

Self-generated knowledge is also a significant way to integrate and refine new teaching practices. In addition to action plans, some of the self-assessment procedures in Chapter Five, such as post-writes, journals, and summarizing questions, can deepen our understanding of the changes we are making. Also, we highly recommend action research (Elliott, 1991) and experimental inquiry (Chapter Four) as a means to generate knowledge about one's teaching.

Share Your Work with Others

Sharing your work with others is critical to continuing the dialogue and evolution of culturally responsive pedagogy. We learn from and with each other. The voices of the many teachers in this book— Beverly Daniel Tatum, Ira Shor, Paulo Freire, Gerald Weinstein, Maurianne Adams, and Linda Marchesani—have informed and inspired us. We also need to communicate about our own work, because—for the sake of our learners as well as our society—we need to move it from the fringes to regular practice. Institutional transformation occurs most effectively when dynamic change evolves on both the inside and the outside of its structure. By writing about our work in newsletters as well as in books and journals, by bringing our ideas to brown-bag lunches as well as to conferences and seminars, by forming collegial cooperative groups as well as national networks and organizations, we respond to the huge ethnic demographic shifts that are occurring in this country at this moment. We also normalize culturally responsive pedagogy. As James Banks (Brandt, 1994) has said of multicultural teachers, "we make a strong, unequivocal commitment to democracy, to basic American values of justice and equality" (p. 31). In philosophy and intent, culturally responsive pedagogy is a classic notion whose time is past due.

Faculty Development

Our experience with the topic of cultural diversity in the area of professional development is that often with many faculty groups there is an apprehension, an idea at the outset that they may be doing something wrong, are guilty of some form of "ism," or will be accused of some kind of ineptitude. There is frequently an air of tension in the group that can preclude any real dialogue and constructive learning. Not surprisingly, culturally responsive teaching approaches tend to work well in such settings. Transformation comes from finding language and means to help faculty examine their values, creating a safe and respectful learning climate, and responding to their concerns and needs for pragmatic procedures.

We have found that there are many faculty development programs in the areas of multiculturalism and culturally responsive teaching being established on campuses across the country, a good number of which are described or referenced in the literature (Border and Van Note Chism, 1992; Schmitz, 1992; Adams, 1992a; Butler and Walter, 1991; Greene, 1989). As a result of examining this literature and interviewing a number of the people who authored it and worked in their own faculty development programs, we find the following inventory of good practices in faculty development programs (adapted from Schmitz, 1992, p. 76) to be an instructive and representative list of exemplary work in this area:

- Design a high-quality program of faculty development with the collaboration of faculty members themselves at the start of the planning process. (Faculty feel they shape and own the program.)

- Examine programs that have worked well on campuses with similar curricular plans. (Helps to reduce initial errors, saves planning time, and encourages greater confidence.)

- Assess the developmental needs of faculty members. Increase perspective sharing.

- Set clear expectations for faculty participation and outcomes at each stage of the process.

- Design specific activities for the planning, pilot, implementation, and assessment phases of the program. Plan for extensive use of collaborative activities.

- Include both theoretical and practical components in the program.

- Use the expertise available among faculty members at the institution as well as outside experts.
- Design the scope and intensity of activities according to the expectations placed on faculty members.
- Make clear to faculty that the program is of benefit to students, the institution, and their own renewal.
- Provide enough resources to compensate faculty members for the amount and kind of work expected of them. (This can include stipends, release time, course reassignments, travel, and so forth. Such matters seem individualized to each campus.)

Although we have not addressed curricular reform, we agree the task is daunting and want to emphasize how important it is to consider how inseparable content and pedagogy really are. The kind of culturally responsive procedures available to a research course may be quite different from those accessible to a language course. Also, even if the same procedures were to be used in both disciplines, their form and texture might markedly vary. Faculty appreciate development programs that are sensitive to and inclusive of the content of their disciplines.

Both reports from the literature and past experience indicate that few faculty development programs will be successful without support from all sectors of the campus (Schmitz, Paul, and Greenberg, 1992; Schmitz, 1992; Madison, 1993; Hayes, 1994). According to Schmitz, Paul, and Greenberg, "The ideal level of support includes an institutional mission statement that emphasizes the creation of a multicultural campus community, financial resources to set up permanent programs for faculty and TA development (including resources for permanent staff), a faculty culture that values professional development and teaching improvement and endorses the need for a positive multicultural environment, and student support for improved intergroup actions, on campus and in the classroom" (p. 82). Although few institutions have this level of support, the literature does describe how a number of effective programs have evolved from very different directions. Each institutional culture is unique, therefore change strategies will vary. Washington State University accelerated its efforts with the appointment of a Commission on the Status of Minorities to enhance ethnic and racial diversity and combat racism on campus (Madison, 1993). Their study led to a comprehensive plan of action including minority faculty and staff recruitment as well as extensive faculty development. To sustain its multicultural core curriculum, the University of North Carolina, Asheville, developed a very successful internship program (Schmitz, 1992). More ideas are found in the references and institutions cited in this section.

Insisting There Is More to Higher Education Than We Have Yet Imagined

We wrote this book because we believed, through practice and scholarship, that a pedagogy that was effective across cultures was inseparable from motivational theories about human nature. As we further explored this relationship in college education we saw more clearly how this highly competitive system directly transmits knowledge to students, grading and ranking them for eligibility to privileged occupations and educational opportunities. With a transmissional pedagogy tightly linked to coveted incentives, higher education, wittingly or unwittingly, is ideally organized to convey a dominant orientation to the world and reality. This framework is supported by an understanding of motivation that sees all people as most responsive to extrinsic rewards and punishments that are legitimized and distributed by educational authorities.

Multiculturalism questions and confronts how equitable and just this educational universe is to all people. We propose that an intrinsic theory of motivation more adequately represents and serves people across cultures, especially in educational settings. We have presented and documented eight criteria as essential to creating situations that elicit any person's intrinsic motivation to learn. When people feel *respected* and *connected* in the learning setting, when people have a voice in *self-determining* learning they find *relevant*, and when people *engage* in *challenging* and *authentic* experiences that enhance their *effectiveness* in what they value, people learn. Because authority of the teacher must, to some extent, be shared and because knowledge must be constructed from multiple cultural perspectives, this is a more complex and subtle way to teach. Yet this kind of pedagogy is the only approach that we have found that heralds our common endowment as human beings, respects the cultures from which we come, and acknowledges the ways in which each of us is an individual. And in those instances where we have attained this kind of learning with our students, the validation and the joy for the teacher appears to be as powerful as it is for the learners.

We are part of a world ravaged by divisive interests. How can higher education be structured so that its graduates directly contribute to a society in which more people are compassionate with one another and serve their collective interests? As we reflect on this question we realize how rare it is to be in a college course and among diverse learners who have dialogues of respect and who feel neither victim nor oppressor but sincerely and critically curious. As human beings, most of us have memories of challenges in which we have not been heroic or courageous. We have not had much guidance in learning to be open and critical at the same time, in having honest and respectful conversations about cultural issues that threaten us, in seeking and telling our own truth knowing there are other truths for other people, and in knowing that as a multicultural society, we can explore and create a future together. To live such experiences so we can carry them in our souls to transform society, colleges must become places where inquiry, reflection, respect, and equal participation among diverse people are the norm.

312   Diversity and Motivation

Although distant, and more vivid in our imaginations than on the campuses of this country, this ideal is what we believe a college education can be and ought to be. As an institution, higher education enjoys remarkable status and influence in this country. It can change the consciousness of society. We deeply want it to be an agent of genuine social and economic improvement rather than a pretense of equity in an increasingly unequal world.

Multiculturalism is a wave of indelible influence on education. What is uncertain is the degree to which colleges will resist or accommodate its force. Colleges know they must accept increasing diversity, and most know it is the right thing to do. Now they need to take the more important step of rethinking instruction to tap into the great benefits of student diversity. On the matter of culturally responsive teaching, we have offered our ideas with careful consideration, if not to be used, then to at least deepen the dialogue and continue the momentum toward transformation. For those of us who teach, we live out one of life's oldest stories: to have work to do in this world and to learn what the world is from doing it well. To this we owe fidelity.

Resource A

Facilitating Equitable Class Discussions Within the Multicultural Classroom

Topically focused class discussions potentially offer English learners rich exposure to new vocabulary and usage in their second language, along with opportunities to interact in a variety of academic situations—reporting information, summarizing, synthesizing, and debating. Frequently, however, linguistically and culturally diverse students remain passive participants in whole-class discussions for varied reasons, including insecurity about their listening comprehension, pronunciation, word choice, and culturally appropriate interactional strategies. Instructors may employ the following strategies to lead carefully orchestrated class discussions that provide language-promoting assistance and facilitate more active participation for English learners:

1. Create a supportive classroom environment for less confident English users by encouraging all students to talk in turn, to listen actively while others talk, and to offer assistance rather than impatience and intolerance for classmates who need help in understanding or responding.

2. Show your students that you expect them all to participate in oral activities by consistently inviting every member of the class to participate.

3. Allow students to first share and rehearse their responses to a key question or comments on a topic with a partner to increase learning and ESL student confidence and motivation to contribute to a unified class discussion.

4. Be sensitive to the linguistic and conceptual demands of discussion questions and activities. Don't inhibit participation by pushing students to communicate too far beyond their current level of English proficiency.

5. The easiest content for less proficient English users to handle is often related to their everyday lives and activities. Make a concerted effort to build in opportunities for language minority students to share information about their cultures, communities, families, and special interests.

6. Pair less proficient English users with a sensitive classmate who can ideally clarify concepts, vocabulary, and instructions in the primary language and also coach the classmate in responding.

7. Attempt to activate students' relevant background knowledge on topics, and provide through "schema"-building activities (e.g., brainstorming, mapping, advance organizers) requisite linguistic, conceptual, and cultural information that would otherwise prevent them from active learning and participation.

8. Move purposefully around the room to enable as many students as possible to enjoy having close proximity to the teacher, which should also encourage students to remain more alert and willing to ask and answer questions.

9. Do not constantly pose questions to the group at large, allowing a minority of more confident or impulsive students to dominate the discussion.

10. Ask a question before naming the respondent to encourage active learning by allowing all students to "attend" and decide how they would answer.

11. Draw in less confident students by asking them to respond to an open-ended question after they have heard a variety of responses from their classmates.

12. Call on English learners to answer not only safe yes/no questions but also more challenging, open-ended questions that provide opportunities for thoughtful and extended usage of their second language.

13. Increase wait time (3–9 seconds) after asking a question to allow adequate time for the student to successfully process the question and formulate a thoughtful response.

14. When calling on a specific ESL student, it often helps to first pose the question and make eye contact with the student while stating his/her name; then pause a few seconds and restate the question verbatim.

15. Discourage classmates from blurting out responses and intimidating less confident English users from taking risks with their second language.

16. Do not interrupt a student's thought processes after asking an initial question by immediately posing one or more follow-up questions; these tandem questions confuse rather than assist English learners who may not realize that the teacher is actually rephrasing the same question.

17. Encourage students to talk through nonverbal means, such as waiting patiently, smiling, and nodding in approval.

18. Make any corrections indirectly by mirroring in correct form what the student has said. For example, suppose a student says, "*Majority immigrants San Francisco from Pacific Rim.*" You can repeat, "*That is correct. A majority of the immigrants in San Francisco come from the Pacific Rim.*"

19. Use these conversational features regularly and in so doing model for your students how to use them in class discussions, lectures, and small-group work:

confirmation checks	*Is this what you are saying?* *So you believe that . . .*
clarification requests	*Will you explain your point so that I can be sure I understand?* *Could you give me an example of that?*
comprehension checks	*Is my use of language understandable to you?*
interrupting	*Excuse me, but . . .* *Sorry for interrupting, but . . .*

Source: Kinsella, 1993, p. 16. Used by permission.

Effective Lecturing Within the Multicultural Classroom

Although occasionally necessary, lectures present particular difficulties for students who are still in the process of acquiring full English proficiency and who may be largely unfamiliar with the specialized terminology of academic disciplines and effective note-taking strategies.

Content area teachers may utilize the following strategies while presenting critical information orally during lessons to facilitate listening comprehension, active engagement, and note-taking ability for non-native speakers of English and other students who may not have a strong auditory learning modality:

1. Begin the lecture with a brief review of the main ideas covered in the previous class session. You can also ask students to summarize the main points of the previous lesson first in pairs, then as a unified class.

2. Early in the semester, teach your students a manageable note-taking system that is particularly useful for your content area, such as the "Recall Clue Note-Taking System." Spend adequate time modeling this system and sharing examples of well-taken notes.

3. Encourage native English-speaking students or fluent bilinguals who take effective, comprehensible notes to share these with students who speak English as a second language (ESL).

4. Provide a partially completed outline of the lecture following the system that you have taught to lighten the listening load for students who are less proficient users of English. Utilize a handout for lengthy presentations of information, and the board or overhead projector for simpler outlines that students may easily copy.

5. Build in accountability for taking effective lecture notes by randomly collecting and commenting on them and allowing students to use their notes during exams.

6. Clarify the topic and key objectives of your lecture at the very beginning.

7. Write as legibly as possible on the board or on overhead transparencies, keeping in mind that students educated abroad may be unfamiliar with cursive writing.

8. Allow students to use a tape recorder or record your lectures and class discussions on tape so that ESL students can listen to them as many times as they need to comprehend and retain information.

9. Before and during the lecture, identify key terms and write all important vocabulary and points on the board, overhead transparency, or handout.

10. Modify your normal conversational style to make your delivery as comprehensible as possible: use a slightly slower speech rate, enunciate clearly, limit idiomatic expressions, and pause adequately at the end of a statement to allow time for thought processing and note taking.

11. Follow an orderly progression of ideas and stick to your outline, thereby enabling students with less academic English proficiency to readily identify essential lesson information and reduce potential "linguistic clutter."

12. Complement challenging information relayed orally with visual aids: illustrations, charts, advance organizers, concept maps, demonstrations.

13. Use many concrete examples and analogies so that students can conceptualize concepts within a more familiar context, and also elicit relevant examples from student volunteers.

14. Build in considerable redundancy with repetitions, examples, anecdotes, expansions, and paraphrases.

15. Relate information to assigned readings whenever possible and give the precise place within the text or selection, enabling students to write these page numbers in their notes and find the information later for study or review.

16. Highlight major points and transitions with broad gestures, facial expressions, purposeful movement, exaggerated intonation, and obvious verbal signals.

17. Focus your students' listening and note taking by using consistent verbal signals or cues (e.g., furthermore, in summary) that indicate the structure and progression of ideas in your lecture. Distribute a chart with transitional expressions organized by function that are commonly used in formal speaking and writing in university classes and professional settings.

18. Make regular eye contact with all your students.

19. Check for comprehension regularly rather than at the end of the lecture. Predetermine critical transitions and ask students to summarize key points first in pairs then as a unified class. You can also ask students to review their notes up to that point and write down any questions they would like answered.

20. Try to answer all questions that the students ask but avoid overly detailed explanation, which may further confuse them. Simple answers that get right to the point will be understood best, particularly if you use relevant visual aids and examples or demonstrate actions to help get the meaning across.

21. Save adequate time at the end to clarify the main points of the lecture.

22. Allow students to compare their notes in small groups or pairs, and then formulate any final questions for the unified class and/or instructor that they could not answer within their group.

Source: Kinsella, 1993, p. 13. Used by permission.

Resource B
Cooperative Lesson Worksheet

Step 1   Select an activity and desired outcome(s).

_____

_____

Step 2   Make decisions.

a. Group size: _____

b. Assignment to groups: _____

_____

c. Room arrangement: _____

_____

d. Materials needed for each group: _____

_____

e. Roles: _____

_____

Step 3   State the learning component in language your
students understand.

a. Task: _____

_____

b. Positive interdependence: _____

_____

      c. Individual accountability: _____

_____

      d. Criteria for success: _____

_____

      e. Specific behaviors to encourage: _____

_____

Step 4   Monitor progress.

      a. Evidence of cooperative and encouraged behaviors:

_____

      b. Task assistance needed: _____

_____

Step 5   Evaluate outcomes.

      a. Task achievement: _____

_____

      b. Group functioning: _____

_____

      c. Notes on individuals: _____

_____

      d. Feedback to give: _____

_____

      e. Suggestions for next time: _____

_____

_____

_____

Source: Adapted from Johnson, Johnson, and Smith, 1991, pp. 4:35–36.

Resource C
Evaluator Assessment

———⟨⟨⟨⟩⟩⟩———

Student: _____ Advisor: _____

Evaluator: _____

Address: _____

Assessment	Outstanding	Excellent	Very good	Good	Satisfactory w/concerns	Unsatisfactory	Not applicable
Participation in learning activities							
Knowledge of theory and content							
Documentation of Learning							
1. Writing skills							
2. Oral skills							
3. Communicating skills							
4. Intellectual skills							
Met contracted learning objectives							
Application/integration of knowledge							
Narrative							

Signature of Evaluator   Date

Note: More extensive area for narrative on original document, with additional page optional.
Source: Antioch University, Seattle, Washington. Used with permission.

Resource D
Evaluative Descriptors
for Narrative Assessment

Course requirements	Unsatisfactory	Satisfactory w/concerns	Satisfactory	Very good	Excellent	Outstanding
Participation in learning activites	Student gave no sign in learning activity of attending to what went on and/or participated in ways that were inappropriate and disruptive to the learning process of others.	Student was present at learning activity and appeared to be attending to what took place but either did not participate actively or participated in an inappropriate way. Some reworking (specify) needs to be arranged.	Student occasionally raised questions and/or offered some contributions to key issues. Participation was appropriate and helpful to the learning of others.	Student was active and made useful contributions that included real engagement with key issues represented in the syllabus or study guide. Student gave evidence of considering the learning needs of other learners in addition to his/her own learning process.	Student raised points that were original and engaged others in dialogue that broke new ground. Student was regularly helpful to the learning needs of other learners in addition to his/her own process.	Instructor could, in all good conscience, have asked student to conduct a portion of the learning activity.
Connecting theory to practice (application of knowledge)	Student either gave evidence of not grasping basic theoretical concepts at all or could only repeat back what was presented without giving evidence of understanding application.	Student gave evidence of being able to connect theory and practice in the learning acticity materials at the overview level, although he/she did not do so in an effective way. Some reworking (specify) is needed.	Student gave occasional evidence of successfully applying many of the learning activity's key concepts to classroom, professional, and/or life situations.	Student applied most of the learning activity's key concepts to illuminate classroom, professional, and/or life situations.	Student consistently used key concepts of the learning activity to illuminate clinical and life situations in an original way, which led to new learning for the instructor.	Student's application of learning activity material to classroom and life situations ws invariably apt, original, and worth passing on to future students.
Knowledge of theory and content	Student's work was characterized by such major problems (specify) that no credit for the learning activity can be given.	Student's work in the learning activity was minimally acceptable; there were some major problems (identify), though not severe enough to be considered "unsatisfactory." Some corrective action/reworking (specify) needs to be arranged.	Student's work was acceptable with no major problems.	Student's work solidly fulfilled learning activity requirements and integrated material in a particularly clear and effective manner.	Student's work showed originality over and above solid competence; instructor learned from student's contributions to the learning process.	Student's work was so competent and original that instructor experienced student as if he/she were a colleague or peer.

Quality of documentation	Means of expression unacceptable with respect to content, organization, and/or style (specify).	Means of expression minimally acceptable with respect to content, organization, and style; there were some problems in one or more of these areas (specify). Some reworking (specify) needs to be arranged.	Means of expression was adequate with respect to content, organization, and style.	Means of expression was particularly clear, well organized, and/or well written.	Means of expression was competent (or better) in execution and original/creative in approach to the topic; materials (papers, projects) could be used as a model for other students.	Means of expression showed particularly clear and creative approach to the topic, an approach that's rarely seen and is of publishable quality.
Met contracted learning objectives	Student did not meet objectives as stated.	Student met objectives at basic level. Minimum required work was completed but with little demonstration of depth or extension of self.	Student met objectives in satisfactory manner. All work fulfilled stated objectives in an acceptable manner.	Student attained objectives. Demonstrated a desire to go beyond the minimum and used the objectives as guidelines rather than prescriptions.	Student exceeded objectives. Demonstrated ability to use objectives as suggestions to stimulate more extensive learning.	Student demonstrated complete mastery of topic far exceeding objectives.

Source: Antioch University, Seattle, Washington. Used with permission.

References

Adams, M. "Cultural Inclusion in the American College Classroom." In L.L.B. Border and N. Van Note Chism (eds.), *Teaching for Diversity*. New Directions for Teaching and Learning, no. 49. San Francisco: Jossey-Bass, 1992a.

Adams, M. (ed.). *Promoting Diversity in College Classrooms: Innovative Responses for the Curriculum, Faculty, and Institutions*. New Directions for Teaching and Learning, no. 52. San Francisco: Jossey-Bass, 1992b.

Adams, M., and Marchesani, L. S. "Curricular Innovations: Social Diversity as Course Content." In M. Adams (ed.), *Promoting Diversity in College Classrooms: Innovative Responses for the Curriculum, Faculty, and Institutions*. New Directions for Teaching and Learning, No. 52. San Francisco: Jossey-Bass, 1992.

Agee, J., and Evans, W. *Let Us Now Praise Famous Men: Three Tenant Families*. Boston: Houghton Mifflin, 1941.

Allen, M. S., and Roswell, B. S. "Self-Evaluation as Holistic Assessment." Paper presented at the annual meeting of the Conference on College Composition and Communication, March 1989. (ED 303 809)

Alley, R. "Simulation Development." In D. S. Hoopes and P. Ventura (eds.), *Intercultural Sourcebook: Cross-Cultural Training Methodologies*. Washington, D.C.: Intercultural Network, 1979.

Alverno College Faculty. *Assessments at Alverno College*. Milwaukee, Wis.: Alverno Publications, 1979.

American Association of University Women Educational Foundation. *The AAUW Report: How Schools Shortchange Girls*. Washington, D.C.: National Education Association, 1992.

American Council on Education. *The 11th Annual Status Report on Minorities in Higher Education*. Washington, D.C.: American Council on Education, 1993.

329

American Psychological Association. *Learner Centered Psychological Principles: Guidelines for School Redesign and Reform*. Washington, D.C.: American Psychological Association, 1993.

Amir, Y. "Contact Hypothesis in Ethnic Relations." *Psychological Bulletin*, 1969, 71, 319-341.

Anderson, J. "Cognitive Styles and Multicultural Populations." *Journal of Teacher Education*, 1988, 39(1), 2-9.

Anderson, J. A., and Adams, M. "Acknowledging the Learning Styles of Diverse Student Populations: Implications for Instructional Design." In L.L.B. Border and N. Van Note Chism (eds.), *Teaching for Diversity*. New Directions for Teaching and Learning, no. 49. San Francisco: Jossey-Bass, 1992.

Angelo, T.A., and Cross, K.P. Classroom Assessment Techniques: A *Handbook for College Teachers*. (2nd ed.) San Francisco: Jossey-Bass, 1993.

Apple, M. *Education and Power*. Boston: Routledge & Kegan Paul, 1982.

Aronson, E., and others. *The Jigsaw Classroom* Newbury Park, Calif.: Sage, 1978.

Aspy, D. N., Aspy, C. B., and Quinby, P. M. "What Doctors Can Teach Teachers About Problem-Based Learning." *Educational Leadership*, 1993, 50(7), 22-24.

Astin, A. W. *Minorities in American Higher Education*. San Francisco: Jossey-Bass, 1982.

Astin, A. W. "The Future of Higher Education: Competition or Cooperation. *Cooperative Learning*, 1993a, 13(3), 2-5.

Astin, A. W. *What Matters in College?* Four Critical Years Revisited. San Francisco: Jossey-Bass, 1993b.

Astin, A. W., Green, K. C., and Korn, W. S *The American Freshman: Twenty-Year Trends* 1966-1985. Los Angeles: Higher Education Research Institute, Graduate School of Education, University of California, 1987.

Au, K. H., and Kawakami, A. J. "Cultural Congruence in Instruction." In E. R. Hollins, J. E. King, and W. C. Hayman (eds.), *Teaching Diverse Populations: Formulation a Knowledge Base*. Albany: State University of New York Press, 1994.

Auletta, G. S., and Jones, T. "Unmasking the Myths of Racism." In D. F. Halpern and Associates (eds.), *Changing College Classrooms: New Teaching and Learning Stragegies for an Increasingly Complex World*. San Francisco: Jossey-Bass, 1994.

Bagdikian, B. *The Media Monopoly*. Boston: Beacon Press, 1987.

Banathy, B. H. "New Horizons Through Systems Design." *Educational Horizons* 1991, pp. 83-89.

Banathy, B.H. A *Systems View of Education*. Englewood Cliffs, N.J.: Educational Technology Publications, 1992.

Bandura, A. "Self-Efficacy Mechanism in Human Agency." *American Psychologist*, 1982, *37*(2), 122–147.

Banks, J. A. "The Canon Debate, Knowledge Construction, and Multicultural Education." *Educational Researcher*, 1993, *22*(5), 4–14.

Banks, J. A., and McGee Banks, C. A. *Multicultural Education: Issues and Perspectives*. (2nd ed.) Needham Heights, Mass.: Allyn & Bacon, 1993.

Barkley Brown, E. "African-American Women Quilting: A Framework for Conceptualizing and Teaching African-American Women's History." In M. R. Malson, E. Mudimbe-Boyi, J. F. O'Barr, and M. Wyer (eds.), *Black Women in America: Social Science Perspectives*. Chicago: University of Chicago Press, 1990.

Baron, J. *Thinking and Deciding*. New York: Cambridge University Press, 1988.

Barringer, F. "When English Is a Foreign Tongue: Census Finds a Sharp Rise in 80's." *New York Times*, Apr. 28, 1993, p. A-1.

Baum, S., Gable, R. K., and List, K. *Chi Square Pie Charts and Me*. Monroe, N.Y.: Trillium Press, 1987.

Baxter Magolda, M. B. "Gender Difference in Cognitive Development: An Analysis of Cognitive Complexity and Learning Styles." *Journal of College Student Development*, 1989, *30*(3), 213–220.

Baxter Magolda, M. B. "Gender Differences in Epistemological Development." *Journal of College Student Development*, 1990, *31*(4), 555–561.

Belenky, M., Clinchy, B., Goldberger, N., and Tarule, J. *Women's Ways of Knowing: The Development of Self, Voice, and Mind*. New York: Basic Books, 1986.

Bensimon, E. M. (ed.). *Multicultural Teaching and Learning*. University Park: National Center on Postsecondary Teaching, Learning, and Assessment, Pennsylvania State University, 1994.

Beyer, B. K. *Developing a Thinking Skills Program*. Needham Heights, Mass.: Allyn & Bacon, 1988.

Blanc, R. A., DeBuhr, L. E., and Martin, D. C. "Breaking the Attrition Cycle." *Journal of Higher Education*, 1983, *54*(1), 80–89.

Bohm, D. *Unfolding Meanings: A Weekend of Dialogue with David Bohm*. London: Ark Paperbacks, 1987.

Bonham, L. A. "Learning Style Use: In Need of Perspective." *Lifelong Learning*, 1988, *11*(5), 14–17.

Bonsangue, M. "Long Term Effects of the Calculus Workshop Model." *Cooperative Learning*, 1993, *13*(3), 19–20.

Bonstingl, J. J. *Schools of Quality*. Alexandria, Va.: Association for Supervision and Curriculum Development, 1992.

Border, L.L.B., and Van Note Chism, N., (eds.). *Teaching for Diversity*. New Directions for Teaching and Learning, no. 49. San Francisco: Jossey-Bass, 1992.

Bowser, B. P., and Hunt, R. C. (eds.). *Impact of Racism on White Americans*. Newbury Park, Calif.: Sage, 1981.

Brandt, R. "On Educating for Diversity: A Conversation with James A. Banks." *Educational Leadership*, 1994, *51*(8), 28–31.

Brannon, L. "To Serve, with Love: Liberation Theory and the Mystification of Teaching." In P. Kahaney, L. Perry, and J. Janangelo (eds.), *Theoretical and Critical Perspectives on Teacher Change*. Norwood, N.J.: Ablex, 1993.

Bredo, E. "Reconstructing Educational Psychology: Situated Cognition and Deweyian Pragmatism." *Educational Psychologist*, 1994, *29*(1), 23–35.

Bronfenbrenner, U. *The Ecology of Human Development: Experiments by Nature and Design*. Cambridge, Mass.: Harvard University Press, 1979.

Brookfield, S. D. *Understanding and Facilitating Adult Learning: A Comprehensive Analysis of Principles and Effective Practices*. San Francisco: Jossey-Bass, 1986.

Brookfield, S. D. *Developing Critical Thinkers: Challenging Adults to Explore Alternative Ways of Thinking and Acting*. San Francisco: Jossey-Bass, 1987.

Brookfield, S. D. *The Skillful Teacher: On Technique, Trust, and Responsiveness in the Classroom*. San Francisco: Jossey-Bass, 1990.

Brooks, J. G., and Brooks, M. G. *The Case for Constructivist Classrooms*. Alexandria, Va.: Association for Supervision and Curriculum Development, 1993.

Brown, L. S., and Ballou, M. (eds.). *Personality and Psychopathology: Feminist Appraisals*. New York: Guilford Press, 1992.

Butler, J. E. "Transforming the Curriculum: Teaching About Women of Color." In J. A. Banks and C. A. Banks (eds.), *Multicultural Education: Issues and Perspectives*. (2nd ed.) Needham Heights, Mass.: Allyn & Bacon, 1993.

Butler, J. E., and Walter, J. C. (eds.). *Transforming the Curriculum: Ethnic Studies and Women's Studies*. Albany: State University of New York Press, 1991.

Caine, R. N., and Caine, G. *Making Connections: Teaching and the Human Brain*. Alexandria, Va.: Association for Supervision and Curriculum Development, 1991.

Canter, L., and Canter, M. *Assertive Discipline: A Take-Charge Approach for Today's Educator*. Los Angeles: Lee Canter and Associates, 1976.

Carter, D. J., and Wilson, R. *Ninth Annual Status Report on Minorities in Higher Education*. Washington, D.C.: American Council on Education, 1991.

Celis, W. "Colleges Battle Culture and Poverty to Swell Hispanic Enrollments." *New York Times*, Feb. 24, 1993, p. A-13.

Center for Academic Development. *Supplemental Instruction: Review of Research Concerning the Effectiveness of SI from the University of Missouri—Kansas City and Other Institutions from Across the United States*. Kansas City: University of Missouri, 1991.

Center on Learning, Assessment, and School Structure, Rochester, N.Y., 1991.

Cheek, G. D., and Campbell, C. "The Transfer of Learning Process: Before, During, and After Educational Programs." *Adult Learning*, 1994, 5(4), 27–28.

Cherrin, S. "Teaching Controversial Issues." *Teaching Excellence*, 1993, 5(1), 1–2; Professional and Organizational Development Network in Higher Education, Ames, Iowa.

Christensen, C. R., and Hansen, A. J. *Teaching and the Case Method.* Boston: Harvard Business School Press, 1987.

Churchman, D. "The Cooperative Thesis." *Cooperative Learning*, 1993, 13(3), 39–40.

Clark, M. C. "Transformational Learning." In S. B. Merriam (ed.), *An Update on Adult Learning Theory.* New Directions for Adult and Continuing Education, no. 57. San Francisco, Jossey-Bass, 1993.

Clifford, J. "Introduction: Partial Truths." In J. Clifford and G. E. Marcus (eds.), *Writing Culture: The Poetics and Politics of Ethnography.* Berkeley: University of California Press, 1986.

Code, L. *What Can She Know? Feminist Theory and the Construction of Knowledge.* Ithaca, N.Y.: Cornell University Press, 1991.

Collins, M. *Adult Education as Vocation: A Critical Role for the Adult Educator.* New York: Routledge & Kegan Paul, 1991.

Combs, A. W., and Snygg, D. *Individual Behavior: A Perceptual Approach to Behavior.* New York: HarperCollins, 1949.

Comer, J. "Creating Learning Communities: The Comer Process." Experimental session of the annual conference of the Association for Supervision and Curriculum Development, Washington, D.C., 1993.

Cones, J. H., Janha, D., and Noonan, J. F. "Exploring Racial Assumptions with Faculty." In J. H. Cones, J. F. Noonan, and D. Janha (eds.), *Teaching Minority Students.* New Directions for Teaching and Learning, no. 16. San Francisco: Jossey-Bass, 1983.

Cooper, J., and Mueck, R. "Student Involvement in Learning and College Instruction." In A. Goodsell, M. Maher, and V. Tinto (eds.), *Collaborative Learning: A Sourcebook for Higher Education.* University Park: National Center on Postsecondary Teaching, Learning, and Assessment, Pennsylvania State University, 1992.

Corion, R. P. "Patient and Therapist Variables in the Treatment of Low Income Patients." *Psychological Bulletin*, 1974, 81, 344–354.

Corno, L., and Mandinach, E. B. "The Role of Cognitive Engagement in Classroom Learning and Motivation." *Educational Psychologist*, 1983, 18(2), 88–108.

Costa, A. L., and Kallick, B. "Reassessing Assessment." In A. L.Costa, J. Bellanca, and R. Fogarty (eds.), *If Minds Matter: A Forward to the Future.* Palatine, Ill.: Skylight, 1992.

Courtney, S. *Why Adults Learn: Toward a Theory of Participation in Adult Education.* New York: Routledge, Chapman & Hall, 1991.

Cross, K. P., and Angelo, T. A. *Classroom Assessment Techniques: A Handbook for Faculty.* Ann Arbor: National Center for Research to Improve Postsecondary Teaching and Learning, University of Michigan, 1988.

Cross, W. E., Jr. *Shades of Black: Diversity in African-American Identity.* Philadelphia: Temple University Press, 1991.

Csikszentmihalyi, M. "The Flow Experience and Its Significance for Human Psychology." In M. Csikszentmihalyi and I. S. Csikszentmihalyi (eds.), *Optimal Experience: Psychological Studies of Flow in Consciousness.* New York: Cambridge University Press, 1988.

Csikszentmihalyi, M. *Flow: The Psychology of Optimal Experience.* New York: HarperCollins, 1990.

Csikszentmihalyi, M., and Csikszentmihalyi, I. S. *Optimal Experience: Psychological Studies of Flow in Consciousness.* New York: Cambridge University Press, 1988.

Cummins, J. "The Role of Primary Language Development in Promoting Educational Success for Language Minority Students." In California Office of Bilingual Bicultural Education, *Schooling and Language Minority Students: A Theoretical Framework.* Sacramento: California Department of Education, 1981.

Cummins, J. "Empowering Minority Students: A Framework for Intervention." *Harvard Educational Review,* 1986, 56(1), 18–36.

Curtis, M. S., and Herrington, A. J. "Diversity in Required Writing Courses." In M. Adams (ed.), *Promoting Diversity in College Classrooms: Innovative Responses for Curriculum, Faculty, and Institutions.* New Directions for Teaching and Learning, no. 52. San Francisco: Jossey-Bass, 1992.

Cuseo, J. "Cooperative Learning: A Pedagogy for Diversity." *Cooperative Learning,* 1993, 13(3), 6–9.

Darling-Hammond, L. "Symposium: Equity and Educational Assessment." *Harvard Educational Review,* 1994, 64(1), 5–30.

DeAngelis, T. "Homeless Families: Stark Reality of the 90's." *APA Monitor,* 1994, 25(5), pp. 1, 38.

de Charms, R. *Personal Causation: The Internal Affective Determinants of Behavior.* San Diego, Calif.: Academic Press, 1968.

Deci, E. L., and Ryan, R. M. *Intrinsic Motivation and Self-Determination in Human Behavior.* New York: Plenum, 1985.

Deci, E. L., and Ryan, R. M. "A Motivational Approach to Self: Integration in Personality." In R. Dienstbier (ed.), *Nebraska Symposium on Motivation.* Vol. 38: *Perspectives on Motivation.* Lincoln: University of Nebraska Press, 1991.

Deci, E. L., Vallerand, R. J., Pelletier, L. C., and Ryan, R. M. "Motivation and Education: The Self-Determination Perspective." *Educational Psychologist*, 1991, 26(3,4), 325–346.

Delpit, L. D. "The Silenced Dialogue: Power and Pedagogy in Educating Other People's Children." *Harvard Educational Review*, 1988, 58(3), 280–298.

Dillon, J. T. *Questioning and Teaching: A Manual of Practice*. New York: Teachers College Press, 1988.

Eisner, E. W. *The Educational Imagination*. (2nd ed.) New York: Macmillan, 1985.

Elbow, P. *Embracing Contraries: Explorations in Learning and Teaching*. New York: Oxford University Press, 1986.

Elleson, V. J. "Competition: A Cultural Imperative?" *The Personnel and Guidance Journal*, Dec. 1983, pp. 195–198.

Elliott, J. *Action Research for Educational Change*. Philadelphia: Open University Press, 1991.

Ellis, A. "Rational-Emotive Therapy." In R. J. Corsini (ed.), *Current Psychotherapies*. Itasca, Ill.: Peacock, 1984.

Ellsworth, E. "Why Doesn't This Feel Empowering? Working Through the Repressive Myths of Critical Pedagogy." *Harvard Educational Review*, 1989, 59(3), 297–324.

Ennis, R. H. "A Taxonomy of Critical Thinking Dispositions and Abilities." In J. B. Barow and R. S. Sternberg (eds.), *Teaching Thinking Skills: Theory and Practice*. New York: W. H. Freeman, 1986.

Ewell, P. T. "To Capture the Ineffable: New Forms of Assessment in Higher Education." *Review of Research in Education*, 1991, 17, 75–127.

Fellows, K., and Zimpher, N. L. "Reflectivity and the Instructional Process: A Definitional Comparison Between Theory and Practice." In H. C. Waxman, H. J. Freiberg, J. C. Vaughan, and M. Weil (eds.), *Images of Reflection in Teacher Education*. Reston, Va.: Association of Teacher Educators, 1988.

Flannery, D. D. "Changing Dominant Understandings of Adults as Learners." In E. Hayes and S.A.J. Colin, III (eds.), *Confronting Racism and Sexism*. New Directions for Adult and Continuing Education, no. 61. San Francisco: Jossey-Bass, 1994.

Foucault, M. *The Archaeology of Knowledge and the Discourse on Language*. New York: Pantheon, 1982.

Freire, P. *Pedagogy of the Oppressed*. New York: Seabury Press, 1970.

Freire, P. *The Politics of Education: Culture, Power, and Liberation*. South Hadley, Miss.: Bergin and Garvey, 1985.

Gabelnick, F., MacGregor, J., Matthews, R. S., and Smith, B. L. *Learning Communities: Creating Connections Among Students, Faculty, and Disciplines*. New Directions for Teaching and Learning, no. 41. San Francisco: Jossey-Bass, 1990.

Gardner, H. *Frames of Mind: The Theory of Multiple Intelligences*. New York: Basic Books, 1982.

Gardner, H. *The Unschooled Mind*. New York: Basic Books, 1991.

Gardner, H. "Assessment in Context: The Alternative to Standardized Testing." In B. R. Gifford and M. C. O'Connor (eds.), *Future Assessments: Changing Views of Aptitude, Achievement, and Instruction*. Boston: Kluwer, 1992.

Gardner, H. *Multiple Intelligences: The Theory in Practice*. New York: Basic Books, 1993.

Gardner, H., and Boix-Mansilla, V. "Teaching for Understanding—Within and Across Disciplines." *Educational Leadership*, 1994, *51*(5), 14–18.

Gardner, H., and Hatch, T. "Multiple Intelligences Go to School." *Educational Researcher*, 1989, *1*(8), 4–10.

Gardner, J. W. *On Leadership*. New York: Free Press, 1990.

Geertz, C. *The Interpretation of Cultures*. New York: Basic Books, 1973.

Geismar, K., and Nicoleau, G. (eds.). "Teaching for Change: Addressing Issues of Difference in the College Classroom." *Harvard Educational Review*, Reprint Series, no. 25, 1993.

Gere, A. *Writing Groups: History, Theory, and Implications*. Carbondale: Southern Illinois University Press, 1987.

Gibson, M. "The School Performance of Immigrant Minorities: A Comparative View." *Anthropology and Education Quarterly*, 1987, *18*(4), 262–275.

Gilligan, C. *In a Different Voice: Psychological Theory and Women's Development*. Cambridge, Mass.: Harvard University Press, 1982.

Giroux, H. A. "Writing and Critical Thinking in the Social Studies." *Curriculum Inquiry*, 1978, 8, 291–310.

Giroux, H. A. *Border Crossings: Cultural Workers and the Politics of Education*. New York: Routledge & Kegan Paul, 1992.

Giroux, H. A., and McLaren, P. "Teacher Education and the Politics of Engagement: The Case for Democratic Schooling." *Harvard Educational Review*, 1986, *56*(3), 213–238.

Good, T., and Brophy, J. *Looking in Classrooms*. (5th ed.) New York: HarperCollins, 1991.

Goodlad, J. *A Place Called School: Prospects for the Future*. New York: McGraw-Hill, 1984.

Goodlad, J. *Teachers for Our Nation's Schools*. San Francisco: Jossey-Bass, 1990.

Goodsell, A., Maher, M., and Tinto, V. (eds.). *Collaborative Learning: A Sourcebook for Higher Education*. University Park: National Center on Postsecondary Teaching, Learning, and Assessment, Pennsylvania State University, 1992.

Goswami, D., and Stillman P. R. (eds.). *Reclaiming the Classroom: Teacher Research as an Agency for Change*. Portsmouth, N.H.: Boyton/Cook, 1987.

Greene, M. F. (ed.). *Minorities on Campus: A Handbook for Enhancing Diversity*. Washington, D.C.: American Council on Education, 1989.

Greenwald, B. "Teaching Technical Material." In C. R. Christensen, D. A. Garvin, and A. Sweet (eds.), *Education for Judgment: The Artistry of Discussion Leadership*. Boston: Harvard Business School Press, 1991.

Gronlund, N. E. *Stating Objectives for Classroom Instruction*. New York: Macmillan, 1978.

Gruenberg, M. M., and Morris, P. E. *Applied Problems in Memory*. San Diego, Calif.: Academic Press, 1979.

Hall, R., and Sandler, B. *The Classroom Climate: A Chilly One for Women?* Washington, D.C.: Project on the Status and Education of Women, Association of American Colleges, 1982.

Hardiman, R., and Jackson, B. W. "Racial Identity Development: Understanding Racial Dynamics in College Classrooms on Campus." In M. Adams (ed.), *Promoting Diversity in College Classrooms*. New Directions for Teaching and Learning, no. 52. San Francisco: Jossey-Bass, 1992.

Hart, L. *Human Brain, Human Learning*. White Plains, N.Y.: Longman, 1983.

Hayes, E. "Developing a Personal and Professional Agenda for Change." In E. Hayes and S.A.J. Colin, III (eds.), *Confronting Racism and Sexism*. New Directions for Adult and Continuing Education, no. 61. San Francisco: Jossey-Bass, 1994.

Heckhausen, H. *Motivation and Action*. Berlin: Springer-Verlag, 1991.

Helms, J. E. *Black and White Racial Identity: Theory, Research and Practice*. Westport, Conn.: Greenwood Press, 1990.

Herman, J. L., Aschbacher, P. R., and Winters, L. *A Practical Guide to Alternative Assessment*. Alexandria, Va.: Association for Supervision and Curriculum Development, 1992.

Hiemstra, R., and Sisco, B. *Individualizing Instruction: Making Learning Personal, Empowering, and Successful*. San Francisco: Jossey-Bass, 1990.

Highwater, J. "Imagination as a Political Force." General session address given at the annual conference of the Association of Supervision and Curriculum Development, Chicago, March 1994.

Hill, P. J. "Multiculturalism: The Crucial Philosophical and Organizational Issues." *Change*, July/Aug. 1991, pp. 38–47.

Hilliard, A. G. III, "Teachers and Cultural Styles in a Pluralistic Society." *NEA Today*, 1989, 7(6), 65–69.

Hillocks, G. "What Works in Teaching Composition: A Meta-Analysis of Experimental Treatment Studies." *American Journal of Education*, 1984, 93(1), 133–170.

Hofstede, G. "Cultural Differences in Teaching and Learning." *International Journal of Intercultural Relations*, 1986, 10(3), 301–320.

Hollins, E. R., King, J. E., and Hayman, W. C. (eds.). *Teaching Diverse Populations: Formulating a Knowledge Base*. Albany: State University of New York Press, 1994.

Holmes, S. A. "AIDS Is Likely to Reverse Gains in Life Expectancy." *New York Times*, May 1, 1994, Section 4, p. 2.

hooks, b. *Talking Back*. Boston: South End Press, 1989.

hooks, b., and West, C. *Breaking Bread: Insurgent Black Intellectual Life*. Boston: South End Press, 1991.

Huffman, T. E., Sill, M. L., and Brokenleg, M. "College Achievement Among Sioux and White South Dakota Students." *Journal of American Indian Education*, 1986, 25(2), 32–38.

Humphreys, L. *Tearoom Trade: Impersonal Sex in Public Places*. Chicago: Aldine, 1970.

Hutchings, P. *Using Cases to Improve College Teaching: A Guide to More Reflective Practice*. Washington, D.C.: American Association for Higher Education, 1993.

Jackson, B. W., and Hardiman, R. "Oppression: Conceptual and Developmental Analysis." In M. Adams and L. S. Marchesani (eds.), *Radical and Cultural Diversity, Curriculae Content and Classroom Dynamics: A Manual for College Teachers*. Amherst: University of Massachusetts, 1988.

Jacobs, W. J., and Nadel, L. "Stress-Induced Recovery of Fears and Phobias." *Psychological Review*, 1985, 92, 512–531.

Jensen, A. R. "How Biased Are Culture-Loaded Tests?" *Genetic Psychology Monographs*, 1974, 90, 185–244.

Johnson, D. W., and Johnson, R. T. *Cooperation and Competition: Theory and Research*. Edina, Minn.: Interaction, 1989.

Johnson, D. W., and Johnson, R. T. *Learning Together and Alone*. Englewood Cliffs, N.J.: Prentice-Hall, 1991.

Johnson, D. W., and Johnson, R. T. "What We Know About Cooperative Learning at the College Level." *Cooperative Learning*, 1993, 13(3), 17–18.

Johnson, D. W., and Johnson, R. T. *Cooperative, Competitive, and Individualistic Procedures for Educating Adults: A Comparative Analysis*. Minneapolis: Cooperative Learning Center, University of Minnesota, forthcoming.

Johnson, D. W., Johnson, R. T., and Smith, K. A. *Active Learning: Cooperation in the College Classroom*. Edina, Minn.: Interaction, 1991.

Jonassen, D. H. "Objectivism Versus Constructivism: Do We Need a New Philosophical Paradigm?" *Educational Training and Development*, 1992, 39(3), 5–14.

Jordan, C. "Translating Culture: From Ethnographic Information to Educational Program." *Anthropology of Education Quarterly*, 1985, 16, 105–123.

Joseph, S. "Multiculturalism: Cautions from Cross-Cultural Experiences." *Multicultural Education*, 1994, *1*(5), 14–16.

Joyce, B., and Showers, R. *Student Achievement Through Staff Development*. White Plains, N.Y.: Longman, 1988.

Katz, J. "White Faculty Struggling with the Effects of Racism." In J. H. Cones, J. F. Noonan, and D. Janha (eds.), *Teaching Minority Students*. New Directions for Teaching and Learning, no. 16. San Francisco: Jossey-Bass, 1983.

Keller, J. M. "Motivational Systems." In H. D. Stolovitch and E. J. Keeps (eds.), *Handbook of Human Performance Technology: A Comprehensive Guide for Analyzing and Solving Performance Problems in Organizations*. San Francisco: Jossey-Bass, 1992.

Kerry, T. "Classroom Questioning in England." *Questioning Exchange*, 1987, *1*(1), 32–33.

Kim, Y. Y. "Intercultural Communication Competence." In S. Ting-Toomey and F. Korzenny (eds.), *Cross Cultural Interpersonal Communication*. Newbury Park, Calif.: Sage, 1991.

Kim, Y. Y., and Ruben, B. D. "Intercultural Transformation." In Y. Y. Kim and W. B. Gudykunst (eds.), *Theories in Intercultural Communication*. Newbury Park, Calif.: Sage, 1988.

King, A. "Inquiry as a Tool in Critical Thinking." In D. F. Halpern and Associates (eds.), *Changing College Classrooms: New Teaching and Learning Strategies for an Increasingly Complex World*. San Francisco: Jossey-Bass, 1994.

Kinsella, K. "Instructional Strategies Which Promote Participation and Learning for Non-Native Speakers of English in University Classes." *Exchanges*, 1993, *5*(1), 12; Institute for Teaching and Learning, California State University System.

Kitayama, S., and Markus, H. R. (eds.). *Emotion and Culture: Empirical Studies of Mutual Influence*. Washington, D.C.: American Psychological Association, 1994.

Kleinfeld, J., and Nelson, P. "Adapting Instruction to Native American Learning Style: An Iconoclastic View." In W. J. Lonner and V. O. Tyler, Jr. (eds.), *Cultural and Ethnic Factors in Learning and Motivation: Implications for Education*. The Twelfth Western Symposium on Learning. Bellingham: Western Washington University, 1988.

Knowles, M. S. *The Modern Practice of Adult Education: From Pedagogy to Andragogy*. (Rev. ed.) Chicago: Follett, 1980.

Knowles, M. S. *Using Learning Contracts: Practical Approaches to Individualizing and Structuring Learning*. San Francisco: Jossey-Bass, 1986.

Kohn, A. *The Brighter Side of Human Nature: Altruism and Empathy in Everyday Life*. New York: Basic Books, 1990.

Kohn, A. *Punished by Rewards*. Boston: Houghton Mifflin, 1993.

Kornhaber, M., Krechevsky, M., and Gardner, H. "Engaging Intelligence." *Educational Psychologist,* 1990, 25(3,4), 177–199.

Kumar, Y. K., and Treadwell, T. W. "Culture-Fairness in Testing." Paper presented at the American Educational Research Association, New York, March 1982.

Ladson-Billings, G. "Culturally Relevant Teaching: The Key to Making Multicultural Education Work." In C. A. Grant (ed.), *Research and Multicultural Education: From the Margins to the Mainstream.* Washington, D.C.: Falmer Press, 1992.

Langer, S. *Philosophy in a New Key.* Cambridge, Mass.: Harvard University Press, 1942.

Lather, P. *Getting Smart: Feminist Research and Pedagogy with/in the Postmodern.* New York: Routledge & Kegan Paul, 1991.

Lave, J. *Cognition in Practice.* Cambridge, England: Cambridge University Press, 1988.

Levin, H. M. "Accelerated Schools for Disadvantaged Students." *Educational Leadership,* 1987, 44, 19–21.

Levin, T., and Long, R. *Effective Instruction.* Alexandria, Va.: Association for Supervision and Curriculum Development, 1981.

Levine, A. *Shaping Higher Education's Future: Demographic Realities and Opportunities, 1990–2000.* San Francisco: Jossey-Bass, 1989.

Light, R. *The Harvard Assessment Seminars: Explorations with Students and Faculty about Teaching, Learning and Student Life, First Report.* Cambridge, Mass.: Harvard University School of Education, 1990.

Locke, D. C. *Increasing Multicultural Understanding: A Comprehensive Model.* Newbury Park, Calif.: Sage, 1992.

Lyons, N. "Two Perspectives on Self, Relationships and Morality." *Harvard Educational Review,* 1983, 53, 125–145.

Maccoby, E., and Jacklin, C. *The Psychology of Sex Differences.* Palo Alto, Calif.: Stanford University Press, 1974.

McCombs, B. L. "Motivation and Lifelong Learning." *Educational Psychologist,* 1991, 26(2), 117–127.

McCombs, B. L., and others. *Learner-Centered Psychological Principles: Guidelines for School Design and Reform.* Washington, D.C.: American Psychological Association and Mid-continent Regional Educational Laboratory, 1993.

McDonald, J. P., and others. *Graduation by Exhibition: Assessing Genuine Achievement.* Alexandria, Va.: Association for Supervision and Curriculum Development, 1993.

MacGregor, J. "What Differences Do Learning Communities Make?" *Washington Center News,* 1991, 6(1), 4–9.

MacGregor, J. "Learning Self-Evaluation: Challenges for Students." In J. Mac-Gregor (ed.), *Student Self-Evaluation: Fostering Reflective Learning*. New Directions for Teaching and Learning, no. 56. San Francisco: Jossey-Bass, 1994.

McIntosh, P. "Curricular Re-Vision: The New Knowledge for a New Age." In C. S. Pearson, D. L. Shavlick, and J. G. Touchton (eds.), *Educating the Majority: Women Challenge Tradition in Higher Education*. New York: American Council on Education/Macmillan, 1989.

McLaren, P., and Leonard, P. (eds.). *Paulo Freire: A Critical Encounter*. New York: Routledge & Kegan Paul, 1993.

Madison, E. "Managing Diversity: Strategies for Change." *College and University Personnal Association Journal*, 1993, 44(4), 23–27.

Marable, M. *The Crisis of Color and Democracy: Essays on Race, Class and Power*. Monroe, Md.: Common Courage Press, 1992.

Marchesani, L. S., and Adams, M. "Dynamics of Diversity in the Teaching-Learning Process: A Faculty Development Model for Analysis and Action." In M. Adams (ed.), *Promoting Diversity in College Classrooms*. New Directions for Teaching and Learning, no. 51. San Francisco: Jossey-Bass, 1992.

Marzano, R. J. *A Different Kind of Classroom: Teaching with Dimensions of Learning*. Alexandria, Va.: Association for Supervision and Curriculum Development, 1992.

Massimini, F., Csikszentmihalyi, M., and Delle Fave, A. "Flow and Biocultural Evolution." In M. Csikszentmihalyi and I. S. Csikszentmihalyi (eds.), *Optimal Experience: Psychological Studies of Flow in Consciousness*. New York: Cambridge University Press, 1988.

Meier, D. "The Kindergarten Tradition in High School." In K. Jervis and C. Montag (eds.), *Progressive Education for the 1990's: Transforming Practice*. New York: Teachers College Press, 1991.

Merriam, S. B., and Caffarella, R. S. *Learning in Adulthood: A Comprehensive Guide*. San Francisco: Jossey-Bass, 1991.

Mesa-Bains, A., and Shulman, J. H. *Facilitator's Guide to Diversity in the Classroom: A Casebook for Teachers and Teacher Educators*. Hillsdale, N.J.: Erlbaum, 1994.

Messick, S. "Personality Consistencies in Cognition and Creativity." In S. Messick and Associates, *Individuality in Learning: Implications of Cognitive Styles and Creativity in Human Development*. San Francisco: Jossey-Bass, 1976.

Meyers, C., and Jones, T. B. *Promoting Active Learning: Strategies for the College Classroom*. San Francisco: Jossey-Bass, 1993.

Mills, R. C. "A New Understanding of Self: The Role of Affect, State of Mind,

Self-Understanding and Intrinsic Motivation." *The Journal of Experimental Education*, 1991, 60, 67–81.

Mills, R. C., Pransky, G. S., and Sedgeman, J. A. "Psychology of Mind: The Founders' Monograph." Paper presented at the annual conference of the Psychology of Mind, Burlington, Vermont, July 1993.

Milton, O., Pollio, H. R., and Eison, J. A. *Making Sense of College Grades*. San Francisco: Jossey-Bass, 1986.

Molnar, A. "Guidelines for Business Involvement in the Schools." *Educational Leadership*, 1989–1990, pp. 84–86.

Molnar, A., and Lindquist, B. *Changing Problem Behavior in Schools*. San Francisco: Jossey-Bass, 1989.

Moore, W. S., and Hunter, S. "Mildly Interesting Facts: Student Self-Evaluation and Assessment Outcomes." In J. MacGregor (ed.), *Student Self-Evaluation: Fostering Reflective Learning*. New Directions for Teaching and Learning, no. 56. San Francisco: Jossey-Bass, 1994.

Mortenson, T. G., and Wu, Z. *High School Graduation and College Preparation of Young Adults, by Family Income and Background, 1970–1989*. Report no. 90-3. Iowa City, Iowa: American College Testing Program, 1990.

Myrdal, G. *An American Dilemma: The Negro Problem in Modern Democracy*. New York: HarperCollins, 1944.

Nelson, A. *Undergraduate Academic Achievement in College as an Indicator of Occupational Success*. Bureau of Policies and Standards, P.S. 75–5, Washington, D.C.: United States Civil Service Commission, 1975.

Newmann, F. M., and Wehlage, G. C. "Five Standards of Authentic Instruction." *Educational Leadership*, 1993, 50(7), 8–12.

Nieto, S. *Affirming Diversity: The Sociopolitical Context of Multicultural Education*. White Plains, N.Y.: Longman, 1992.

Noonan, J. F. "Discussing Racial Topics in Class." In M. Adams and L. Marchensan (eds.), *Racial and Cultural Diversity, Curricular Content, and Classroom Dynamics: A Manual for College Teachers*. Amherst: University of Massachusetts, 1988.

O'Donnell, J. M., and Caffarella, R. S. "Learning Contracts." In M. W. Galbraith (ed.), *Adult Learning Methods*. Malabar, Fla.: Kreiger, 1990.

Ogbu, J. U. "Variability in Minority School Performance: A Problem in Search of an Explanation." *Anthropology and Education Quarterly*, 1987, 18, 312–335.

Oldfather, P. "Epistemological Empowerment: A Constructivist Concept of Motivation for Literacy Learning." Paper presented at the National Reading Conference, San Antonio, Texas, December 1992.

Ovando, C. J., and Collier, V. P. *Bilingual and ESL Classrooms*. New York: McGraw-Hill, 1985.

Paris, S. G., and Byrnes, J. P. "The Constructivist Approach to Self-Regulation and Learning in the Classroom." In B. J. Zimmerman and D. H. Schunk (eds.), *Self-Regulated Learning and Academic Achievement: Theory, Research, and Practice.* New York: Springer-Verlag, 1989.

Paul, R. "Critical Thinking: Fundamental to Education for a Free Society." *Educational Leadership,* 1984, *42*(1), 4–14.

Paul, R. "Socratic Questioning." In R. Paul (ed.), *Critical Thinking: What Every Person Needs to Survive in a Rapidly Changing World.* Rohnert Park, Calif.: Center for Critical Thinking and Moral Critique, Sonoma State University, 1990.

Pearlman, M. "Trends in Women's Total Score and Item Performance on Verbal Measures." Paper presented at the annual meeting of the American Educational Research Associates, Washington, D.C., April 1987.

Pedersen, P. "Multiculturalism as a Generic Approach to Counseling." *Journal of Counseling and Development,* 1991, *70*, 6–12.

Pedersen, P. *A Handbook for Developing Multicultural Awareness.* (2nd ed.) Alexandria, Va.: American Counseling Association, 1994.

Pedersen, P., and Ivey, A. *Culture-Centered Counseling and Interviewing Skills.* Westport, Conn.: Greenwood Press, 1993.

Perkins, D. N. "Educating for Insight." *Educational Leadership,* 1991, *49*(2), 4–8.

Perkins, D. N., Allen, R., and Hafner, J. "Differences in Everyday Reasoning." In W. Maxwell (ed.), *Thinking: The Frontier Expands.* Hillsdale, N.J.: Erlbaum, 1983.

Perkins, D. N., Faraday, M., and Bushey, B. "Everyday Reasoning and the Roots of Intelligence." In J. F. Voss, D. N. Perkins, and J. W. Segal (eds.), *Informal Reasoning and Education.* Hillsdale, N.J.: Erlbaum, 1991.

Perrone, V. *Expanding Student Assessment,* Alexandria, Va.: Association for Supervision and Curriculum Development, 1991.

Perry, W. G. *Forms of Intellectual and Ethical Development in the College Years.* Troy, Mo.: Holt, Rinehart & Winston, 1970.

Peterson, P., and Fennema, E. "Effective Teaching, Student Engagement in Classroom Activities, and Sex-Related Differences in Learning Mathematics." *American Educational Research Journal,* 1985, *22*, 309–335.

Phillips, S. U. *The Invisible Culture: Communication in Classroom and Community on the Warm Springs Indian Reservation.* White Plains, N.Y.: Longman, 1983.

Phinney, J. S. "Ethnic Identity in Adolescents and Adults: Review of Research." *Psychological Bulletin,* 1990, *108*(3), 499–514.

Pierce, L. V., and O'Malley, J. M. *Performance and Portfolio Assessment for Language Minority Students.* Washington, D.C.: National Clearinghouse for Bilingual Education, 1992.

344   References

Plutchic, R. *Emotion: A Psychoevolutionary Synthesis*. New York: HarperCollins, 1980.

Popham, W. J. "The Merits of Measurement Driven Instruction." *Phi Delta Kappan*, 1987, 68, 679–682.

Pransky, G. S. "Psychology of Mind: Its Origins, Discoveries and Its Vision for the Mental Health Field." Paper presented at the annual conference of the Psychology of Mind, Burlington, Vermont, July 1993.

Presseisen, B. Z. "Thinking Skills: Meanings and Models." In A. L. Costa (ed.), *Developing Minds*. Alexandria, Va.: Association for Supervision and Curriculum Development, 1985.

Quann, C. J. *Grades and Grading: Historical Perspectives and the 1982 AACRO Study*. Washington, D.C.: American Association of Collegiate Registrars and Admission Officers, 1984.

Quann, C. J. "Grading by Narrative Evaluation: Present Tense." *College and University*, 1993, 69(1), 22–31.

Reyhner, J. (ed.). *Teaching the Indian Child: A Bilingual/Multicultural Approach*. Billings: Eastern Montana College, 1986.

Rogoff, B., and Lave, J. (eds.). *Everyday Cognition: Its Development in Social Context*. Cambridge, Mass.: Harvard University Press, 1984.

Ryan, R. M., Mims, V., and Koestner, R. "Relation of Reward Contingency and Interpersonal Context to Intrinsic Motivation: A Review and Test Using Cognitive Evaluation Theory." *Journal of Personality and Social Psychology*, 1983, 45(4), 736–750.

Sadker, M., and Sadker, D. "Confronting Sexism in the College Classroom." In S. Gabriel and S. Smithoon (eds.), *Gender in the Classroom*. Champaign: University of Illinois Press, 1990.

Sadker, M., and Sadker, D. "Ensuring Equitable Participation in College Classes." In L.L.B. Border and N. Van Note Chism (eds.), *Teaching for Diversity*. New Directions for Teaching and Learning, no. 49. San Francisco: Jossey-Bass, 1992.

Sadker, M., and Sadker, D. *Failing at Fairness: How America's Schools Cheat Girls*. New York: Charles Scribner's Sons, 1994.

Sampson, E. E. "Identity Politics: Challenges to Psychology's Understanding." *American Psychologist*, 1993, 48(12), 1219–230.

Sandler, B. "The Classroom Climate: Still a Chilly One for Women." In C. Lasser (ed.), *Educating Men and Women Together: Coeducation in a Changing World*. Champaign: University of Illinois Press, 1987.

Schein, E. H. *Organizational Culture and Leadership*. San Francisco: Jossey-Bass, 1992.

Schkade, L. L., Romani, S., and Uzawa, M. "Human Information Processing and Environmental Complexity: An Experiment in Four Cultures." *ASCI Journal of Management*, 1978, 8, 56–63.

Schmitz, B. *Core Curriculum and Cultural Pluralism*. Washington, D.C.: Association of American Colleges, 1992.

Schmitz, B., Paul, S. P., and Greenberg, J. D. "Creating Multicultural Classrooms: An Experience Derived Faculty Development Program." In L.L.B. Border and N. Van Note Chism (eds.), *Teaching for Diversity*. New Directions for Teaching and Learning, no. 49. San Francisco: Jossey-Bass, 1992.

Schneider, S. F. "Psychology at a Crossroads." *American Psychologist*, 1990, *45*, 521–529.

Schön, D. A. *Educating the Reflective Practitioner: Toward a New Design for Teaching and Learning in the Professions*. San Francisco: Jossey-Bass, 1987.

Schuster, M., and VanDyne, S. "Placing Women in the Liberal Arts: Stages of Curriculum Transformation." *Harvard Educational Review*, 1984, *54*(4), 413–428.

Scribner, S., and Cole, M. *The Psychology of Literacy*. Cambridge, Mass.: Harvard University Press, 1981.

Secretary's Commission on Achieving Necessary Skills (SCANS). *What Work Requires of Schools: A Scans Report for America 2000*. Washington, D.C.: U.S. Department of Labor, 1992.

Segall, M. H., Dasen, P. R., Berry, J. W., and Poortinga, Y. H. *Human Behavior in Global Perspective: An Introduction to Cross-Cultural Psychology*. Elmsford, N.Y.: Pergamon Press, 1990.

Senge, P. M. *The Fifth Discipline: The Art and Practice of the Learning Organization*. New York: Doubleday/Currency, 1990.

Shade, B.J.R. "Afro-American Cognitive Style: A Variable in School Success?" *Review of Educational Research*, 1982, *52*(2), 219–244.

Shade, B.J.R. (ed.). *Culture, Style, and the Educative Process*. Springfield, Ill.: Thomas, 1989.

Shannon, T. M. "Introducing Simulation and Role Play." In S. F. Schomberg (ed.), *Strategies for Active Learning in University Classrooms*. Minneapolis: University of Minnesota Press, 1986.

Sheared, V. "Giving Voice: An Inclusive Model of Instruction—A Womanist Perspective." In E. Hayes and S.A.J. Colin, III (eds.), *Confronting Racism and Sexism*. New Directions for Teaching and Learning, no. 61. San Francisco: Jossey-Bass, 1994.

Shepard, L. A. "Why We Need Better Assessments." *Educational Leadership*, 1989, *46*(7), 4–9.

Shepard, L. A. "Evaluating Test Validity." In L. Darling-Hammond (ed.), *Review of Research in Education*. Vol. 19. Washington, D.C.: American Educational Research Association, 1993.

Shirts, G. *BaFa' BaFa': A Cross-Cultural Simulation*. Del Mar, Calif.: Simulation Training Assistance, 1977.

Shor, I. *Empowering Education: Critical Teaching for Social Change*. Chicago: University of Chicago Press, 1992.

Shor, I. "Education Is Politics: Paulo Freire's Critical Pedagogy." In P. McLaren and P. Leonard (eds.), *Paulo Freire: A Critical Encounter*. New York: Routledge & Kegan Paul, 1993.

Shulman, J. H., and others. "Case Writing as a Site for Collaboration." *Teacher Education Quarterly*, Winter 1990, pp. 63–78.

Sigel, I. E., Brodzinsky, D. M., and Golinkoff, R. M. (eds.). *New Directions in Pragetian Theory and Practice*. Hillsdale, N.J.: Erlbaum, 1981.

Sleeter, C. "White Racism." *Multi-cultural Education*, Spring 1994, pp. 5–8, 39.

Smith, B. L., and MacGregor, J. T. "What Is Collaborative Learning?" In A. Goodsell, M. Maher, and V. Tinto (eds.), *Collaborative Learning: A Sourcebook for Higher Education*. University Park: National Center on Postsecondary Teaching, Learning, and Assessment, Pennsylvania State University, 1992.

Smith, D. G. *The Challenge of Diversity: Involvement or Alienation in the Academy?* ASHE-ERIC Higher Education Report, no. 5. Washington, D.C.: Association for the Study of Higher Education, 1989.

Smith, D. M., and Kolb, D. A. *User's Guide for the Learning Style Inventory: A Manual for Teachers and Trainers*. Boston: McBer, 1986.

Solorzano, D. "Teaching and Social Change: Reflections on a Freirean Approach in a College Classroom." *Teaching Sociology*, 1989, *17*, 218–225.

Spear, K. *Sharing Writing: Peer Resource Group in English Classes*. Portsmouth, N.H.: Boyton/Cook, 1988.

Sternberg, R. J. "How Much Gall Is Too Much Gall?" (review of *Frames of Mind: Theory of Multiple Intelligences*). *Contemporary Education Review*, 1993, *12*(3), 215–224.

Stiggins, R. J. "Revitalizing Classroom Assessment: The Highest Instructional Priority." *Phi Delta Kappan*, Jan. 1988, pp. 363–368.

Sue, D. W., and Sue, D. *Counseling the Culturally Different: Theory and Practice*. (2nd ed.) New York: Wiley, 1990.

Sue, S. "Ethnicity and Culture in Psychological Research and Practice." In J. D. Goodchilds (ed.), *Psychological Perspectives on Human Diversity in America*. Washington, D.C.: American Psychological Association, 1991.

Svinicki, M. D., and Dixon, N. M. "The Kolb Model Modified for Classroom Activities." *College Teaching*, 1987, *35*(4), 141–146.

Swartz, E. "Multicultural Education: From a Compensatory to a Scholarly Foundation." In C. A. Grant (ed.), *Research and Multicultural Education: From the Margins to the Mainstream*. Washington, D.C.: Falmer Press, 1992.

Swisher, K., and Deyhle, D. "Styles of Learning and Learning for Style: Educational Conflicts for American Indian/Alaskan Native Youth." *Journal of Multilingual and Multicultural Development*, 1987, 8(4), 345–360.

Tannen, D. "Teachers' Classroom Strategies Should Recognize That Men and Women Use Language Differently." *Chronicle of Higher Education*, June 19, 1991, pp. B-1–B-3.

Tatum, B. D. "Talking About Race, Learning About Racism: The Application of Racial Identity Development Theory in the Classroom." *Harvard Educational Review*, 1992, 62(1), 1–24.

Taylor, E. W. "Intercultural Competency: A Transformative Learning Process." *Adult Education Quarterly*, 1994, 44(3), 154–174.

Tharp, R. G. "Psychocultural Variables and Constants: Effects on Teaching and Learning in Schools." *American Psychologist*, 1989, 44(2), 349–359.

Tinto, V. *Leaving College: Rethinking the Causes and Cures for Student Attrition*. Chicago: University of Chicago Press, 1987.

Tinto, V., Goodsell-Love, A., and Russo, P. *Building Learning Communities for New College Students*. University Park: National Center on Postsecondary Teaching, Learning, and Assessment, Pennsylvania State University, 1994.

Touchton, J. G., and Davis, L. *Fact Book on Women in Higher Education*. New York: American Council on Education/Macmillan, 1991.

Treisman, U. "A Study of the Mathematics Performance of Black Students at the University of California, Berkeley." Unpublished doctoral dissertation, Department of Mathematics, University of California, Berkeley, 1985.

Treuba, H., and Delgado-Gaitan, C. "Socialization of Mexican Children for Cooperation and Competition: Sharing and Copying." *Journal of Educational Equity and Leadership*, 1985, 5(3), 189–204.

Uguroglu, M., and Walberg, H. J. "Motivation and Achievement: A Quantitative Synthesis." *American Educational Research Journal*, 1979, 16, 375–389.

Vasquez, J. A. "Teaching to the Distinctive Traits of Minority Students." *The Clearing House*, 1990, 63(7), 299–304.

Ventura, M. "Standing at the Wall." *The Sun*, Mar. 1994, pp. 4–6.

Villegas, A. M. *Culturally Responsive Pedagogy for the 1990's and Beyond*. Princeton, N.J.: Educational Testing Service, 1991.

Voss, J. F. "Problem Solving and the Educational Process." In A. Lesgold and R. Glaser (eds.), *Foundations for a Psychology of Education*. Hillsdale, N. J.: Erlbaum, 1989.

Vygotsky, L. *Thought and Language*. Cambridge, Mass.: MIT Press, 1962.

Vygotsky, L. *Mind and Society*. Cambridge, Mass.: Harvard University Press, 1978.

Waluconis, C. J. "Self-Evaluation: Settings and Uses." In J. MacGregor (ed.), *Student Self-Evaluation: Fostering Reflective Learning*. New Directions for Teaching and Learning, no. 56. San Francisco: Jossey-Bass, 1994.

Warren, J. *College Grading Practices: An Overview*. Washington, D.C.: ERIC, report no. 9, 1971.

Watson, J. S., and Ramey, C. G. "Reactions to Response-Contingent Stimulation in Early Infancy." *Merrill Palmer Quarterly,* 1972, *18,* 219–228.

Weaver, F. S. *Liberal Education: Critical Essays on Professions, Pedagogy, and Structure.* New York: Teachers College Press, 1991.

Webster's Ninth New Collegiate Dictionary. Springfield, Mass.: Merriam Webster, 1986.

Webster's Third New International Dictionary. Springfield, Mass.: Merriam Webster, 1993.

Weinstein, G., and Obear, K. "Bias Issues in the Classroom: Encounters with the Teaching Self." In M. Adams (ed.), *Promoting Diversity in College Classrooms: Innovative Responses for the Curriculum, Faculty, and Institutions.* New Directions for Teaching and Learning, no. 52. San Francisco: Jossey-Bass, 1992.

Wendler, C., and Carlton, S. "An Examination of SAT Verbal Items for Differential Performance by Women and Men: An Exploratory Study." Paper presented at the annual meeting of the American Educational Research Association, Washington, D.C., April 1987.

Wetherell, M., and Potter, J. *Mapping the Language of Racism: Discourse and the Legitimation of Exploitation.* London: Harvester Wheatsheaf, 1992.

Whitehead, A. N. *Process and Reality.* New York: Free Press, 1979.

Whitman, N. *Peer Teaching: To Teach Is to Learn Twice.* ASHE-ERIC Higher Education Report, no. 4. Washington, D.C.: ERIC Clearinghouse on Higher Education, 1988.

Wiggins, G. "A True Test: Toward More Authentic and Equitable Assessment." *Phi Delta Kappan,* May 1989, pp. 703–713.

Wiggins, G. "Standards, Not Standardization: Evoking Quality Student Work." *Educational Leadership,* 1991, 48(5), 18–25.

Wiggins, G. "On Performance Assessment: A Conversation with Grant Wiggins." *Educational Leadership,* 1992, *49,* 35–37.

Williams, R. M., Jr. *American Society: A Sociological Interpretation.* (3rd ed.) New York: Knopf, 1970.

Wilson, A. L. "The Promise of Situated Cognition." In S. B. Merriam (ed.), *An Update on Adult Learning Theory.* New Directions for Adult and Continuing Education, no. 57. San Francisco: Jossey-Bass, 1993.

Wilson, R. C. "Improving Faculty Teaching: Effective Use of Student Evaluations and Consultants." *Journal of Higher Education,* 1986, 57(2), 196–211.

Wlodkowski, R. J. *Enhancing Adult Motivation to Learn: A Guide to Improving Instruction and Increasing Learner Achievement.* San Francisco: Jossey-Bass, 1985.

Wlodkowski, R. J. "An Analysis of the History, Status, and Impact of Peer Coaching at the British Columbia Institute of Technology." Report to the Learning Skills Center of the British Columbia Institute of Technology, Vancouver, 1992.

Wlodkowski, R. J., and Ginsberg, M. B. "I'm Normal; You're Not." *In These Times*, Apr. 5, 1993, pp. 29–30.

Wolfe, A. "How We Live Now." *New York Times Book Review*, July 25, 1993, p. 30.

Wyatt, J. D. "Native Involvement in Curriculum Development: The Native Teacher as Cultural Broker." *Interchange*, 1978–1979, 9, 17–28.

Zaharna, R. S. "Self-Shock: The Double-Binding Challenge of Identity." *International Journal of Intercultural Relations*, 1989, *13*(4), 501–525.

Zessoules, R., Wolf, D. P., and Gardner, H. "A Better Balance: Arts PROPEL as an Alternative to Discipline-Based Arts Education." In J. Burton, A. Lederman, and P. London (eds.), *Beyond Debate: The Case for Multiple Visions of Art Education*. Dartmouth, Mass.: University Council on Art Education, 1988.

Zinn, H. *A People's History of the United States*. New York: HarperCollins, 1980.

Name Index

Cones, J. H., 43
Cooper, J., 81
Corno, L., 168
Costa, A. L., 256
Courtney, S., 19
Cross, K. P., 96, 98, 247, 266
Cross, W. E., Jr., 47
Csikszentmihalyi, I. S., 20, 164
Csikszentmihalyi, M., 20, 163, 164, 168, 169–170, 176, 178, 179, 192
Cummins, J., 20, 116, 117, 192, 302
Curtis, M. S., 89
Cuseo, J., 67, 69

D

Darling-Hammond, L., 257
Dasen, P. R., 23
DeAngelis, T., 203, 205
DeBuhr, L. E., 90
de Charms, R., 113
Deci, E. L., 20, 24, 26, 63, 112, 113, 123, 169, 232, 236
de la Cruz, J., 161
Delle Fave, A., 170, 179
Delpit, L. D., 2–3
Dillon, J. T., 180
Dixon, N. M., 150–151, 153, 154n

E

Eisner, E. W., 125, 126
Eison, J. A., 275, 278, 280
Elbow, P., 271–272
Elliott, J., 206, 209, 306
Ellison, R., 184
Ellsworth, E., 58
Ennis, R. H., 180
Ewell, P. T., 239, 247

F

Faraday, M., 184
Fellows, K., 175
Fideler, E., 218–219
Flannery, D. D., 171
Freire, P., 65, 66, 170, 185, 226, 289, 263, 307

G

Gabelnick, F., 103, 104
Gable, R. K., 209
Garcia Marquez, G., 137
Gardner, H., 61, 119, 120, 136–137,

138n, 139–140, 142, 145, 149, 173, 225, 234, 239, 253, 260
Geertz, C., 7
Geismar, K., 9
Gere, A., 88
Gibson, M., 111
Giles, J., 153–159
Gilligan, C., 54, 66, 239
Ginsberg, M. B., 22
Giroux, H. A., 19, 168, 201
Goldberger, N., 53–54, 66, 180, 239
Golinkoff, R. M., 264
Good, T., 147
Goodlad, J., 291
Goodsell, A., 81
Goodsell-Love, A., 104
Goswami, D., 209
Green, K. C., 240
Greenberg, J. D., 309–310
Greene, M. F., 308
Greenwald, B., 223
Gronlund, N. E., 124

H

Hafner, J., 180
Hall, R., 74
Hansen, A. J., 216
Hardiman, R., 47–51, 264
Hatch, T., 138n
Hayes, E., 309
Hayman, W. C., 143, 145
Helms, J. E., 47
Herman, J. L., 239, 263
Herrington, A. J., 89
Hiemstra, R., 145
Highwater, J., 209
Hill, P. J., 18, 283, 284
Hilliard, A. G., III, 142, 144, 145, 147
Hillocks, G., 88
Hofstede, G., 56, 185
Hollins, E. R., 143, 145
Holmes, S. A., 196n
Hunt, R. C., 4
Hunter, S., 256
Hutchings, P., 216, 219n, 221, 222

I

Ivey, A., 57

J

Jacklin, C., 145

Subject Index